SEARCH FOR BIG CHUB

TONY MILES

The Crowood Press

First published in 1996 by
The Crowood Press Ltd
Ramsbury, Marlborough
Wiltshire SN8 2HR

British Library Cataloguing in Publication Data

A catalogue record for this book is available from the British Library.

ISBN 1 85223 959 X

All photographs by Tony Miles.

Line drawings by Paul Groombridge.

Photograph previous page: the temperature was hovering around zero all day, but this 5lb 14oz Cherwell fish still gulped a big chunk of crust for the author.

Typeset and designed by:
D & N Publishing
DTP & Editorial Services
Crowood Lane, Ramsbury
Marlborough, Wiltshire SN8 2HR

Typefaces used: main text and captions M Plantin; labels, Gill Sans.

Phototypeset by HPS Ltd, Havant.
Printed and bound by BPC Consumer Books, Aylesbury.

CONTENTS

ACKNOWLEDGEMENTS

It would be an impossible task to try and thank individually all those anglers and friends who have so enriched my angling life as to have made this book possible. To each and every one of you I extend my warmest regards and wishes for many more chub to grace your landing nets.

Naturally, there will be those to whom I must pay special thanks. First, there is Trefor West, surely one of the greatest chub and barbel anglers who has ever lived. The debt I owe Trefor, in the understanding of my chub fishing, but above all in friendship, is incalculable. Then there is Merv Wilkinson, the first man to join me in the Coventry Specimen Group in the sixties, and still a great angler. It was Merv's guidance in those early days that enabled the rest of the group to develop into the anglers we are today. Two other members were Phil Smith and Mick Nicholls. Rarely do we hear of Mick's catches, as he prefers to keep a low profile, but those of us who know him well recognize him as an angler of outstanding natural ability. Phil Smith, of course, needs little introduction, in his present position as Chairman of NASA (National Association of Specialist Anglers).

Countless enthralling chubbing days have been spent in the company of Dave Plummer, and once again I take the opportunity of expressing my gratitude to him and to Linda for so often converting their comfortable lounge into a bedroom for me.

Another angler of truly outstanding ability, and now firm friend, is Bob James, a man whose ability to produce fish for the cameras is almost magical. To Bob I extend my gratitude for the opportunity of wonderful fishing on the Longford estate waters of the Avon.

Then there is that great thinking angler Stef Horak. Many hours have been spent discussing chub tactics with Stef, particularly on the Southern rivers, and his experiences and advice have led me to chub captures that I may not have achieved otherwise.

Another enormously gifted angler and now close friend is Matt Hayes, and to Matt I extend my warmest thanks for his assistance over the last season. The same applies to that richly talented angler from Stoke on Trent, Graham Marsden. Graham and I are now fishing together as often as possible and, as with Matt Hayes, I really relish his company.

In the last two seasons, I have made a firm friend of Matthew Bodily from Northampton, who is young enough to be my son, but who reminds me of myself at the same age. Matthew, your enthusiasm is infectious, and my chub and barbel fishing in your company carries an extra edge of enjoyment.

Another good friend is Marsh Pratley, now doing sterling work as Secretary of NASA. Start talking to Marsh about chub and his eyes glaze – the sign of a true believer.

There are many anglers of like mind to myself who have been firm friends for years and who have inspired me, yet we have rarely fished together. These would include Simon Lush, Chris Turnbull, Len Arbery and two men who have made many NASA conferences so enjoyable, Alf Tapley and Bob Karn.

Inspirational indeed is another man for whom I have special regard and to whom I give special thanks, Martin James. In every way Martin is outstanding, not least of all in the courage and bravery in the way he deals with multiple sclerosis. Spend some time in Martin's company and you will appreciate what a great ambassador for angling he really is.

I must also take this opportunity formally to thank Simon Roff of Metrocrest, who publish *Coarse Fisherman,* and the directors of Burlington Publishing, who published *Practical Coarse Fishing,* for permission to reproduce extracts of articles of mine that have appeared over the years.

I must also pay tribute to those in the tackle trade who now produce such outstanding equipment. They would include Bruce Vaughan of Wychwood Tackle, Simon Henton of Relum Ltd, Simon Bond of Shimano, Phil Hawker of Sharpes Rods, Martin Kowal of SBS baits, Terry Eustace of Gold Label, Dave Swallow of Ringwood Tackle, and all those connected with Leeda, Keenets, JRC and Fox International.

Lastly, I would like to thank John Bailey for his invaluable assistance in ensuring that this book became a reality.

In February 1995, my wife and I celebrated thirty years of marriage, and it is a matter of no small wonderment to me how Fran has tolerated my fishing over all those years with such remarkably good humour. She has been and still is the most wonderfully supportive wife any man could wish for and to her, yet again, I dedicate this book.

A 5lb 4oz fish caught at the end of the season.

INTRODUCTION

The first chub of my angling career came when I was fifteen, when I took two fish of a pound and a half each on float-fished cheese from the Warwickshire Leam. Those fish were the result of a lucky accident. Having left my maggots at home and having run out of worms, I was forced to cannibalize my cheese sandwiches!

Those chub had a profound effect on me, and they quickly established themselves among my favourite fish. During the next two years, I went on to catch many more from the Leam, never taking any of much over 3lb. And then 1961 saw me begin my fabulous relationship with the Claydon Brook, a delightful tributary of the Upper Great Ouse, only a few miles from Dick Walker's famous fishery at Beachampton.

During the sixties, the chub fishing was phenomenal. The average fish was over four pounds in weight, with several fives each season and three fish over six pounds. At the time of writing, I am still awaiting another six-pounder.

After my formation of the Coventry Specimen Group in 1967, and the beginning of my long association with anglers of the calibre of Trefor West, Mervyn Wilkinson, Phil Smith and Mick Nicholls, we all started to spread our wings in our searches for big chub. The next few years saw us take many great fish from several different rivers. The Cherwell, Upper Ouse and Dorset Stour became special favourites of Trefor and myself, and the seventies harbour so many fabulous chubbing memories it would take several books to do them all justice.

During this period, our home river, the Leam, had been neglected, as it had always been known for a large head of very average fish. But in the late seventies that all changed. For reasons that have never been clear, there was quite a sudden decline in the chub population, although the size of individual fish boomed. Most days saw me struggle for bites, two or three being the norm, but the fish were almost always over 4lb. When Trefor joined me, we were to enjoy a few years of tremendous Leam chubbing, with both of us taking five-pounders, culminating in my 5lb 10oz fish in the early eighties.

At about that time, another chapter in my chub career was commencing, with my introduction to the Wensum by that tremendous angler and great friend Dave Plummer. For the next decade, Trefor and I were regular visitors to Norfolk, fishing first for the chub and, during the latter years, the barbel. In that time, I had well over twenty Wensum five-pounders, strangely most of them on large meat baits intended for barbel. I will never forget one incredible winter when I took thirteen fives in this way, all on one-inch cubes of luncheon meat. Treasured memories indeed!

Thirty-six years have now passed since my first chub in 1959, years that have been good to me in that I have been privileged to land seventy-nine fish over the magical five pounds in weight. For the last thirty-two of those years, I have been attempting to beat a very special fish, a chub that remains my personal best by a very comfortable margin. Let me set the tone for this book by relaying a fresh account of my capture of this leviathan among chub, the thrill of which will only leave me on the day I die.

During the summer months of the sixties on the Claydon Brook, I used to divide my time between the big perch and chub the river contained. Invariably, I would fish hard for the perch at first light for a few hours and then, when the light intensity became too much and the perch went off the feed, I would switch to freeline chubbing with natural baits. On a never-to-be-forgotten day in June 1962, I arrived at a shallow glide between beds of dense rushes in late morning, a swim which always contained a number of chub. At that time, my biggest from the swim was just under five pounds although I had twice seen a fish that looked well over, perhaps five and a half. I was prepared with 6lb line, a size 4 and a big, black slug and, as I peered carefully over the rushes, I spotted a chub I could scarcely believe: in mid-river, barely five yards away, was a monstrous fish, possibly as much as seven pounds.

There was, however, to be no fairy tale ending. For several minutes, I had my heart in my mouth as the chub examined the bait from every angle. I felt it was only to be a matter of time, but fate intervened in the shape of a small pike that snatched the slug almost from under the chub's nose. After the jack had dashed round with great abandon, creating a level of disturbance that was completely disproportionate to its size, the chub had vanished. I was not to see it again that day.

There was to be a repeat performance in July, when a small chub beat the big one in a race for my double lobworm offering, but, in October, I was finally locked in combat with the fish of my dreams. I had found him in late afternoon, and he took my lobs without hesitation as soon as they hit the water. On feeling the hook, he rocketed across river, there to bury himself deep in the marginal rushes and settle down into an immovable sulk.

I was not unduly worried. The river was still low and clear, and so I went in after him. As I ploughed through the dense rush bed, freeing the line as I went, I was confident of success. The chub, however, had other ideas. When I was almost on top of him, he shot through the rushes again. This time, as the fish had obviously been completely tangled in the vegetation, and I was

The little road bridge from which I first spotted my 6lb 12oz chub in the early sixties.

now on a short line with very little stretch, the inevitable happened. There was a sickening crack, and the line broke.

After that experience, catching that big chub became a burning passion and every trip to the river was with the sole intention of achieving that end. Nearly a year passed and then, in August 1963, my persistence was rewarded. Just after dawn, I peeped over the parapet of the small road bridge, and spotted immediately six chub lying in a huddle over the gravel at the head of the run, where a dwarf willow gave some shade. In the middle of the group was the monster.

I must have watched those fish for an hour or more while I pondered my tactics. I knew the odds were stacked against me with five much smaller chub in attendance, and so I made the difficult decision to leave the fish in peace and look again later, when the big one might be alone or at least a little apart from the others. I had learned the lesson well from the previous season when a small chub had ruined my chances.

By early afternoon, I was in a state of barely contained excitement, as I confirmed that the big chub was still in position, but that now only one other fish was with him, and the two were quite well separated. I would not get a better opportunity than this so I flicked out double lobworm on a size 2 hook on 8lb line, aiming for the bait to settle a yard or so upstream of my quarry. When the bait landed, my heart sank. My nervous anticipation had led to a very tentative cast, such that the lobs fell well short of the intended area, alighting equidistant between the two chub. This time, however, fortune favoured me. Although both fish darted to intercept the worms, the big one won, and within seconds I was holding on grimly as the massive fish strained to gain sanctuary in some lilies to my left. Not for nothing, however, had I elected to use 8lb line, and I was determined to keep the fish out of snags at all costs. In that I was successful, and eventually the chub gave it up and tried for the opposite rush bed. Again, I was having none of that and soon, having applied intense pressure from the word go, I was able to haul my prize into the net. It was not pretty, but it was effective.

Real anglers will appreciate the overwhelming elation when that chub was heaved clear, tempered very slightly when I confirmed that the fish was in poor condition. It was obviously quite old, with several scales missing and an ugly scar on the tail root. In its prime, I reckon that chub had weighed well over seven pounds. As it was, it took my scales down to an immensely satisfying 6lb 12oz. I have never come close to a chub of that size since.

An early five-pounder from Claydon Brook. I even had hair then.

1 THE CHUB

IDENTIFICATION

Although there have been many cases of inexperienced anglers confusing chub with roach, and claiming monster roach captures as a result, there really is no excuse for this confusion. The large, black edged scales, large mouth adorned with distinctive white lips and the big, blunt head, hence the nickname 'loggerhead' make the chub, *Leuciscus cephalus*, one of the most instantly recognizable of all our coarse fish.

There are, however, two circumstances where mistakes are possible on the bank. The first is hybridization with other species. In truth, this is something I have never come across in more than thirty-five years of chubbing, but there have been cases of chub-roach hybrids reported by others. Apparently, these fish have so obviously been hybrids that all but the most inexperienced could not confuse them with true chub. If you are unsure, the chub has forty-two to forty-nine scales along the lateral line, and the anal fin has seven to nine branched rays, as has the dorsal.

The most common identification mistakes occur with immature chub, which can be confused with large dace. The give away here is that the anal fin of the chub is convex, unlike the markedly concave equivalent of the dace.

When spotting chub in the water, there are two mistakes that can be made by the most experienced anglers, specially if viewing conditions are poor. Even I, on a quick glance, have initially mistaken small common carp for big chub. A good look obviously soon corrects this error, the very distinctive long carp dorsal being unmistakable. In coastal areas, grey mullet are also very

The blunt head of the chub is unmistakable.

The white lips are like beacons to the chub hunter.

easily mistaken for chub, sharing with chub the same general appearance, colouring and white lips. I remember my first trip to Throop in 1961, casting baits to mullet for hours, thinking that they were chub, and wondering why I could not get a bite!

Chub occasionally exhibit a lack of the pigment melanin, which gives the black colouration of the tail, the black scale edges and the overall silvery grey body tone. Twice in my career, however, from the river Leam in Warwickshire, I have caught chub that had golden flanks, rich navy backs and fins that were crimson instead of the usual pale orange. They were undoubtedly true chub, all characteristics apart from colouration being perfect. I wish all chub were like that; they really were beautiful creatures.

BIG CHUB HISTORY

Until very recently, when the present record of 8lb 10oz was taken from the Tees by Peter Smith, the record was held by a fish of 8lb 4oz taken in December 1913, also by a Mr Smith, Mr G. F. Smith to be precise, who travelled from his home in Putney regularly to fish the Hampshire Avon at Christchurch, where the capture was made. The fish was caught on one of the old time favourite chub baits, pith, better known today as beef marrow. It is an interesting fact that in those days a local slaughter-house used to dump its unwanted offal in the river, obviously frowned

upon today. Naturally, this would include bone marrow, which the fish loved.

By a strange coincidence, the fish that held the record before the 8lb 4oz fish was taken by a third Mr Smith, this time Mr F. W. Smith, who landed a fish of 7lb 6½oz in 1906 from the famous Royalty. As well as that specimen there were other seven-pounders from the Avon: Mr E. J. Walker took fish of 7lb and 7lb 5oz, Dr Lewis-Smith one of 7lb 6oz, and of course the legendary Bill Warren had specimens of 7lb 3oz and 7lb 6oz. Bill's catches from the Royalty were stunning, and almost inconceivable today. Figures I have gleaned from my old friend and fellow chub fanatic Len Arbery show that in the 1953/54 season alone, Bill Warren took no fewer than 18 chub over 5lb in weight, and in his career recorded the staggering total of 234 five-pounders and 25 six-pounders, as well as the two sevens.

While in no way trying to minimize those achievements, it has to be said that the Avon, until the mid-sixties, was the most unbelievable chub river, with fish of remarkably high average weight. When I first fished the Royalty in 1967, the first signs of decline were becoming evident, but I remember a conversation I had with the late Peter Rayment about a catch of fish made in 1965 by his old friend Don Stockton. Trotting maggots, and feeding heavily all day with gallons of bait, he took a tremendous catch of big chub which included two six-pounders and six more over five.

A study of the top 50 chub list reveals that the Hampshire Avon has always figured highly, there being thirteen other fish listed between 7lb 4oz and 8lb 4oz. There are several highly suspect captures in that list, but one fish that is well documented is the 7lb 4oz capture in 1913 by Trent maestro F. W. K. Wallis who had, ten years earlier, had a fish only two ounces lighter from the Trent itself. Another totally authenticated fish is the magnificent 7lb 8oz capture of Roger Newman from the Avon at Fordingbridge, taken on trotted breadflake, which was weighed and witnessed by Len Arbery. Away from the Avon, many rivers have figured in reports of giant chub, the most famous of which has to be the reputed

10lb 8oz Annan capture of Dr Cameron. There seems little doubt among those who have investigated this claim that the weight of the fish is extremely doubtful. However, there is no doubt that the Annan contains big chub. Other rivers that have yielded apparently genuine 7lb-plus specimens in the past are the Thames, Trent, Wye, Ribble, Yorkshire Ouse, Swale, Derwent and Ure, Wensum, Waveney, Severn, Welland, Dorset Stour, Kennet, Wissey, Medway and Upper Great Ouse. Reported seven-pounders I have more doubts over are fish from the Cherwell, Sussex Arun, Yorkshire Hull, Surrey Wey and Windrush. I am not saying these were not genuine, just that I have seen no evidence supporting them.

The writings of Richard Walker, of course, confirmed what a superb chub river the Upper Great Ouse was, and include reports of big fish either caught, seen or found dead. Two reports of the latter are the freshly dead fish of 8lb 2oz from Dick's own stretch at Beachampton and an estimated ten-pounder at Offord. This was apparently too rotten to weigh, but at 27in (67.5cm) in length had obviously been a colossal chub in its day. Dick himself told me of a chub he had lost on crayfish which he put at possibly as big as nine pounds, and I believe my own 6lb 12oz best, from an Ouse tributary only three miles from Dick's fishery, had weighed well over seven pounds in its prime. When I caught it, it was obviously seriously in decline, but was still a mightily impressive specimen even then. Apart from that fish, I remember seeing two chub in a shallow mill race one close season. They were both exceptional, but I would put a year's salary on the bigger of the two exceeding eight pounds. That was in the early sixties.

In more modern times, of course, the big chub scene has witnessed the increasing influence of stillwaters, particularly gravel pits. The first personal experience I had of these was in the early seventies at Hardwick in Oxfordshire, a water I fished extensively for pike at the time. Trefor and I frequently saw big chub cruising on the surface some way out, but never conducted a campaign to catch one. An occasional accidental capture

came to pike baits, and although the two chub I caught were only three-pounders, I witnessed a fish one day of 6lb 7oz, taken on a sprat. I also saw a photograph of a huge chub taken on a live-bait in the close season, by one of the caravan owners, fishing from a boat. The reported weight was 9lb 7oz, and although there is no way of substantiating that, the photograph showed very clearly a massive chub.

Taken quite deliberately from the same water, on sardine, by living angling legend Peter Stone, was a superb and well-deserved fish of 7lb 4oz, in 1982. At about the same time, seven-pounders were also taken by Kevin Pimm and Phil Tew, to be followed a few years later, from another Oxford pit, by a fish of 7lb 7oz captured by Rolf Wobbeking. Peter Stone, and others who fish these pits extensively, tell me that they have spotted fish they feel are into double figures.

RIVER CHUBBING TODAY

It was not that many years ago that a six-pound river chub was one of the rarest and most difficult of all specimens to catch. Certainly, throughout most of the eighties, big river chub were in decline and above a ceiling of around 5lb 10oz, captures were very few and far between.

I remember an article I wrote at the time in which I said that I could see no possibility whatever of my ever beating my 6lb 12oz personal best, taken in 1964.

In the last few years, however, something dramatic and very sudden has happened to push up average chub weights substantially. Two or three rivers with which I am familiar have seen the average chub over a pound heavier now than a few years ago, and the number of six-pounders being caught today is quite mind blowing. Many captures are not being reported to the angling press, and I have privileged information of three catches I know to be genuine and which demonstrate quite how exciting the prospects are. As I wish to protect the anonymity of the anglers concerned, I shall only give the briefest details. The catches were: nineteen fish over 5lb 8oz from December

My biggest Leam chub, an immaculate, stocky 5lb 10oz.

to March, including three six-pounders to 6lb 10oz; a catch of twenty-four chub, including seven fives and two sixes in a single weekend; and, most mind boggling of all, three fish on consecutive casts on flake, which weighed 6lb 2oz, 6lb 4oz and 6lb 9oz respectively. Those are obviously quite mouth-watering statistics.

Even more exciting is the fact that this upsurge in chub weights is not confined to one or two rivers but seems to hold true generally across the country. The Hampshire Avon, ignored by chub men, including myself, for many years, is now throwing up an incredible number of sixes and has produced at least two genuine sevens in the last three years. The same goes for the Dorset Stour. The Great Ouse, for many years merely a shadow of its former glory, is again producing six-pounders, with one fish I know of weighing an ounce under seven. Then there are the rivers Waveney and Wensum in Norfolk, both of which have produced sixes and one seven in the last two years, and the Yorkshire rivers Ouse and Swale. Who could have failed to note the incredible string of big Swale fish? In the Midlands, the Warwickshire Avon produced a 6lb 10oz fish last winter, and the Cherwell two chub of six and a

quarter. On one stretch of the Cherwell I know very well, I have fished for years and the biggest chub I have ever managed is 4lb 14oz. During the final fortnight of last season, eight different fives came out, all in pristine condition and as fat as butter. The biggest, at 5lb 14oz, should have weighed about three and a half pounds on any weight-for-length measure but its girth was truly amazing. So, what exactly has happened and what does it all mean for our chubbing over the next few seasons?

Recognizing the fact that it is not just isolated fish we are talking about, but many big fish of high average weight, I believe there are two factors to take into account. Firstly, as the growing period of most cyprinids is thirteen to fourteen years, when they reach their maximum skeletal size, many of the young, short and fat chub now being taken are probably progeny of the tremendous 1976 spawning year having come to maturity in 1989 and 1990. Secondly, that would coincide with exceptionally mild winters, giving the fish opportunity for uninterrupted feeding, during which they would obviously pack on weight.

Once a chub, or any other cyprinid for that matter, has reached its maximum skeletal size, its

Dave South with a magnificent 6lb 4oz Cherwell fish.

weight then varies about a mean in response to changing climatic factors and associated feeding opportunities. This is commonly known as weight freewheeling and in certain circumstances weight changes can be very dramatic, as they can in humans. The current situation is extremely exciting for the specimen hunter because many of the current crop of five- and six-pound chub are short, fat fish, individuals that would weigh perhaps three and a half to four and a half pounds normally. They are the fish of average skeletal size and it takes little imagination to realize the potential of one of today's chub which has a much larger body shell than average. In any group of fish there will be the odd individual who grows more rapidly than the others, and it is these that were the rare six-pounders of a few years ago. Those same individuals could now be the rare seven- and even eight-pounders of today. I said earlier that the average big fish at the moment seems to be short and fat. When someone catches one that is both long and fat we could see a new record.

2 TACKLE AND EQUIPMENT

The first general point to make before going into the specifics of this section is that there is an enormous amount of excellent tackle these days from which the chub angler can choose. All I can do is tell you what I have found satisfactory and have no hesitation in recommending.

RODS

For the past three seasons, I have been using rods exclusively from my own Supreme range, marketed by J. Weaver & Son, under the Sharpes Scottie Rods banner.

For my summer freelining, I use the Barbel Supreme, which is an 11ft through action rod of about 1¼lb test curve, and with sufficient power to deal with a very big chub in a snaggy situation. This rod is equipped with a threaded tip ring to take a screw-in betalight if necessary.

For trotting, summer or winter, I use my three-piece 13ft Specimen Float rod, but I have to say that the bulk of my winter chubbing is carried out with my Quiver Supreme, the lighter version of the barbel rod with spliced-in quivertip. The medium-strength quiver allows sensitive downstream bite indication as well as giving a good deflection in an upstreaming situation. The quivertip is fitted with a sleeve which acts both as a sight bob and as a holder for a Drennan mini night light for after-dark fishing. Those night lights really are the business for night fishing, especially if, like me, you have dodgy eyesight and need glasses for fishing.

There is a multitude of good rods from which to choose, and the choice always must come down to personal preference, what you feel most comfortable with, the type of chubbing you will be doing and, not least, the price you can afford to pay, as carbon rods are not cheap these days. As a general rule, a through action rod of about a pound test curve will handle the majority of chub you come across. If, like me, your chubbing is geared more towards bigger than average fish from snaggy waters, you will occasionally require something stronger.

For fun chubbing with light gear, perhaps for average fish or in snag-free water, I often use a delightful quiver rod, the Shimano Aero Quivertip. The overall test curve rating is around 14oz, and the rod is equipped with three push-on quivertips, with tip ratings of ¾oz, 1oz and 1½oz. This gives the rod tremendous versatility to cope with most situations.

REELS

For approaching twenty years, all my chub fishing has been carried out using Cardinal 54 reels, and they really are superb. Sadly, of the three in my possession, only one still has its original clutch mechanism. This reel is now used solely for my barbel fishing and it will be a sad day when that, too, has to be retired.

Although the other two reels have been reconditioned and are generally in good working order, the clutches are not as silky smooth as they were originally. I understand that one metal component is now unavailable and has been replaced with a plastic one. The result is that there is not the fine adjustment available that is necessary if you fish off a correctly set clutch, and often in snaggy water. If a clutch does not have your total confidence, it is useless and you are better off backwinding.

The truly superb Shimano 4010.

When I reluctantly came to the conclusion that my trusty old Cardinal 54 reels were getting a bit long in the tooth, I was very careful when choosing replacements. I had heard terrific reports of the Shimano 4010, but my first reaction to the double handle was that it looked likely to prove a little clumsy, especially when fishing in the dark. My fears were proved totally unfounded: the double handle dyna balance system is in fact a delight to use, giving a silky smooth retrieve, totally vibration free. Casting is also super smooth, courtesy of the tapered spools and the two-speed crosswind line lay system. I also appreciated the two spare spools provided with each reel. Like all Shimano reels, the overall finish of the product is excellent and very robust, promising years of trouble-free service.

The GTM 4010 is fitted with Shimano's fighting drag system, which is basically a two-stage clutch tension. This will be of no interest to anglers who never use the clutch and rely on back-winding, however, and in this case it would be pointless purchasing this particular feature.

For those who, like me, play big chub off the clutch, the system is excellent and the clutch super sensitive and very smooth indeed. The fighting drag system has many devotees, but I prefer to use the normal drag pre-set at the tension I require, and then control the fight by finger pressure on the spool. I would stress, however, that this is a personal quirk of mine based on thirty years' experience of playing fish this way, and is in no way a criticism of the 'fighting drag' system.

All in all, the Shimano GTM 4010 exhibits the high quality we have come to expect from Shimano, and fulfils all the promises made by the manufacturers. It is a pleasure to use.

Also from Shimano is the Stradic 2000, which I use in conjunction with the Aero Quivertip rod.

It is a very light, well-balanced reel and has the most delightful clutch.

For float fishing, which I am doing much more of these days, I use both fixed spools and centrepins. For general float fishing work, say laying on, a lovely reel to use is the Quantum SX4 from Leeda. It is silky smooth, and perfect for effortless casting of light float tackle. For the technically minded, I am told that the bihelical line wrapping feature of the reel minimizes friction for casting ease. For trotting work, I prefer the centrepin, but as I am not an expert at the art I always carry a closed-face fixed spool if strong winds make conditions difficult. I have little knowledge of closed-face reels generally, but Dave Plummer recommended a Daiwa 125M several years ago and I have had no cause to regret that advice.

When I decided to get into centrepin trotting for chub, I took advice from two men who are well versed in the art, Bob James and Dave Swallow. Dave manufactures superb centrepins and I have a matched pair equipped with audible checks. This ensures that I can use the reels both for their intended use in trotting and for static fishing with bolt rigs and boilies, which I am now doing more often for very big chub work. The check provides an unmistakable bite alarm.

One of the problems with using a centrepin for trotting is the tendency for lighter lines to bed in, and to prevent this it is important to resist the temptation to overload the spool. The maximum efficient range of trotting I suppose is in the range of about 60yds (54m), so there is little point in having much more than sixty yards of line on the spool. The less line on the spool and the wider the drum, the less bedding in will be a problem and the sweeter the reel will perform.

NETS

It should go without saying that whatever your choice in landing nets and, if you use them, keep nets, they should be constructed of the softest material available so as to prevent damage to the chub. I can do no better than recommend the superb products marketed by Keenets. There is a large choice of landing nets to suit every taste, but the two I use are the big mesh Mega Spoon and, when I am on a barbel river and wish to hedge my bets, the triangular Carp Mix Big Fish Net, which features a duplex mesh, allowing for easy draining generally but with a finer bottom mesh so that the end rig does not fall through too

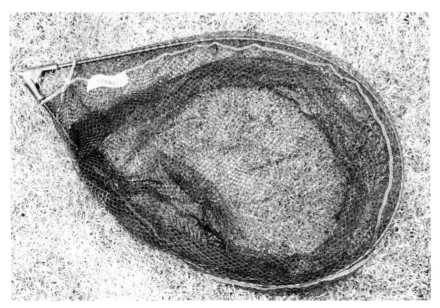

My favourite chub net, the Keenets Mega Spoon.

easily. This net is available in three sizes, but mine is the version with 36in (90cm) arms.

As far as landing net handles are concerned I would recommend a telescopic version, as you are bound to be faced with the high bank or wide rush margin eventually. I use the Keenets carbon telescopic which extends to 10ft. Coupled with the lightweight Mega Spoon frame, the whole landing net is simple to wield single-handed. Heed one word of warning, though, with carbon telescopic handles. Although light and strong, they do not take kindly to being trodden on. So watch where you are putting your feet.

Although I never use keep nets myself, I have no problems with those anglers who do wish to use them, so long as they are used responsibly.

SACKS, TUBES AND WEIGH SLINGS

These days, most specialist anglers will retain a fish they wish to photograph in a carp sack, and here there are some excellent products available. I cannot fault the sacks and slings marketed by Relum, Wychwood and Drennan, and I use products of all three suppliers.

Most useful in mobile fishing like chubbing are the sack/weigh sling combinations and all three of the suppliers mentioned produce first-class versions. They are compact and soft enough to stuff into small spaces in seat boxes or rucksacks, and I generally have at least four with me on most

trips. I also always have handy a couple of old guy ropes and bivvy pegs, to ensure a fish can be retained in sufficiently deep water.

I never keep more than one fish in each sack, but where you may wish to retain several fish, the ET pike tube, marketed by Relum, doubles up as a superb horizontal keep sack for several chub. There is a version with a zip top for ease of access. This was designed by Eddy Turner with pike retention over the side of a boat in mind, but is ideal for chubbing applications. The principle is identical to the Queenford Retention System, designed for the safe retention of giant bream and marketed by Bob Church.

HOOKS

For my heavier chubbing with big hooks, almost all my fishing is carried out with Au Lion d'Or, pattern 1534, which I have now been using for over twenty-five years. These were first recommended to me for my carping by Jim Gibbinson in the late sixties. In all that time, I have only ever known two to break and have never had one open up on a fish. You must obtain the heavy forged hooks, however, in the red packets. The manufacturers do produce a lighter wire version, and these are much weaker. For the bulk of my chubbing, I use a size 6, but will revert to a 4 for meat after dark or for fishing large naturals in summer.

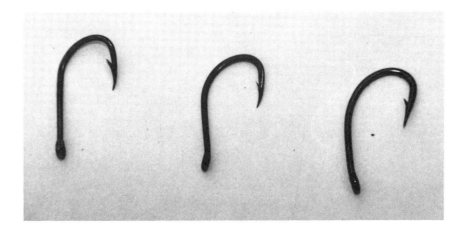

My three favourite large chub hooks: left (straight eye), Au Lion d'Or, middle, Drennan Boilie and right Gold Label Penetrator.

Drennan Carbon Specimen Hooks, my favourite small pattern.

Although I am a firm fan of Au Lion d'Or, I have used Drennan boilie hooks in the large sizes and Terry Eustace Gold Label Penetrators. Both of those patterns are also superb.

Strangely enough, I do not use Au Lion d'Or in the smaller sizes, as in my experience these have shown a tendency to open. For fishing with sizes 10 to 14, both Drennan Carbon Specimen and Drennan Starpoint hooks are superb. Where I want to fish finer than normal, say for feeder fishing for educated chub, possibly at Throop or certain stretches of the Avon, Drennan Super Spades give a brilliant presentation. Two top-class Avon anglers, Pete Reading and Stef Horak, who have caught many great chub between them, swear by Drennan ready-tied Super Spades to nylon, in sizes as small as 20 in feeder-fishing application.

LINES

I am very conservative with main lines for my fishing, being a great believer in the adage that you should stick with something if it does not let you down. For this reason, I have always had total faith in Maxima, or latterly the Peter Drennan equivalent, Drennan Specimen Plus. This line has stood the test of time. If it has a fault, it is that it is a little more springy than some of its competitors, and these days, if I am using a monofilament hooklink, I tend to opt for Berkley Trilene XL, which is very soft and limp. For very snaggy fishing, although Maxima and Specimen Plus are pretty abrasion resistant, they can chafe, leading to unexpected breakage. For this application, perhaps a better bet is Berkley Trilene XT, which is a tough brute of a line. At the time of writing, I have recently taken five double-figure barbel from under dense tree roots on XT, which entailed much heaving and hauling through the snags, after which the line appeared as good as new.

I have no time for pre-stretched lines for my chubbing, and this is more to do with me than with the lines themselves. Playing fish from the clutch, and being naturally a little heavy handed, my angling style and lines with low shock resistance simply are not compatible!

Trefor summed it up very succinctly on the Cherwell several years ago, when we were trying

All my chubbing is carried out using these lines.

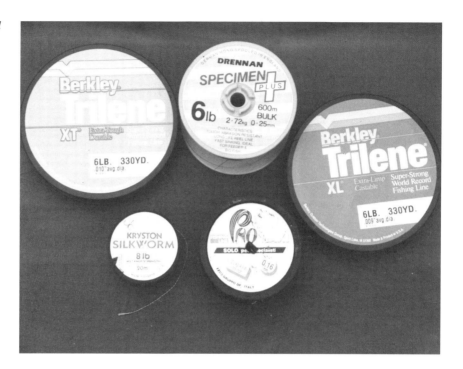

out Drennan Double Strength for our chubbing (a line incidentally which is excellent in the correct application). Trefor said that the way we fished for chub, we were in danger of getting smashed up tying the hook on!

HOOKLINK MATERIALS

For most of my chubbing with heavier gear I now use soft braided hooklinks, although I have to say that I am not convinced whether it really makes

Relum's innovative lead-cored braid from Rod Hutchinson.

that much difference. Good braids I have faith in are Kryston Silkworm, Drennan Carp Silk and Rod Hutchinson's The Edge, which is now marketed through Relum.

If you are fishing in woody snags, all braids can have a problem if the fibres are continually picked at by wood splinters, progressively weakening the material. I lost a good barbel in flood water for this reason last winter. In these situations, I revert to monofilament or Drennan solid black Dacron.

Although not strictly a hooklink, I am very impressed with another product from Relum, Rod Hutchinson's Edge Plus, which is a braid with a fine lead core. This is mainly for summer applications, using several feet of the product above the hooklink itself. This ensures that the main line is nailed to the riverbed in the critical area, thereby eliminating the problem of line bites.

SEATS AND SEAT BOXES

For the past two seasons, I have been using my JRC XL Supreme Low Chair for my longer chub sessions. Even for a big, heavy individual like me, the chair is the ultimate in comfort, being fully sprung and featuring high density foam inserts for total cushioning. As well as the general seat padding, the chair features generously padded head, leg and arm supports, to prevent the metal frame causing any discomfort.

For ease of transport, the chair features legs that fold flat and it is surprisingly light for such a strong product. All four legs are completely adjustable for coping with uneven banks, each being fitted with a non-slip rubber boot. The adjustment of each leg is also much easier than on some earlier products, important on those raw

The extremely comfortable chair from JRC.

winter days when tight, push-spring stops can be such a trial with numb fingers. With the JRC chair, extending the leg is simply a case of pulling the leg shaft to the required position. Friction locking then keeps it in place. Contracting the leg at the end of the session requires a quick flick on a spring release lever and the leg slides back into position.

One thing that is important with all low chairs is preventing the feet sinking into very soft mud, of which we find a lot in a typical English winter. The JRC chair, and its main rival the equally good Fox Ultra, both feature anti-sink wide feet, which work well most of the time. For those occasions, however, when the banks are very soft, I carry four old carpet tiles to place under the feet, which work like a dream.

For very mobile winter chubbing, where I can be moving swims every fifteen minutes throughout the day, I use a seat box rather than a chair to cut down the amount of gear. Comfort is now of secondary importance since I am not set in one place long enough to get stiff. There are many basic seat boxes on the market which do the job well enough at a reasonable price, but if you want the best seat in combination with a rucksack, look no further than the Fox Ruckbox. One of the drawbacks with many boxes is having to get up when you want something from the interior. With the Fox Ruckbox, exterior pockets for tackle items, sandwiches and so on, make access much quicker, as well as giving extra capacity without sacrificing portability.

For those short, summer chubbing sessions, where I am on the move constantly with natural baits or floaters, and carrying the absolute minimum of gear, I can recommend the Relum Fishing Seat/Rucksack, which features a small folding stool with a small rucksack attached. This bit of kit is ideal for the two- or three-hour session, where all you want is a small Stewart box for the disposable tackle items, and a few assorted baits.

RUCKSACKS AND OTHER LUGGAGE

For the specialist angler, one of the very best sources of top-quality luggage is undoubtedly Wychwood, run by Bruce Vaughan, himself a chub angler of no mean ability. For my chubbing, I use two Wychwood rucksacks, the Ruckman for all those sessions where I carry a separate chair, and the Stalker where I am moving about with naturals or wading and fishing floaters.

One tackle item I never use when chubbing is a holdall. I take all the ancillary items such as bank sticks, landing net, umbrella, camera tripod, and so on in a rod quiver. Again, the very top quality is available from Wychwood, and I use the K2 carp quiver. For ease of transporting rods, two made-up rods can be clipped to the side of the Quiver, the tips being protected by a special sleeve. Relum also supply a really superb quiver in their Rod Hutchinson range, with all the same features of the Wychwood version.

UMBRELLAS AND SHELTERS

For most of my chub fishing, summer or winter, I dispense with an umbrella, as it is an encumbrance for essentially mobile techniques. I rely instead on proper protective clothing to keep me warm and dry whatever the elements may throw at me. However, if I am employing more static methods, say building up a long winter glide or fishing for big fish with boilies on a sluggish stretch, I will then go fishing with my own personal comfort more in mind. Obviously, by fishing more statically, you are more likely to feel the chill, especially at night, and then angling efficiency suffers. Until this season, a normal umbrella provided the shelter, and it still does if I am fishing on a very sloping bank. However, where the banks are even, a far better proposition, and far lighter to transport, is a small pop-up bivvy. I am now using an absolutely superb product, the Day Broddie from Relum. It pops up as fast as you can erect an umbrella, you knock in a few pegs and you are all set. All the gear can be kept nice and dry, and you can sit in the doorway out of the worst elements the English winter can throw at you. Some of my more static chubbing is for very big fish after dark in the winter from slower stretches, which can be a waiting game. The

Relum Broddie ensures that I can fish all night if needs be in maximum comfort, but, being so easily and quickly erected and dismantled, it need be no bar to moving swims if necessary.

PROTECTIVE CLOTHING

For the bulk of my angling life I was a committed advocate of Barbour clothing. However, good as Barbour products undoubtedly still are, waxed cotton has now been superseded by superior products for angling use. The best equipment these days is far lighter, certainly far more flexible, and, most important, more waterproof.

Clothing for angling is an area where you can still be caught out with inferior products if you are not careful, particularly with regard to their water resistance. Much of the gear on the market, some of it with well-known names and at high prices, is little more than shower proof. I have been into this topic in some depth over the last few years, and I can unreservedly recommend two companies for offering angling clothing of the very best quality. Once again, those companies are Wychwood and Relum.

Wychwood market a whole range of suits, jackets and trousers in their Aquatex material, and my choice is for the bib and brace coupled with the three-quarter jacket. This gives complete versatility, whatever the weather conditions. The jacket is hooded, the hood being zipped and detachable. I recommend buying these items at least one size too big, to allow for wearing a one-piece thermal suit underneath in the depths of winter. Also from Wychwood, I have the multi-pocketed waistcoat for summer fishing mobility.

Of similar excellent quality is Rod Hutchinson's Ambience clothing, featuring waterproof Membratex, marketed by Relum. The range of options is very similar to Wychwood, but again my choice is the three-quarter jacket plus bib and brace. One interesting feature of the Ambience three-quarter jacket is that you can buy a separate zip-out quilted jacket, which can either be worn independently or as a thermal lining. The winter cold and damp are more likely to get at you via the head, hands and feet. In my van at all times is a selection of headgear, depending on weather conditions. I have two wide-brimmed trilby hats, one totally waterproof, but both equipped with chin straps to stop them flying away in a strong wind. If I want to wear a hat under my hood in very wet weather, but still retain a brim to keep rain off my glasses, I revert to either a Barbour-style narrow brimmed trilby or, better still, a baseball-type cap with a deep brim. For those very cold days, a selection of woolly hats and a heavy balaclava complete the arsenal.

I detest wearing gloves for mobile fishing, but when I am forced to I use a pair of Relum neoprene waterproof angler's gloves, with the top end of the thumb and first finger missing.

As far as footwear is concerned, the variety of weather, water and temperature conditions demand a selection of alternatives for maximum efficiency and comfort. My van contains a pair of moonboots with separate linings, a pair of Derri-boots, a pair of thigh waders, a pair of thermal thigh waders, and a pair of chest waders. Several spare pairs of socks, some thermal, are always on hand, as are a couple of towels. Wet or cold feet spell the end of a serious fishing session for me.

ODDS AND ENDS

Apart from the major tackle items, my chubbing equipment will contain a multitude of other items, many of which will be in small containers in my pockets. The list will include the following:

1. Range of leads from $\frac{1}{4}$oz to 2oz, at least two of each size
2. Container of split shot
3. Heavy metal putty
4. Two packets of Drennan mini night lights
5. Two screw-in beta light adaptors
6. Different strength screw-in Drennan quivertips
7. Snap links
8. Rod Hutchinson loop-eyed swivels
9. Rig beads
10. Hair rig needle and Drennan hair rig dumbell stops

Drennan mini night-lights. Small enough for a quivertip, yet very bright indeed.

11. Silicon tubing for making semi-fixed bolt rigs
12. Scissors
13. Forceps
14. Small container of poly-pops
15. Bob Jones flotsam for floating baits
16. Line grease or silicone floatant
17. Small bottle washing-up liquid for degreasing
18. Superglue
19. Leger stops
20. Float stops
21. Rod Hutchinson Phantasm PVA string and PVA tubes
22. Hook-sharpening stone
23. Small wallet with spare hooklinks
24. Head lamp torch, plus spare batteries and bulbs
25. Cable release and air bulb for self portraits
26. Small roll of insulating tape
27. Few assorted rubber bands
28. Half a dozen swimfeeders
29. Drennan floats
30. Screw-in scythe blade
31. Small, sharp knife
32. Small spool of light line for making hair rigs
33. Two bait droppers
34. Thermometer with lanyard
35. Small notepad and pencil

36. Two Wychwood Reddicat catapults, one for loose feed, one for bait items
37. Waterproof wallet containing rod licence/club books
38. Avon scales
39. Small hand towel
40. Spool of Power Gum
41. Syringe for air-injecting lobs
42. Bob Jones counterbalance

As well as all of the above, plus possibly a few other bits and pieces I have not brought to mind, I also carry at all times my camera and filters. Even if I were not an angling writer, this would always be an essential part of my kit, as I derive much enjoyment from going through my slides at home. The camera I use is a Canon EOS 100, which is fully automatic including auto focus, essential for me now that I have impaired vision in one eye. My filter bag contains a selection of Cokin filters for that special shot, and the bag will also include spare films and batteries for the camera, plus the tripod camera adaptor.

Also at the bottom of my bag or seat box is a small emergency kit, containing plasters, a bandage and paracetamol. Two or three times, that kit has been welcomed by friends. Lastly, and a sign of the times, I now always carry my mobile phone. Three times that has got me out of a mess, when I had car trouble miles off the beaten track.

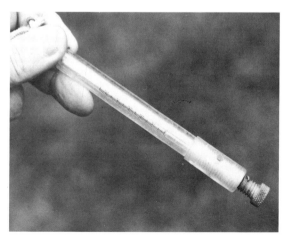

My thermometer is essential equipment. I would feel naked going fishing without one.

3 BAITS AND GROUNDBAITS

Without a doubt, there are few things edible that chub will not eat with relish. The list of baits for chub, summer and winter alike, is, therefore, almost limitless.

NATURAL BAITS

During the summer months, some of the most effective fishing can be carried out with simple freelining, using heavy natural baits. Natural bait fishing is mobile for the most part, moving from swim to swim on the look out for new targets, and is undoubtedly my favourite form of summer chubbing.

Crayfish

I have been guilty in the past of writing about chubbing with crayfish. Along with Trefor West, I had many exciting years and hundreds of good chub on these freshwater crustacea. However, this is one instance where I have to implore readers to ignore this particular advice from now on. In the last few years, there has been a catastrophic decline in the population of native 'crays'. Because of stockings with larger North American signal crays, which have carried a disease to which they are immune but which is lethal to our native stocks, British crayfish are virtually extinct on many waters. Those that have survived do not need anglers further decimating stocks. In

It would take a good chub to tackle this full-grown signal crayfish.

Freelined crayfish plotted this four-pounder's downfall.

fact, it is now a criminal offence to take native crayfish, as they are a protected species.

I can see nothing wrong with using immature signal crays as chub bait, and they are easily recognizable by the reddish tints on their bodies and claws. Native crays are almost all dark brown or black with dirty white undersides.

I have accidentally caught fully adult signal crays on the Ouse weighing as much as a pound and fully nine inches long. If you want to use one of those for chub bait, good luck to you. One thing is for sure, if a chub ever does take one it is going to be a hell of a fish! These days, therefore, the only time I would ever use a crayfish on a hook is if I catch an immature signal accidentally. That would be fished on a weightless line, using a size 4 hook, hooking the crustacean through the third tail segment. The bait is fished on the move constantly, as I fish slugs, casting at individual fish and then using line movements to simulate the natural swimming action of the bait.

There is a school of thought that the dramatic weight increase of Kennet chub over the last few years may be due in part to the upsurge in the signal crayfish population. It may be that the chub are taking advantage of the signal baby boom!

Slugs

Now that I can longer use crayfish for my summer chubbing, my favourite natural, without a doubt, is the slug, and the bigger and blacker the better. The only problem with slugs is that they can be very uncertain in supply and, once obtained, are difficult to keep fresh for long. It is best if you can collect them the evening before going fishing, or, better still, at dawn on the day itself. On a nice dewy morning, you will discover loads of juicy slugs in the dampness of the bankside vegetation, especially around the roots of rushes and burdocks. The only thing about collecting slugs that gives me the horrors is actually touching the things. Most things I can handle

A big, black, juicy slug, the premier summer chub bait.

This chub is probably regretting tackling that slug.

with my bare hands without the slightest problem but I am happy to make an exception for slugs. I use a pair of old sugar tongs to pick up the slimy beasts! Keep them in a large bait box, with plenty of room, and plenty of damp greenstuff. Wet lettuce leaves are absolutely ideal. You must keep the bait box cool and out of the sun at all times, or you will have a very unpleasant mess on your hands, believe me!

Slugs are best fished on the move. If a chub is spotted lying in a little clearing, I will land a slug with a good loud plop about a yard upstream of his head, taking care not to show myself. A fish that has not been spooked will generally be on to the bait immediately. If, however, the fish ignores it but shows no signs of being alarmed, try inducing a bite. When the slug has settled, allow it to lie still for a short while and then jerk it upstream a few inches. If it makes a puff of silt rise, so much the better. Chub can rarely resist such movements and the reaction can be savage in the extreme. Do not keep the line too taut after you have moved the bait, or you could be broken on the bite!

Lobworms, Redworms and Brandlings
The lobworm is one of the most universally effective baits for most species, and yet surprisingly few anglers seem to use them these days. As a

chub bait, the humble lob has few equals. As a natural bait in the summer months, it can be free-lined and fished on the move in exactly the same way as the slug. Because the lob is a less dense bait, I often fish two or even three full-sized lobs on a large hook for this fishing. Chub find these 'octopus' offerings irresistible. Unlike slugs, which I have found poor for static chubbing, lobs are an excellent choice in the summer where you wish to present a static or ambush bait. The bait's attractiveness can be further enhanced by injecting a little air into the tail, making them waver off bottom enticingly. If doing this, however, be careful not to inject yourself with air. An air

Injecting a lob with air. Do NOT do this in your fingers.

A Cherwell five-pounder to freelined lobworm.

embolism in the bloodstream can be fatal, and there is also the risk of other infection from the dirty needle. I always hold the lob firmly with forceps and inject it on the top of a bait box, having my hands nowhere near the syringe, just in case.

In the winter months, of course, especially in coloured water or flood conditions, lobs are the most valuable baits of them all. Collecting lobworms is simplicity itself, although it can lead to a backache you will not forget quickly. Choose a mild night after steady rain, preferably with little wind, and go to some close-cropped grass no earlier than about two hours after dark. Use a torch as dim as possible and wear soft-soled shoes. If you have waited long enough, you will see many worms lying completely out of their holes, ready for the night-time mating ritual, and many more half in and half out. Grip the worm's body adjacent to where it leaves its hole and pull gently. Do not snatch the worm or you will break it. Broken

worms do not survive long in a bait box or wormery, and if you intend keeping a supply for long, a dead worm will lead to the rest of the stock also dying quickly.

There have been many media recommended for keeping lobworms, but these days I simply use ordinary garden soil, kept moist but not soaking. Every few days, I place vegetable waste on the soil, and cover with some old, damp sacking. So long as you do not make the mistake of overcrowding, and so long as the container is kept cool and damp, worms will keep in good condition for months.

Redworms are another excellent chub bait, although I find myself using them less and less these days. Where they do score is as a change bait on a smaller hook when feeder fishing with maggots. In the same situation, they are excellent fished as cocktail baits with maggots or casters. The best place to obtain redworms is by digging in mature compost heaps, where you find them by the thousand.

I have little to say about brandlings, except that I do not use them for any of my fishing. As well as being unpleasant to use, as they exude a nasty yellow juice that irritates the fingers, they are also vastly inferior to other worms.

Small Fish

Small fish are excellent baits for summer chubbing, especially minnows, loach and bullheads.

When using tiny fish as chub baits, they can either be legered, pinching a large shot about a foot from the hook, or fished under a balsa float. A presentation I like for this fishing is to trot minnows alongside a steep bank overhung with foliage or along the side walls of weirs. I have had loads of good summer chub fishing in this manner as well as a satisfying number of big bonus perch.

There are two methods to use for catching these small fish for bait. For minnows, the good old minnow trap still takes some beating. For this you want an old wine bottle of the type that has

a deeply concave bottom. Knock out this bottom recess, tie a piece of string around the neck, and you have your trap. Then bait the trap with bread and place the bottle on the shallows with the neck upstream. After a while, you will notice minnows entering the trap through the bottom recess, but they then have difficulty finding their way out again. When there are several minnows inside, remove the bottle and transfer the occupants to your bait bucket.

For catching fish such as loach and bullheads, the best method is similar to that I have written about in the past for catching crayfish. Search for the fish on stony shallows, ideally where there are about eighteen inches of steadily moving water to disperse disturbed silt quickly. As for crayfish, carefully search under the stones by lifting them in turn. Unlike with crays, however, you are a better man than I am if you can catch bullheads by hand. I use a small triangular net and place the long flat on the river bed downstream of the stone I am about to disturb. As it is lifted, the disturbed silt obviously washes downstream, and any loach

This chunky chub breakfasted on freelined minnow.

or bullhead in residence will dart downstream with it, hopefully straight into the waiting net mesh.

Where chubbing with small fish really comes into its own is in the very early season, just after spawning, when the fish are cleaning themselves on the gravel shallows, especially where there is a brisk flow. At this time of year, the chub are more predatory than usual, and trotting minnows under a stubby little chub float is a lethal method. I particularly like the run out from a weir, where chub will gather in their dozens after spawning. I have fond memories of some multiple chub catches from Thames weirs many years ago fishing in this manner.

Maggots and Casters

Chub are no different from the majority of coarse fish, in that maggots and casters are among the most lethally effective baits you can use, summer and winter. Much of their application will be in conjunction with the swimfeeder and Chapter 8 is devoted to feeder techniques.

During the summer months, however, maggots and casters are brilliant when fished as a mass bait, in the same way as hemp, presenting a bunch of them on a large hook. The swim to select is one with a gentle flow so the bait will not be dispersed far and wide. It is also vitally important to loose feed with a bait dropper. The feed needs to be concentrated on the gravel at the selected fishing position, and the dropper guarantees this. For maggot fishing, so great is their pulling power that I am content to use them alone, so long as I have sufficient quantity to achieve a level of preoccupation. I would generally want a minimum of half a gallon to fish this method most effectively.

If I am using casters, I would usually use them in conjunction with hemp, and fish them as I do any other particle bait. The only difference in approach would be that with some particles I severely restrict the number of free offerings in the hemp, whereas with casters I would use a pint for every four pints of hemp. Obviously mass baiting with casters alone would be effective, but the limitation to this approach is its cost.

A freelined cockle is a devastating summer bait.

Cockles, Prawns and Shrimps

I first caught good chub on prawns and shrimps over twenty-five years ago on the Claydon Brook, and these are undoubtedly a terrific bait. The problem with the baits, though, is that they are extremely fragile, as well as being expensive, and I always feel that slugs are a better option.

Keeping Koi first alerted me to how cyprinids love cockles. The fish fight over them and, in my first serious session on the Ouse last season, I caught numbers of chub, bream and barbel on them. I fish cockles in much the same way as I present particles, including one or two freebies in each dropper of hemp.

Chub attack cockles viciously, in the same way as they do a lot of natural baits, and some impressive pulls can result. It is unwise to fish them on light tackle. One word of warning, though, is to buy fresh, shelled cockles from a fish market. Do not buy them preserved or bottled, as they are kept in vinegar for human consumption. These are useless as angling baits.

ORTHODOX BAITS

Bread

The most universal of chub baits is bread, used in all its forms, plain or flavoured. My favourite is the tough crust off the outside of a farmhouse loaf. Buy a fresh loaf from a bakery and do not be put off by the crust initially being far too brittle for use as bait. While the loaf is still fresh,

This battle-scarred 4lb 15oz Leam chub accepted plain bread crust.

seal it in a polythene bag and a few hours later the brittleness will have gone and been replaced by crust so tough you have trouble tearing it off the loaf.

If you want to flavour a loaf, adopt the same procedure but before sealing the bag introduce a little of the selected flavour, then freeze the lot before going fishing. As the loaf is thawing in your car on the way to the river the thawing process sucks the flavour into the bread. When I am using flavoured crust on the hook I will usually flavour my mashed bread attractor similarly. I use a canvas bucket as a mashed bread container and once I have the correct consistency I then add the required amount of my selected flavour and give it a good stirring.

While the pre-packed white sliced bread is perfect for flake, its crust is totally useless for legering for chub. The 'crust', if it can be honoured with that description, is far too soft and crumbly. The only breadcrust suitable for the job has to be both tough and rubbery, so that it can be bent between the fingers for inserting a hook without cracking. It should also be able to withstand being bounced around in the current without continually dropping off the hook. For hook-baits, tear off a piece of this crust, with a good

This Leam four-pounder took simple breadcrust.

Avon maestro Bob James mixes his liquidized bread, grilled hemp feed.

chunk of flake attaching, and fold it in half with the crust itself on the outside. Pass the hook through one side of the crust and out the other. When the bread is then released, it springs open on the hook. Thus mounted, you will find that the bait withstands any amount of twitching through the swim.

Obviously, you need to use a hook balanced with the bait you wish to use. You are asking for trouble if you insist on mounting a ten pence-sized piece of breadcrust on a size 16. For that size of bait, I would normally choose a size 6 for chubbing.

As well as mashed bread for loose feeding, I also use handfuls of fresh, squeezed bread crumbs for keeping a swim primed. This is used when I assess that the fish will be feeding well, and actively looking for food. A ball of fresh, squeezed crumb disperses rapidly into an attractive cloud as soon as it hits the water. As it sinks, it breaks into a wide band, thereby increasing the attraction.

If I am fishing a flavour, I take the trouble of preparing a bag of flavoured crumb the day before, in exactly the same way as described for the flavoured loaf earlier.

For an even finer cloud, with minimal food value, liquidized bread really comes into its own. For this, remove the crusts from fresh, sliced bread and liquidize it in your home blender. Bags can then be stored in the freezer, after first flavouring if desired. Liquidized bread is good for fishing in conjunction with a feeder, using bread-flake hookbaits. A terrific additive to liquidized bread in this application is ground, grilled hemp, a firm favourite with that master Avon angler, Bob James.

For fishing breadflake, which I prefer in feeder applications or when trotting, I use fresh, medium sliced white bread. Tear off a strip about half an inch (1cm) wide by an inch and a half (3½cm) long and fold it round the hook shank, pinching in place but leaving the point exposed. Fresh, sliced bread is also what you need if you decide you require a breadflake offering on a very small hook, where bread punches come into their own. I admit to very rarely using punches myself, generally using bigger bread baits, but they are a very convenient way of preparing tiny bread baits.

Although waning in popularity, as other pastes are readily available, bread paste still has a niche.

It is also much cheaper than buying high protein pastes if your budget is limited. For preparing bread paste, you need sliced bread, without the crusts, at least two days old. Fresh bread results in lumpy, unappealing paste.

To make bread paste, dampen the slices without over soaking them, and squeeze as much of the water out as possible. For kneading the paste, use a clean, white cloth, and your bait will be nice and white. If you knead by hand, the natural retained dirt in your skin pores tends to make the paste an unappealing, grubby off-white colour. The end result should be a smooth, pliant paste of even consistency.

If you fancy a variant from standard bread paste, try adding powdered additives such as custard powder. The list of possibilities is endless. An uncle of mine, now sadly departed, swore by strawberry paste for his chub and roach fishing, and he caught plenty of fish with it. That was simply a mixture of plain bread paste and strawberry blancmange powder.

The main reason why bread is undoubtedly my favourite winter chub bait is its versatility. As I have said *ad nauseam* over the years, in most circumstances a chub will eat anything if it has not been alarmed, and choice of actual hookbait will be determined by the bait presentation required rather than the actual bait itself. In this, bread is supreme. A loaf can provide a buoyant or a sinking bait, or one of neutral density. Alteration of bait size can provide a totally different presentation in an instant. With crust, for example, increasing the bait size can provide a slow sinking offering, where previously the bait had been nailed down to the riverbed. With flake, a buoyant offering can be created by squeezing a disc flat on the hook shank.

Where conditions are suitable for bread for winter chub, which would be all but heavily coloured water, I cannot visualize any situation where a bread bait could not be adapted to provide the ideal presentation.

Cheesepaste

My cheesepaste is made up as follows: A 10oz (250g) pack of frozen shortcrust pastry is rolled flat and to this is added 6oz (150g) of grated mature Cheddar and 4oz (100g) of finely crumbled Danish blue. The pastry is then folded over so that the cheese is inside and the whole again rolled. This is repeated constantly until thorough mixing has occurred, when the paste is formed into a large ball and thoroughly kneaded by hand.

Traditional cheesepaste: still one of the best.

I then introduce 2ml of SBS mature Cheddar flavour into a large freezer food bag, put the ball of paste inside, seal the bag and place it in the freezer. Upon re-thawing, the paste has the most appealing texture and consistency, as well as a powerful cheesy aroma.

You can, of course, use standard bread paste as the base for your cheese paste, but using the frozen pastry mix is far more convenient and far quicker. It also gives a lovely even texture.

During the summer months, when water temperatures are high, you can use cheese on its own, simply moulded into a ball on a large hook. In the winter, however, when the bait would be most used, all cheeses with the consistency necessary for use on a hook harden considerably in cold water, thus impeding hook penetration. This problem is overcome by making a paste in the way I have described. The bait remains lovely and soft, even in the coldest water.

Luncheon Meats

I have lost count of the number of chub I have taken on processed meats of one type or another and luncheon meat is now so widely used that it can be classed as one of the standard baits.

All these meats can be used very successfully straight from the tin, and for chubbing I normally use ¾-inch cubes. I have taken good chub on all varieties of tinned meats, including luncheon meat, bacon grill, chopped ham and pork and so on. It is best to opt for one of the softer varieties, as these leak their flavour into the water quicker and give no problems with hook penetration. You must not, however, fall in to the trap of leaving the same bit of meat on the hook all day if there have been no bites, which is a common mistake to make. Most meats of this type, if they have not been specially flavoured, soon lose their natural smells and become bland and unappealing.

I have lost count of how many big chub have fallen to luncheon meat.

My current favourite meat for both chub and barbel, where it is used as supplied, is Plumrose chopped ham and pork. If I am going to use a flavour, which I now do most of the time, the base meat brand matters less, but the texture is still important. Plumrose luncheon meat is the choice here, as it is cheaper than the ham and pork variety.

Bacon grill can either be brilliant or useless, and in my experience tends to outlive its useful life quite quickly. For two seasons on the Wensum I could do no wrong with big chub on this meat, and then the fish refused it altogether. As with certain carp flavours, perhaps the bacon flavour is one that blows rapidly.

I still see many anglers using luncheon meat baits on ridiculously small hooks for chubbing, and then complaining that the meat keeps falling off. If you are going to use a half-inch or three-quarter-inch cube of meat, use a hook matched to the bait. My minimum will be a size 6. To hook the meat, I push the hook bend through the bait, and then twist and pull the hook point back into the meat along a different line. Using this attachment, the meat will not fly off, but the hook pulls easily through on the strike if you have selected your meat brand correctly.

Sausages

Sausage was certainly a bait much used on the Thames years ago. It was mainly used then as a barbel bait, but many chub were tempted by it. My first ever barbel was taken from the Thames at Rushey Weir, and that accepted half a beef banger!

There are two ways of using sausage for chub and barbel baits, either a portion of sausage or a paste made of the meat. If using the sausage solely, it is best to used the variety with skin, as the skinless ones tend to be too soft and fall apart too easily. When using skinned sausages, however, take care to hook them in such a way that the skin does not impede hook penetration. Do not be afraid of using a big chunk. You get some impressive pulls on half a sausage mounted on a size 4 hook.

Sausage meat paste is a superb bait for lots of species. I make mine up by mixing sausage meat

with the special rusk available from butchers. However, you can mix the meat with any bulk binder that takes your fancy and the delicatessen is full of interesting alternatives for you to try.

Peperami

Sticks of this flavoured meat are available from most supermarkets, and are very convenient change baits to keep in your tackle box as they require no preparation whatever and keep indefinitely while in an unopened packet. Simply break off a chunk, flatten one end slightly to put the hook through and there you have a superb bait. As it has a fairly tough skin, it is a good idea to pare the skin away with a sharp knife where the hook is inserted. Failing this, you can experience problems with bumping fish off on the strike.

MASS BAITS AND PARTICLES

I have no doubt whatever that chub would respond with relish to the whole range of particles that repose in the carp angler's armoury. For the purposes of this book, however, I will confine my comments to those particles I have actually used.

The most universal, of course, is hemp, and there is little to say on this magic seed. I prepare mine in large quantities in a five-gallon galvanized bucket, and freeze that which is not immediately required. Having brought the water to the boil, simmer the seeds for an hour or so until they split to reveal the creamy interior. Make sure that the seeds are always under water as they absorb it rapidly during the cooking process. I always keep the bait in the liquid in which it was prepared as this is attractive to fish.

Similar baits in texture to hemp, but larger, are tares and, larger still, maple peas, both terrific chub baits. At the time of writing, I have always used these two offerings in conjunction with hemp mass baiting. However, the current steep escalation in hemp prices could be the spur to mass baiting with tares and maples alone. That would be an interesting experiment.

Sweetcorn is one of the most popular particles for chubbing, and again little needs to be said about its preparation. I prefer the tins to the frozen packets, as I believe the sticky liquid enhances the attractiveness of the bait. For chub, corn can be used in large quantities without apparently being detrimental, something that is not always the case with other species.

Two other particles I have used for chubbing successfully, although not in recent years, are boiled rice and wheat. Plain white rice grains are extremely attractive in their own right, but rice is very receptive to colourings and flavourings. A terrific mass bait is rice flavoured and coloured with turmeric.

One bait I see used very infrequently these days is stewed wheat, which you prepare in the same way as you do hemp, simmering it until the grains split to show the creamy interior. I had some tremendous bags of chub and roach from the Ouse on this bait, but its use has to be sparing. It is very dense and filling, so resist the temptation of piling it in, or you will kill the swim.

When I am using wheat, I put in around twenty grains per dropper of hemp initially, and then content myself with a dozen grains every half hour or so. This trickle feed keeps the fish looking for more.

Although I have not used any nuts for chubbing myself, I am told by those chub anglers who are constantly pestered by eels that tiger nuts are a terrific bait which eels apparently ignore. If you do decide to use any nuts, please be careful to cook them properly. I always pressure cook mine for carping. Nuts take flavours well, and they are effective chub offerings flavoured with spices such as curry and garlic.

PASTES

As well as using hard boilies, the same mixtures can also be used as very successful hook baits in their soft paste form, although not all boilie mixes

SBS Strawberry Jam EA, a terrific ready-mixed paste.

are smooth enough to form a paste suitable for a hook bait. Some fish meal mixes are a little coarse in texture; they are great once boiled but they fall apart very easily in their soft form.

I admit to using these pastes for chub very rarely indeed, but I have experimented with some of the ready-made boilie mixes, for the fun of it, and caught chub on all of them. So far, this has been confined to the SBS Catcher range of base mixes, and Rod Hutchinson's Seafoodblend. To date, I have taken chub on SBS Scopex, Strawberry Jam EA, Tutti Frutti EA and Chocolate Malt mixes. As well as being used on their own, they also make good neutral buoyancy cocktails when fished with crust.

BOILIES

In recent seasons, there has been a growing tendency to fish for chub and barbel with scaled-down carp tactics, using bolt rigs and boilies, and whether we like it or not, there is no denying that these tactics can be ruthlessly effective.

In streamy water, I do not see myself changing from my mobile approach with standard leger rigs, simply because I find it so enjoyable. However, in very sluggish stretches, or where there is a low population density of bigger fish, the matched rod, bolt rig approach has some merit.

On some of these slower stretches, both barbel and chub can be very nomadic, and carp tactics

All these mini-boilies have produced chub.

of laying down a bed of boilies and waiting for the fish to home in on them allows for very relaxing fishing. The static approach also allows the use of two rods, presenting baits in two distinct areas. Trying to use two rods in the mobile approach is more hassle than it is worth.

To date, I have taken chub on Richworth's Tutti Frutti and Salmon Supreme boilies, as well as on their neutrals flavoured with Tutti Frutti and Nectar. I have also caught chub on SBS Strawberry Jam and Red Shrimp boilies. At the time of writing, Martin Kowal of SBS has supplied me with some of the new Frankfurter Sausage boilies; you have to smell it to believe it! When I opened the parcel, my west highland terrier went berserk, trying to get at the baits! I can hardly wait to give them a try.

Of course, several well-known anglers have been using boilies for chubbing for years. Len Arbery and his son Tony have caught many big ones on the method, specially using mini- and midi-boilies.

The first time I seriously used this approach was two winters ago on the Hampshire Avon, and the results were a real eye opener. On a stretch of river where there were both streamy glides and seductive slacks behind rush beds and on the

inside of bends, I baited the slower areas with large quantities of SBS luncheon meat flavoured mini-boilies. I found that the action was fairly slow on the first day, taking one four-pound chub and pulling out of a bigger one, but on the second day, each of the primed swims was full of fish. Several more four-pound chub succumbed, as well as a double-figure carp that gave a memorable scrap in and out of the streamer. But most noticeable was the tremendous number of taps and bumps from dace and small roach. Obviously, once the fish have discovered the bait carpet, it has tremendous holding power.

Chubbing with mini- and midi-boilies has real potential on harder-fished waters, where the fish are becoming wary of more traditional offerings.

Although I have not chub fished with mini-boilies anywhere near enough yet to form any firm ideas about flavours, I have to say that I have caught on every one I have tried. After my initial success with SBS Luncheon Meat, I have caught chub on them since, both in their plain form and dunked in the pungent SBS Frankfurter Sausage flavour. The latter gave me a tremendous day in flood conditions in January. I have also taken nice fish on two other SBS flavours, Sweetcorn and Chubby Cheese. The latter has been used

Even 20mm boilies are no problem for big chub.

Some of my favourite additives.

successfully, both on its own and soaked in SBS Mature Cheddar liquid flavouring. First-class flavours that have also proved their credentials with chub are those stalwarts, Richworth's Tutti Frutti and Salmon Supreme.

Boilie fishing for chub will never replace the more mobile and intimate methods in my affections. However, used in its rightful place, there is no doubt whatsoever that it provides an important addition to my repertoire.

FLAVOURS AND ADDITIVES

What an absolutely fascinating subject this is, and one of course that could fill a book on its own. In a general treatise on chub fishing, this topic can only be discussed generally. Others have devoted more attention to bait flavours than I, but I will pass on my own experiences for consideration.

Bread

I mentioned earlier that when using crust, I flavour the bait loaf at home in the freezer, so that as the loaf thaws it absorbs the flavour evenly. Flavours I have used very successfully are nectar, blue cheese, crayfish, sweetcorn, hemp, maple crème, tutti frutti, strawberry and seafood. My catch of three five-pounders in a day came to strawberry-flavoured crust.

As well as carp flavours, crust can also be enhanced with more common foodstuffs, and over the years I have had good chub on crust smeared with cheese spread, Marmite, honey, beef and salmon spreads, and golden syrup. A fond memory I have is of one recent day on the Leam when I had three good fish in three casts on crust smeared with blackcurrant jam from one of my sandwiches!

When using liquidized bread in a feeder, the opportunity exists to add powdered attractants, and one of the most devastating I ever used was

Fish of 5lb 7oz and 6lb 2oz to Martin James on crust smeared with cheese spread.

Flavatract Anise, from SBS. This was based on aniseed and I will never forget two sessions on the Warwickshire Avon when the chub and roach would not leave me alone. All the other Flavatract powders are well worth a try and so far I have used Sweet Strawberry, Meaty and Fruity with good results. As well as these powders, SBS also produce powdered taste enhancers in their Flavone Plus and Flavone Savoury products. The former is for use with sweet flavours, such as Flavatract Fruity, while the latter would enhance the Flavatract Meaty. I have no doubt all the other bait manufacturers produce similar products, although I have not used them personally.

Ground, grilled hemp is an excellent additive to liquidized bread, as is liver powder, and the attraction of the feed can be further enhanced by adding milk powder to the mixture. This gives a very appealing cloud.

In considering bread pastes, of course, the permutations are literally limitless, and with a little thought you could easily come up with a paste that is unique to you.

Particles

It is fair to say that I have rarely felt the need for flavouring particles for chub fishing, and the only particle I have used flavoured is sweetcorn. I have found on most of my barbel rivers that the barbel quickly spook on large quantities of corn. Last season, when I tried fishing coloured and flavoured corn, the numbers of chub I caught taught me that there was potentially some mileage in this approach. So far I have used red corn in both strawberry and tutti frutti flavours, and have caught chub on both variants.

Flavouring corn is simplicity itself. All you need is a quarter teaspoon of powdered dye or,

A brilliant chub bait: Pescaviva red, strawberry corn.

preferably, a little liquid colouring and some of your chosen flavour added to a tin of corn, and you are ready to go. I prepare this in a bait box the night before I go fishing, so that by morning the flavour has been fully absorbed, but that is not strictly necessary. Alternatively, you can use the ready flavoured and coloured corn marketed by Pescaviva.

Maggots

There is absolutely no doubt that the attractive properties of maggots are enhanced with flavourings, and I believe that the man who has made an exhaustive study of the subject of bait additives and flavours, Archie Braddock, now never fishes plain maggots. I am rapidly heading along that road myself. So often have I fished two rods side

These flavours from Relum have proved a lethal combination.

by side, one armed with plain maggots and one with a flavoured alternative, and found every single time that the flavoured bait outfished the plain one, that I now require no further proof.

Every flavour I have ever used on maggots has produced fish, but among my favourites are Rod Hutchinson's Roach Attractor, Maple Creme, Nectar and Scopex, SBS Strawberry Jam EA, Tutti Frutti EA and Pineapple Cream EA, and Richworth's Vanilla, Cherry and Roast Peanut.

To flavour maggots for the hook, I put a teaspoon of the selected flavour in a small, empty bait box, put on the lid and then give the box a good shake so that the inside walls are coated. The surplus liquid in the box can be used to flavour the bulk of the feeder maggots. I then put a small number of maggots, say about fifty, into the box, making sure there is no sawdust or bran to make a sticky mess. After this, the lid is closed and the box given another good shake. Within a couple of hours, the maggots will be thoroughly impregnated with the flavour.

The rest of the maggots, for use in the feeder or for loose feeding, are flavoured in exactly the same way, but on a larger scale, and I always aim to have the hook baits more strongly flavoured

than the free samples, to encourage those to be sought out selectively.

A fairly new flavour alternative for hook maggots is the Berkley Power Bait, which was originally intended for smearing on trout flies. I received a couple of tubs of this from Terry Eustace, in yellow and fluorescent orange, both in the floating formula. Although I have not as yet used it in my chubbing, I have had some very encouraging results in my early season tenching. Using a smear on the hook with two maggots yielded me a catch of over thirty tench in a two-day session.

Luncheon Meat
So widespread is the use of luncheon meat these days that very rarely do I use it unflavoured. There is absolutely no doubt that my favourite flavour for this is SBS Attract Frankfurter Sausage, which is devastatingly effective. Again, the meat is best prepared some hours before fishing. All I do is section the meat into cubes of the size I want, and then pour the flavour over it so that it is well coated. This gives the most unbelievably pungent sausage aroma, which I have found to be irresistible to chub and barbel.

This one really is the business. A lethal additive.

Although I have used that flavour far more often than any others, I have caught several chub on meat flavoured with two other SBS savoury alternatives, the Green Lipped Mussel EA and Spicy Meat EA. This season, I intend to try Fresh Lobster, Liver Spleen and Squiddly Diddly.

Luncheon meat can also be enhanced with powdered attractants such as garlic, curry, mixed spice or any other combination you can dream up. Again, treating the meat is simple. Just sprinkle your chosen additive over the meat and leave overnight. The next morning, you will find that the natural moisture in the meat will have dissolved the powder and absorbed the resulting liquid. The best powdered attractant I have ever used is that concoction developed by Merv Wilkinson, which he calls 'Wicked'. Lots of chub and barbel have found that irresistible.

Another interesting variation with luncheon meat is to fry it gently in a chosen flavour, and my favourites for this application are tandoori curry and barbecue sauce. I specially rate the barbecue sauce. Two seasons ago, I attacked the Cherwell barbel with barbecue sauce-fried meat over a two-day session, but failed completely because the chub simply would not leave me alone. It got to the stage where they were taking the meat on the drop!

DEADBAITS

Very rarely indeed do I use deadbaits for chub, and then only in the form of a minnow, loach or bullhead for summer fishing. In rivers, where all my chubbing is done, I have never, frankly, felt the need.

However, friends who are into stillwater chubbing tell me that deadbaits are among the most successful offerings, and it would appear that big, stillwater chub have a tendency to be very predatory. This appears especially to be the case with mackerel, and mackerel strip or chunk has caught many fine specimens. I know that some of the very biggest fish from the Oxford pits came to small, whole mackerel. That fine angler, Peter Stone, has had some tremendous success with

stillwater chub deadbaiting. Peter will confirm that it is a method requiring great patience and determination to succeed.

There is obviously no logical reason why you should not be able to catch river chub on mackerel chunk. In fact, my friend Marsh Pratley has taken some great Thames fish in this manner. I am still to be convinced, though, that it offers any significant advantage over other baits; on some of the best chub rivers, which see either a good population of eels or signal crayfish, it could even offer a significant disadvantage.

COCKTAIL BAITS

By 'cocktail baits' I mean putting two or more different baits together, to give a varied presentation to a suspicious fish. It is a variation to keep in your repertoire when the usual approach is giving disappointing results.

There is little else to say on this topic except to list some of the cocktails that I have often used successfully. These would be lobworm/corn, caster/corn, maggot/corn, maggot/tares, maggot/redworm, tare/redworm, corn/meat, maggot/flake, maggot/meat, and lobworm meat.

As well as those, any bait garnished with soft paste can be considered a cocktail, and I have successfully used crust smeared with all varieties of paste, crust balanced with cheesepaste, luncheon meat/cheesepaste, and tiny fragments of cheesepaste with maggots, casters, corn and tares. A great cocktail to try is a ball of cheesepaste with grains of hemp pressed into it. As with flavourings, you can let your imagination run riot with cocktail alternatives.

CHANGE BAITS

During a conversation I had with Bob James a few years ago, he mentioned that he had often found that, after taking a chub on a particular flavour, he had then struggled for further bites. Changing the flavour had brought another immediate response and he had caught fish in the

Red strawberry corn plus red maggots. One of my favourite cocktails.

course of a day on as many as six different flavours. I do not think Bob was making the point that the flavours themselves were doing the damage, but more that it was the bait variation that was important. There is, of course, nothing new in that. We have known for a long time that fish can become spooked on one particular offering, necessitating a bait change in some way. However, this spooking effect usually occurs gradually over several sessions, and I had never before considered the possibility of changing baits after each bite. At the time of the conversation I found the idea very interesting, thought I might try it some day and then promptly forgot about it.

About a year later, I was on the banks of the Dorset Stour and the day's chubbing I enjoyed, although producing nothing spectacular, is well worth recounting.

I had with me a large canvas bucket full of well-mashed bread and hemp and decided to sit it out for the day in one swim, a long glide over bank-

side rushes, the glide eventually disappearing under the sheltering fronds of a large downstream willow. My plan was to introduce regular small balls of bread and hemp throughout the day, a technique that I thought might encourage large numbers of chub. During the day, I would fish with a 4lb hook link, stepping up a little towards dusk to 6lb when the chances of a barbel would be higher.

As bait, I had with me a crusty loaf, cheese-paste, sweetcorn, luncheon meat, and three sticks of Peperami, together with about a dozen sugar cube-sized pieces of chopped ham and pork laced with SBS Frankfurter Sausage flavour. This was left over from a barbel session of the previous evening.

From about 9 o'clock until the early afternoon, I spent a few contented hours fishing away without response, on an extremely pleasant sunny day. It was not until around 2 pm that I had my first bite, to my favourite legered crust. A cast to the midstream crease had been followed by the line cutting into the near bank as I bounced the bait under those inviting willow fronds, and then by a sudden, urgent tightening and a vicious jab on the quivertip.

My answering strike was met with a frantic lunge, and a couple of yards of line zipped off against the clutch as a good chub stormed downstream. Stour chub at the moment are stocky, muscular individuals, and this one was no exception as it fought gamely against the relentless pressure I was applying. However, with no snags to worry about other than a sparse bed of ranunculus, there could only be one victor, and eventually a superbly conditioned fish sagged into the net. Soon, I had confirmed it to be 4lb 3oz, and returned it carefully about a hundred yards upstream in a near bank slack.

I was now full of confidence, being sure that the constant supply of hemp and mash had done its job. Other chub would now follow steadily to my crust baits, I thought.

However, this was not to be. For the next three hours, I searched the swim meticulously, keeping the baits mobile, all the while steadily introducing the loose feed. I could not believe the swim contained only the one chub, and felt that my bait presentation was somehow flawed. I experimented with a lighter link, a longer tail, smaller pieces of crust, and so on. I tried inducing bites by drawing the bait upstream in the way that has yielded me hundreds of chub in the past, but it was all to no avail.

At around 5 pm, I was wondering whether the constant trickle of hemp might have encouraged any barbel in the swim. On impulse, I switched to a 6lb hooklink and a size six Au Lion d'Or and propelled an inch cube of unflavoured luncheon meat under those willow branches. The reaction was immediate and savage. The terminal rig had not properly settled when the rod hammered round to what I initially assumed was a barbel bite, but very soon realized was another decent chub. Again, an enjoyable scrap ensued, and perhaps four minutes later I was lifting another short, fat chub from my landing net, a fish fractionally bigger than the previous one, at 4lb 6oz.

As I returned it, I pondered over the fact that I had had a chub bite on meat in a matter of seconds, from the exact spot that had been searched by my crust baits for the last few hours.

Another meat offering was soon reposing under those branches, but this time there was no such dramatic response, and half an hour passed without incident. As I was thinking over the events of the day, my conversation with Bob James suddenly came to mind. A bait change had worked once, perhaps it would again. So next time my terminal rig came to rest, two grains of corn lay in ambush. Within a minute, I was again on my feet, as another heavy chub rocketed to midstream. This was the fish that gave me the most trouble, twice getting me snagged in midriver streamer, and several times taking line in powerful, short rushes. Throughout the fight, I was convinced that it was substantially bigger than the two I had already landed, so I was very surprised when I landed another chub of almost identical size, just an ounce bigger than its predecessor, taking the scales to 4lb 7oz.

The fact that I had now taken two chub on change baits immediately, after long, biteless periods, I now felt could not be merely coincidental. Once perhaps, but twice was stretching chance rather a long way. I decided to test the theory, and so went back in again with sweetcorn, which I would leave for at least fifteen minutes, assuming no bites, and then try a lump of cheesepaste. Sure enough, there was no further response to the corn, but only moments after replacing it with the cheesepaste, the fourth and biggest chub was battling for its freedom, a worthy adversary of 4lb 14oz.

Sheer bad luck was to rob me of a fifth fish ten minutes later, a chub I had close to the net once and that was certainly well over five pounds. This time, flavoured chopped ham and pork was the successful offering. At that time, throughout my twenty-year association with Au Lion d'Or hooks, I had only ever known one to break, on a big tench at Sywell in the Seventies, but during the playing of that big chub it was to happen for a second time. A few minutes into the fight, with my being apparently in total control, the line suddenly fell slack. I assumed I had simply pulled out, but I soon discovered that the hook point had snapped off just below the barb. It was difficult to understand why. I could not really believe that the hook was faulty, after having landing four other good fish on it.

Perhaps the hook had taken a hold in hard gristle or pharyngeal teeth, and a sudden twist of the fish had proved too much. Or possibly I had inadvertently damaged the hook using my forceps to extract it from an earlier capture. Whatever the truth of the matter, I had just lost possibly my biggest ever Stour chub.

Still keeping faith with the constant bait variation theme, the last hour of daylight saw me try Peperami plus several cocktail offerings. Two good bites came my way during that period, one on Peperami and one on a small piece of luncheon meat garnished with a smear of cheesepaste. Unfortunately, both were missed, which did not surprise me unduly as the fast, savage jabbing nature of the indications confirmed that the remaining chub in the swim were now very nervous indeed.

Once it had become dark, the bites surprisingly ceased abruptly and, after two hours completely devoid of any indication on my quivertip, I was contemplating the delights of a local Chinese takeaway. As I was draining my last cup of tea before packing up, there was a sudden, urgent little tug on my finger. Something was taking an interest in my offering of crust balanced with cheesepaste. Moments later, the starlight slowly arced down towards the dark water surface, where again, battle was joined with a big Stour chub. I was never to get a glimpse of this fish, unfortunately, but had it on long enough to know that it was another specimen I would have been mightily pleased to have landed. It was not to be, however, as the sudden downturn in my day's fortunes continued. Again, I was a few minutes into the fight when the fish inexplicably came off. This time I was to find a hook with the point completely turned over, indicating that I had taken hold in the throat teeth.

That day on the Stour, when I had a total of eight good chub bites on eight different baits or bait combinations, is one of the most interesting chub sessions I have had for a long time, and it has set me thinking about the whole subject of bait afresh. It also brought to mind a fascinating episode a few weeks before, when I had been whiling away a few hours in the middle of a hot day trying to tempt average barbel from a shallow run. One of the first baits I tried was a cockle, after seeing several barbel eat free offerings avidly. The first cockle to drift down on a hook was taken immediately by a five-pounder, but after that the barbel bolted in alarm if they saw one, even over an hour later, when they had recovered their composure after the fish had been landed and were quite happily feeding over hemp and corn. Why was it that a bait that had been acceptable to several fish, and certainly did not appear to alarm the others, suddenly became so frightening after only one fish had been caught on it? Is there some sort of communicative fear factor at work? Having been able to witness that behaviour in barbel in clear water, could exactly the same sequence of events have been occurring with the Stour chub, when I could not actually observe their behaviour? It is interesting to speculate. I know one thing. Sometimes I wonder how we ever manage to catch fish at all and the older I get the more I realize the truth of one of Dick Walker's favourite sayings 'the more we learn about this sport of ours, the more we realize we do not know'.

ARTIFICIALS

I have very little experience of fishing for chub with artificial baits, although I took a couple of fish many years ago on a red-tasselled spinner meant for Leam perch. Although I have never fly fished for them myself, friends tell me that it is a very efficient method. Dry flies, nymphs and lures all take fish. Trefor, who did a lot of small stream trouting last close season, told me that the chub were an absolute nuisance.

One artificial bait that I am now using is the Berkley Power Worm, available from Terry Eustace, and I am grateful to Terry for sending

Chum Mixer, a terrific surface bait.

me them to try. At the time of writing, I have had a couple of small stream chubbing sessions, and both times the fish smashed into these baits with great ferocity. They are impregnated with flavours and enhancers, and I have taken chub on both the Pumpkinseed and Red Shad flavours. They are best fished on the move, and I fish them just as I do slugs, casting at individual chub and then inducing bites, if necessary. One thing I quickly learned is not to strike too quickly. Chub attack the baits viciously and a premature strike will miss the fish. As they appear to hang on to the bait, I wait a couple of seconds before tightening.

FLOATING BAITS

As well as plain bread crust, all other floating baits used by carp anglers are similarly attractive to chub. I have taken fish on high protein floaters, mixed similarly to ordinary boilie mixes but with twice the quantity of eggs to make a runny mix, and then baked like a cake in the oven. These sponge-like floaters are brilliant in texture, and I remember a good catch of fish taken in sub zero conditions on chunks of peanut-flavoured floater, anchored just off bottom. They can also be surface-fished in exactly the same way as crust. Other floating baits that have produced large numbers of fish are trout pellets, on which Bob James must have taken hundreds of Avon fish, Chum Mixer, on which two friends of mine have taken colossal catches of Cherwell chub, and floating Koi pellets, which I have used successfully. Chum Mixer and Koi pellets are brilliant fished anchored. In both cases, fishing them in conjunction with a feeder loaded with powder from ground pellets is a killing method.

4 PRE-BAITING AND LOOSE FEEDING

SUMMER TECHNIQUES

As with all fish, you improve your chances of sport with chub by the intelligent use of pre-baiting or loose feeding. In the summer months, one of the most exciting methods of taking chub is with floating crust and, as with first weaning carp on to floating baits by pre-baiting, it is essential to encourage the chub to rise freely by drifting down loose offerings in advance of the hook bait. Once they are taking confidently, success is assured so long as you are capable of a delicate bait presentation without alarming the fish.

Another summer pre-baiting situation would be with the use of particle baits, especially hempseed, in exactly the same way as for barbel fishing. Priming swims with hemp and hookbait samples, and then fishing them later, is as effective with chub as it is with barbel. Be aware, though, that chub are more intelligent than barbel. Once barbel have been weaned on to that approach, they can become ridiculously easy to catch over and over again. If a chub has had a nasty experience, however, he is far less likely to return for another helping.

There are two principal aims behind pre-baiting a summer chub swim with particles. The first is to achieve a level of preoccupied feeding, and the second is gradually to allay the suspicions of the bigger fish, so that they feed confidently. Let us look at preoccupation first.

Preoccupied feeding means simply that fish are feeding on one particular food item to the exclusion of all others. Some anglers say that when preoccupation becomes total, the fish may not even recognize other baits as food temporarily, although I cannot go along with that entirely.

Its relevance with anglers' baits is that the more individual items of food are available, the more are the fish likely to be preoccupied in feeding on them. These days, preoccupation is talked about mostly in carp fishing circles, when discussing particle baits or mass baits. A simple example to illustrate the principle is to imagine three identical buckets, one filled with standard-sized boilies, one with sweetcorn and one with hemp. There are going to be vastly more separate grains of corn in one bucket than there are boilies, and vastly more grains of hemp than corn. In chub fishing, the simplest examples of preoccupied feeding are seen over beds of hemp and/or sweetcorn, although the fish will take any other baits that they stumble across in the same area.

As with barbel, total chub preoccupation can be achieved by using sufficient quantities of maggots, at which time you will be hard put to get a bite on anything else. This, however, has more relevance when fishing the swimfeeder, which you will read about in Chapter 8.

Over the last few years, as Trefor and I have developed our pre-baiting techniques for barbel fishing, it has become increasingly apparent how devastatingly effective they are for chub too, so much so that we have been forced to devise ways of segregating the two species when a big barbel is the quarry. With big summer chub the target, I now adopt exactly the same procedures as for barbel. The technique is designed to promote preoccupied feeding, and at the same time achieve the secondary objective of very confident feeding by the biggest fish present. Anyone who has bought our book *Quest for Barbel* will have seen the technique explained there. However, so fundamentally important is this pre-baiting approach to consistent success that I make no apologies for repeating it here.

My swim preparation technique is simply one of allowing the chub steadily to adapt themselves to a preoccupied feeding pattern, without any disturbance whatever from me, other than by topping up the free feed periodically. The longer the fish are allowed to feed unmolested in this way, the greater their preoccupation will become. A beneficial side-effect for the specimen hunter is that the bigger chub respond best to this approach.

It is certainly true that they are most easily spooked, but having been given hours of carefree feeding, they, being bigger and greedier, spend longer on the bait than some of their lesser companions. It is very noticeable that, when we top up the bait in a swim which has been left, say, for two hours, the biggest chub in residence is usually the first one to return to the dining table.

Watching the behaviour of feeding chub gives us a clue as to our best approach to catching them. When the fish first discover food in a swim, say a recently introduced carpet of hemp and corn, they are understandably nervous and, although each fish will linger over the bait for a little while, they invariably vacate the swim after a few minutes. It is natural caution.

After an absence of from a few minutes up to half an hour, the fish will drift back into the area, take a few more mouthfuls and go again. This procedure can go on for some time, but if you watch them for several hours, you will notice that their stay in the swim starts to get longer and longer, and the interval between each visit shorter.

The longer that they are allowed to feed in peace in this manner, the more time they will spend in the swim, until there arrives a point where the

Trefor lowers a dropper of hemp and corn into a Bristol Avon streamer bed.

chub are virtually resident in the swim, provided that there is an adequate food supply. When this stage has been reached, much of their natural caution has been submerged under their preoccupation with the loosefeed, and I have often observed chub remaining in the swim while the feed is topped up by bait dropper. This takes hours to achieve, but once it has been achieved, our chances of catching one or two fish are very high. Obviously, I am talking about gentle introductions of the dropper. As with any fish, care should be taken at all times to avoid unduly alarming them.

If we now look at the pre-baiting procedure in detail, the first thing to say is that the premier attractant for chub, as it is for barbel, is undoubtedly hempseed, well simmered so that it has split, showing an attractive creamy white interior. I have not fished a river yet where the chub did not respond to this magic seed, and if there are any fish in the vicinity of the swims I have selected, they will eventually move on to the hemp to feed.

During the initial baiting of a swim, I will generally deposit ten droppers of hemp at exactly one rod length out from the bank. The reason for this

A bait dropper is essential for accurate pre-baiting.

is twofold. First, observation of the fish activity is much easier under the near bank, providing you are capable of keeping low and still, and second, it will be easy, on subsequent visits to the swim, to place further feed in exactly the same spot. The exact position in a swim that the chub will feed can be dictated by you. They will feed where

Hemp and corn. Now a standard baiting ploy.

the food is concentrated, provided they are not alarmed. Also, when we come to the fishing itself, which will often be at night, there will be nothing 'hit and miss' about the placing of the hook bait. As it is exactly one rod length out, the bait can be lowered in the right spot every time, even in pitch darkness.

During the initial hemp baiting, the dropper will also contain samples of whatever I intend to use on the hook, if I am planning to use a particle bait such as corn, tares, casters or mini-boilies. Particle baits are always the choice in daylight in all but very coloured water. Although large baits in clear water do not have the tremendously unsettling effect on chub that they certainly do on barbel, I prefer small baits for this style of chubbing during the day. At dusk and through the dark hours, the larger baits such as luncheon meat and cheesepaste come into their own. For summer chubbing in daylight, I reserve my large baits for casting at individual fish in a mobile approach.

The above theory is based on the certain knowledge, from hundreds of hours' observation, that once chub are avidly feeding over a hemp-primed area, they will accept any edible item in the swim, providing that they are not spooked by it.

Once all the selected swims have received their initial baiting, it is time for patient observation of each one, and this is where you must exercise maximum self-restraint. Not long after the baiting, chub should be observed in at least some of the swims, heads down over the hemp. The worst thing you can now do is start fishing. That is fatal. First of all, spend a few minutes in each swim just watching, logging the numbers of chub involved and the sizes of the individual members of the shoal. Try to observe if there is any preferential pattern to the feeding, and if the chub enter or leave the swim by any particular route. All this information will assist you in eventually deciding exactly where to place the hook bait, in order to stand the greatest chance of hooking the biggest fish.

This observation process is made much easier if you have included in your loose feed highly visible particles, such as sweetcorn, bright mini-boilies or small pellets of cheesepaste. These, or rather their rate of disappearance, will give you an indication of how fast the loosefeed is being consumed, and will therefore dictate at what frequency the feed should be topped up. For the technique to work properly, there must be adequate feed in the swims at all times, otherwise the chub will abandon them.

Generally speaking, I will top up each swim after about two hours, or obviously more frequently if there is heavy activity in one particular area, and each topping up will be with six droppers of hemp containing whatever particles I am introducing. One of the better particles to use is sweetcorn, and here the reaction of chub is very different from that of barbel. Very heavy baiting with corn has often been observed to have a definitely detrimental effect on barbel, with the fish shying away from it. Chub, however, seem happy to tolerate any amount of the stuff. The same can be said about the other most used particles, maggots and casters. It is almost impossible to overdo the baiting with these, the only restriction on their use being cost, and the attention of nuisance fish, particularly the river angler's nightmare, bootlace eels.

Where there is no eel problem, preparing a chub swim with hemp and maggots or hemp and casters is absolutely devastating, but, of course, it can be expensive.

For my summer fishing, where the rivers are generally low and clear and the chub need a long time to become confident, I will often pay four pre-baiting visits to each swim before contemplating fishing, and the mathematicians among you will realize that this entails some eight hours of baiting, without actually wetting a line. It requires self-restraint, but if I am summer chubbing and preparing a few swims like this for after dark, I will combine my pre-baiting activities with visual fishing with large natural baits during the day in other swims.

Taken to its ultimate conclusion, the pre-baiting technique described is used throughout the daylight hours, with no attempt being made to fish at all until the onset of dusk. Even when night fishing is not allowed, so quickly do chub

Maggots are a lethal chub bait, summer or winter.

respond to a hook bait after they have been fed undisturbed all day that several fish can be caught in quick succession in just one hour's fishing time at the end of the day. However, there is no doubt that, when night fishing is available, not introducing a hook bait into a prepared swim until dusk is one of the most devastating ways of fishing for chub of all.

Use of Mini-Boilies

Although the foregoing description discussed primarily the pre-baiting process using hemp as the base attractant, exactly the same procedures can be followed using any other particles. Among the most interesting are mini- or midi-boilies, which chub love. The beauty of these is that, being dense, they can be fed without the bait dropper. I have found that it pays to scatter the feed a little to keep the chub actively milling around the swim for them. One thing to be aware of, though, is that unlike more traditional offerings, it can take some time to wean chub on to boilies if they have not seen them before. Once they have developed a taste for them, however, hectic fishing can result.

There are two methods of pre-baiting with mini-boilies, depending on how many baits you have available. If you only have a small quantity, you can treat them like any other particle, using hemp as the main base, incorporating a few boilies into each dropper load, and feeding a few more by hand.

Far better, though, is to bait with minis alone, using a generous quantity. This gets the chub on to the bait quicker.

WINTER TECHNIQUES

For winter chubbing, if I am fishing statically, say, giving a long glide a couple of hours, I will introduce a small quantity of loose feed at regular intervals, the amount depending on conditions. In low water temperatures, I feed sparingly. Where I am fishing breadcrust, my favourite winter bait in normal conditions, and still one of the most deadly, a small handful of bread mash every fifteen minutes, or a ball of squeezed, fresh breadcrumbs, builds the swim up steadily and slowly draws fish upstream.

For a day spent fishing in a more mobile fashion, which is my normal approach, I will usually pre-bait six swims before starting to fish. This depends on the numbers of anglers about and I realize that 'weekend only' anglers may find this impossible on very popular stretches. If it is possible, however, I can thoroughly recommend it as it gives you a definite edge. Not only does such pre-baiting get the chub in feeding mode, but it is also a great confidence booster to know that you are continually moving into prepared swims. In big fish angling, absolute confidence in what you are doing is vital.

What I do is put three generous handfuls of mashed bread in each swim, either plain or flavoured, or samples of other baits if I am not using bread. Once I have commenced fishing the first swim, I will periodically break off to top up the feed in the other five swims. If I am working a long length of river, say half a mile in a downstream direction, after perhaps fishing swim two and before casting into swim three, I will wander downstream and prepare a further two brand new areas. At the end of a day's mobile chubbing, I will then have had cast a bait into every likely chub spot, knowing that each and every one will have been primed in advance. In this way, I will know the couple of swims on which I should really concentrate at dusk and into the dark hours, the hot time. I will also know which swims possibly to discard on my next trip.

A pre-baiting approach I developed over several years during the eighties is geared primarily at removing as many of the average-sized fish from selected swims as possible, thereby lessening the odds against taking the bigger chub. To explain this selective technique, let me describe a day's fishing in February 1991 that is one of the major highlights of my chubbing career to date.

I had arrived at the river at dawn, and the first job was to walk the entire stretch with a large bagful of well-mashed bread, laced, incidentally with strawberry flavour. I was looking for swims of a very specific type, areas where there was very steady water in close proximity to a good current. The ideal is the small slack that develops behind bankside rushes, as the main flow diverts round

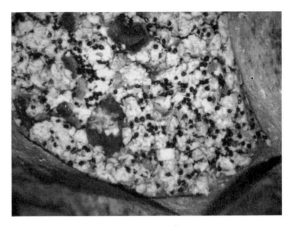

Hemp and bread mash, a terrific winter attractor.

the foliage. It mattered not how small the slacker area was, or how close it was to the near bank. All I wanted was somewhere for the heaviest feed in the mash to settle. This would eventually be my target area.

After about an hour, I had selected four swims that had all the attributes I wanted, and it was time to start the preparatory work. This is without doubt the most important time spent in the search for extra big chub. Just as with barbel, correct swim preparation is critical. Each swim was baited in the same way: two large handfuls of the heavy mash were introduced directly into the slack area, and then two or three much smaller handfuls were introduced at the edge of the main flow and at the tail of the slack, where the current again began to quicken. In the case of the two swims where the slack had been created by near-bank rushes, a handful of mash was also placed upstream of the rushes in the main flow.

On the face of it, this apparently haphazard introduction of feed would appear totally counter-productive, as it would result in the chub present being scattered all over the place. That is exactly the intention. My entire philosophy these days in searching out bigger-than-average chub and barbel is geared around the fact that the bigger individuals are, as well as being the wariest, the greediest and laziest. When I first formulated this swim preparation technique, it was in the belief that the biggest fish would be most likely to prefer to feed in the steady water, and the least likely to chase food fragments all over the river. The point of placing bait in positions where it would drift downstream away from the intended fishing area is to attract away from the area those chub I did not want to interfere with my chances of catching the leviathans; in other words, the more active, small-to-average fish.

It is not sufficient, however, to bait a swim in this manner and then start fishing ten minutes later. For big chub, as with big barbel, feed must be introduced on a regular basis as quietly as possible over several hours. This achieves two things. First, it gradually overcomes their natural caution of the chub, leading to more uninhibited feeding. Second, the more confident the big fish become, the more they assert their rank in the pecking order for the available food. There is then a second reason why the odds of a big chub are improved when a hookbait is eventually introduced: as well as many of the smaller chub having being enticed out of the swim by the programmed baiting, any smaller fish still resident in the swim are likely to be bullied out of the way by old granny when she sees that succulent morsel enter her parlour!

Back to our freezing February morning.

It was my intention to leave my four swims unfished for at least six hours and so, after the initial baiting, I leisurely collected my gear from the van and set up in a lovely, long streamy glide. I would fish that glide for those first six hours, catching anything that came along, breaking off every hour to top up the bait in the four main swims.

By late morning, I was still fishless, having missed my solitary bite, and I was extremely chagrined to see two other anglers arrive and set up in two of my prepared pitches. Not wishing to give anything away, I decided to stick with my glide until they packed up and left. I was prepared to wait until after dark if necessary, but seeing that the anglers were very inadequately dressed for that freezing day I did not believe I would have to wait that long. They showed remarkable fortitude, however, and it was not until about an hour before dusk that I again had the river to myself.

Whenever I first introduce a hookbait into a prepared swim, I am in a state of barely suppressed excitement, and that February afternoon was no exception. With a large piece of strawberry-flavoured crust anchored an inch off the bottom of the first slack, I settled on my low stool, watching the quivertip intently. It cannot have been more than a minute after the bait had settled that the tip was whipping round as a big chub rocketed under the overhanging downstream willow. Two minutes later, I was swinging ashore a fat specimen which proved to weigh 5lb 3oz; a chub in absolutely pristine condition. During the landing of that chub, I had really been in agony from my back, the result of a fall on ice the previous day, and I decided that I would pack up and go home early. First, though, I would take a few self-portrait photographs and so, after sacking the chub, I wandered slowly back to the van for my camera and tripod. I was back perhaps twenty minutes later, just as an icy drizzle was starting, and by the time I had organized the tripod and cable release, it was raining steadily.

I was now in a dilemma. I had no umbrella with me and it would obviously be risking damage to an expensive camera to take shots in the rain. I decided, therefore, to fish a little longer in the hope that the rain would stop. Once again, I lowered a chunk of crust into the little slack and waited on events. A second, virtually instantaneous bite resulted, and once more, a heavy chub surged for the willow roots. Before long, the fish had been confirmed at 4lb 7oz and, with thoughts of a photograph of a nice brace, that chub was also retained until the rain, which was now easing, had stopped completely. I made a third cast, not for a moment expecting any more action, and was absolutely amazed when there was a vicious lunge on the rod top almost before the bait could have settled. Another big chub of 4lb 8oz was soon being weighed and only then did it dawn on me that something very exciting was occurring.

Although the rain had now stopped, my third and last carp sack was brought into commission for the latest capture, and then I made my fourth cast into that exciting near-bank slack. The pain

Ouse chub of 4lb 7oz, 4lb 8oz, 5lb 3oz and 5lb 10oz taken on strawberry-flavoured crust.

from my back, although now agonizing, had been relegated to second place in my mind. This unique evening could well see a very big chub put in an appearance. I decided to fish as long after dark as I could stand.

Ten minutes passed without further action, and I was just on the point of moving to the second prepared swim when the tip twitched and then pulled round in determined fashion. As soon as the hook was set, I knew this fish was special and it gave an account of itself in keeping with its status. It fought a lot like a big barbel, never rushing anywhere but battling deeply and slowly, coming off the bottom very grudgingly.

With a direct pull on a fish from above, however, there should only ever be one winner, and soon a magnificent chub was being reverently placed in my weigh sling. The scales soon confirmed what I already knew, that I had caught a brace of five-pounders in a session for the seventh time in my angling career: 5lb 10oz was the weight of the fourth fish, perfect in every fin and scale.

At that moment I really did decide to pack up and, after spending a few minutes photographing the fish, carefully lowered them back to their home alongside the tangle of willow roots.

On the long walk back to the van, I had to walk past the fourth of my prepared swims, the only

The smile hides the agony in my back as I display Ouse fish of 5lb 3oz and 5lb 10oz.

one that had remained undisturbed for the entire day. Despite the excruciating pain and the return of the heavy rain, I simply could not resist a cast behind the little clump of rushes that had received the baiting hours before. As I settled into the swim I was overcome by that overpowering feeling I get so often. At that moment, I knew that I was only minutes away from another big fish. I can offer no logical explanation for this instinct, which has preceded my catching so many big fish over the years. It did, however, prove as reliable as ever because, no more than five minutes later, the rod crashed round as another mighty chub found my strawberry-laced crust irresistible. After another exhilarating

battle in the dark, my fifth and last chub was finally being admired in the torch beam. At that moment, I knew that I had achieved a first: three fives in a session and, when I read 5lb 5oz, I was in a state of euphoria. Three five pound chub in a matter of a couple of hours. What a truly unforgettable evening.

That catch of big fish, I have no doubt, was a direct consequence of the baiting technique used and the unusually long delay in actually fishing the swims, on account of the activities of the other two anglers. The session gave me much food for thought, and my fishing this coming winter will be very much influenced by lessons learned on that cold, wet and painful February evening.

5 ADVANCED TERMINAL RIGS

Throughout this book, I have indicated the usual terminal rigs employed for the bulk of my chubbing. However, there will be occasions when a situation presents itself that requires a rig modification to achieve the required presentation.

What I would like to do in this chapter, therefore, is outline a few of the rigs I have used over recent seasons. Some of them may only have been used once, perhaps to solve a particular problem, but they are all stored in my memory for the next occasion when I have cause to use them.

USE OF PVA

Stringer Rigs

More often in my chubbing, especially in the more static methods of summer fishing, I am employing the carp angler's ploy of introducing free offerings by stringer. I have to date tried this mainly with sweetcorn and mini-boilies, and once with small chunks of Peperami, but any bait samples can be introduced this way.

One word of warning with this rig, and all rigs using PVA for that matter, is to make sure that the bait being introduced is perfectly dry before making up the stringer. I know that sounds obvious, but I remember watching an angler trying to tie up a PVA stringer by threading the string through a large darning needle. He kept putting the end of the string in his mouth to assist in the threading process, and wondered why he was having problems!

If I am using PVA, I keep some of the freebies, say grains of corn, drying on a towel for a while before making up the rig. Stringers are easily made by using a simple baiting needle, available from all tackle shops.

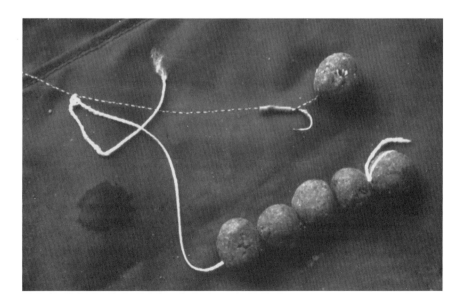

PVA has many uses. A boilie stringer is one.

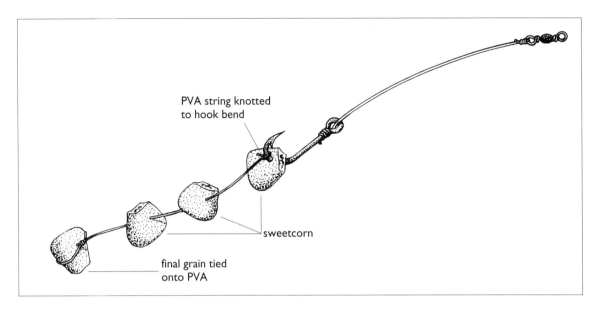

PVA string knotted
to hook bend

sweetcorn

final grain tied
onto PVA

Use of PVA in tying stringers.

The Expander Rig

This is a rig I have used only twice to date, with barbel in mind, but it has caught a very cautious chub and is certainly one I shall employ again when conditions warrant it.

Its use is suited to a situation where you wish to present a bait several feet downstream of the closest point you can actually cast to, and where you feel the fish cannot be persuaded to move upstream to the bait. This has particular relevance to big, suspicious fish lying stubbornly at the rear of a raft of surface flotsam.

I tie up a hooklink to the length I require (the longest I have used is 9ft/2.7m), and carefully coil it before tying the coils with PVA. You have to be careful not to cross the loops of line or it may tangle when the PVA melts. The theory is that when the PVA dissolves, the hooklink unravels and allows the bait to progress naturally downstream. In practice, for the rig to work, you do require a certain minimum amount of flow, and it is almost always necessary to assist the process by making the hook of neutral density by adding sufficient rig foam so that it only

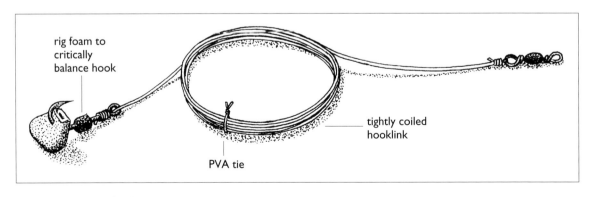

rig foam to
critically
balance hook

tightly coiled
hooklink

PVA tie

Tying up the expander rig.

just sinks. In this way, the current easily lifts the hook and bait when the PVA melts and helps the hooklink to straighten.

The Looped Feeder Rig

Where you wish to present a maggot hookbait tight against the feeder body, but still retain a normal length hooklink to promote confident feeding, this rig works like a charm. I have only used it when blockend feeding maggots, but there is no reason why it could not be used for any other bait in conjunction with an open-ended feeder.

The Condom Rig

In the chapter on feeder fishing, I have made several references to the problem of this method in summer in thick vegetation, where a run from a big chub or barbel can pull the terminal rig into weed roots, thereby leading to snagging. Although the sliding feeder rig largely solves the problem most of the time, there are occasions when you wish to present particle hookbaits in a tight area amongst a bed of freebies when the surrounding vegetation is really dense. Anything on

The expander rig. For those 'awkward to get at' specimens.

the line, even a free sliding feeder, may result in irretrievable snagging.

The answer is the condom rig, which is self explanatory. For this, you need one of those PVA tubes which is marketed by Relum in the PVA Phantasm range. I place a stone in the bottom, as entrapped air makes these tubes float once sealed, before filling the tube with the selected particles and then tying the neck tightly with PVA string. By tying the tube to the terminal rig,

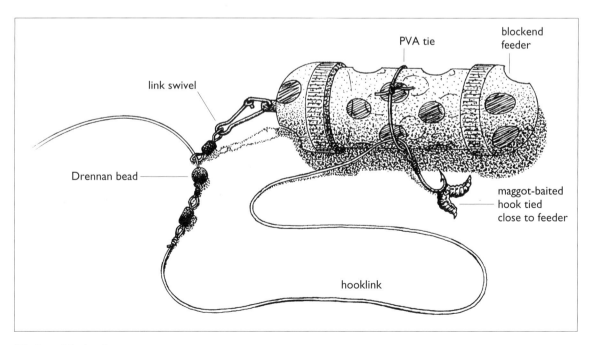

The looped feeder rig.

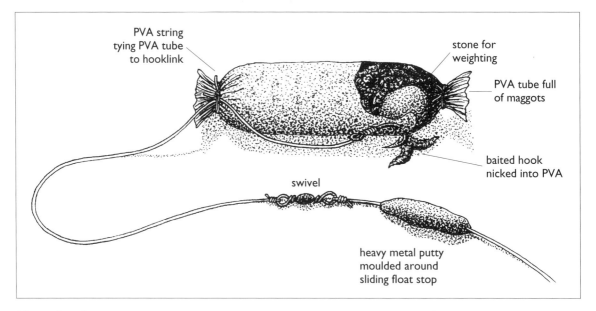

The condom rig.

such that it hangs against the hookbait, it results in a tight area of loose feed right where the hook is lying, and an unencumbered line. I lightly nick the hook into the side of the PVA tube before casting.

I have used this rig often for maggot fishing in thick cabbages, where I wished to present a bait either freelined or just with a small blob of heavy metal putty.

HAIR RIG ALTERNATIVES

Paste Baits
In the last season, I have been doing quite a bit of chubbing using soft pastes, in particular, two proprietary brands of carp mix. These are SBS Strawberry Jam and Rod Hutchinson's Seafoodblend. I have to say that results have been more than encouraging. Several multiple catches have resulted and many more exciting possibilities exist. Although I have caught fish by moulding the paste around a big hook, better results and certainly more hittable bites have resulted from hair rigging in conjunction with a bolt rig. This is easily achieved by adapting a simple leger stop.

Boilies
A standard hair rig, as found in any treatise on carp fishing, is used for chubbing with boilies. Now, I always fish the baits tight against the hook shank, as I have had quite a high incidence of missed bites when using longer hairs.

To hold the boilie in place, I use a thin sliver of plastic drinking straw, which I push through the loop of the hair. This is stiff enough to hold the

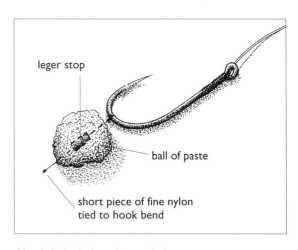

Simple hair rig for soft paste baits.

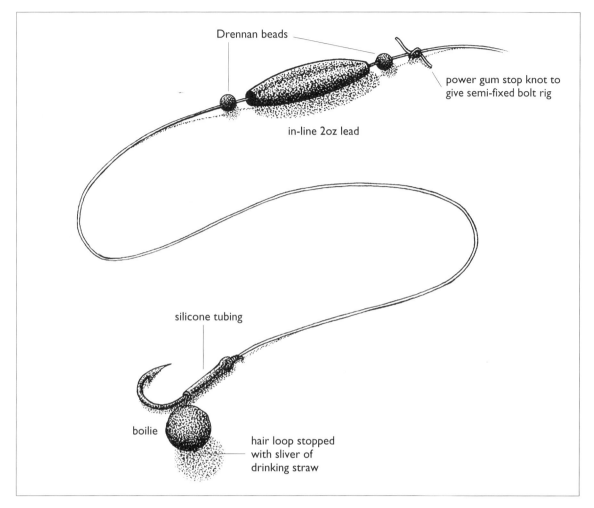

Drennan beads

power gum stop knot to
give semi-fixed bolt rig

in-line 2oz lead

silicone tubing

boilie

hair loop stopped
with sliver of
drinking straw

In-line bolt rig.

bait in place yet it can be trimmed neatly to size once pulled into the bait surface. The dumb-bell hair stops you can buy are fine, but I find them a bit fiddly, especially in cold or damp conditions.

Mini/Midi-Boilies

Chubbing with mini- and midi-boilies has real potential on harder-fished waters where the fish are becoming wary of more traditional offerings. The only problem with their use on a decent sized hook is that they tend to split very easily. They are therefore best fished off the hook in a hair rig arrangement, and Len Arbery and his friends use the highly efficient stiff bristle rig.

Personally, I prefer something a little more flexible and for a while used a standard hair rig. However, this can be very fiddly with a small bait like a mini-boilie and I have therefore devised a simple little rig for fishing two mini-boilies in tandem. The beauty of this set-up is that many baits can be prepared at home before fishing, a godsend on those wet and cold winter days.

To mount a brace of these mini-boilies, I take a short piece of thin rubber band and pierce one end with a fine needle. The same fine needle is used to pierce two mini-boilies. I then use a short length of stiff monofilament (I find that about ½in/12mm Drennan sea line ideal) to impale one

Stage one in making the mini-boilie hair rig.

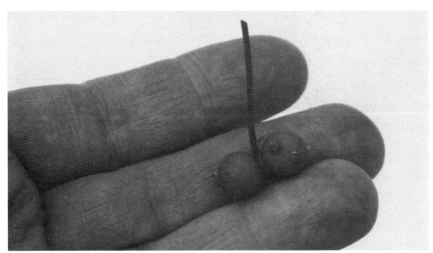

Stage two.

Stage three, the finished article.

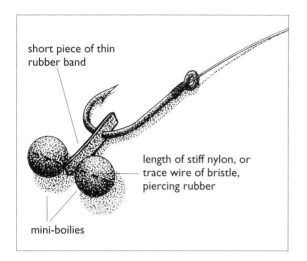

My special mini-boilie tandem rig.

As with any off-the-hook bait presentation, I have found this rig best fished as a bolt arrangement, using a lead far heavier than I would contemplate for orthodox chubbing. It really is scaled down carping, with a size 6 Au Lion d'Or, a six-inch hook length of 8lb Silkworm, and a semi-fixed two-ounce lead. With this arrangement, chub bites are truly awesome, and all the little taps that are inevitable when small fish peck at the baits can be safely ignored. Fishing minis on this rig with a standard light rolling leger produces an unacceptable number of missed bites.

Hemp Multi-Hair Rig

When fishing over hemp loose feed, and the chub cannot be persuaded to take other baits, this rig can provide the solution. I usually use it in conjunction with a PVA tube filled with dried hemp. The simplest way to attach the hemp grains to each individual hair is with superglue. I pick each grain up individually with tweezers, dab the side opposite the split with superglue and hold it in place on the hair for a few seconds. This works much better and quicker if carried out with pre-dried grains. Like all hair rig arrangements, it is best fished as a bolt rig in conjunction with a heavy lead.

boilie, then the rubber, then the other boilie. With the two boilies mounted side by side, the line is trimmed to size and the hook point then passed through the other end of the rubber. My initial experiments with this rig used fine copper wire in place of the stiff monofilament. A little trace wire would also do the job, but I prefer the nylon. This prevents any possibility of a smaller fish getting the wire jammed across its mouth.

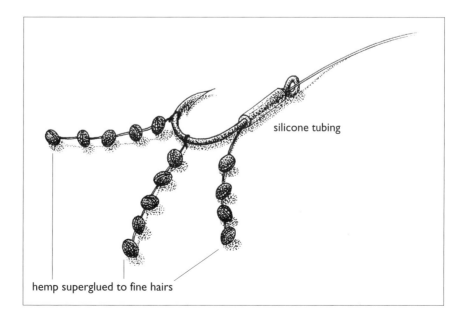

Multi-hair hemp rig.

Maggot/Caster Hair Rig

This particular hair rig variant is absolutely lethal, and has caught lots of chub and barbel, although it is very prone to the attentions of nuisance fish. It is therefore best used where you know there are only big fish present. Simply tie to the hook bend a length of very fine monofilament and trim to the required length. Then apply a dab of superglue to the fat ends of two maggots and hold them together, trapping the end of the hair as you do so. Within seconds, you have the most naturally wriggling bait imaginable.

Adjustable Particle Hair Rig

The most common objection to hair rigging particles is the intensely fiddling process of their production, which I have managed to overcome with my adjustable variant. This can also be

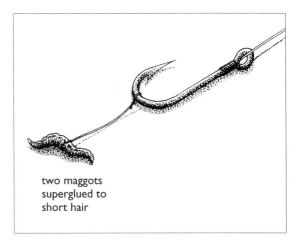

two maggots
superglued to
short hair

Superglued maggots on the hair.

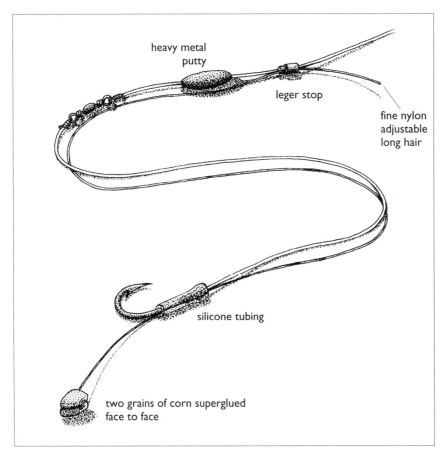

heavy metal
putty

leger stop

fine nylon
adjustable
long hair

silicone tubing

two grains of corn superglued
face to face

The adjustable hair bolt rig.

Pop-up boilie rig.

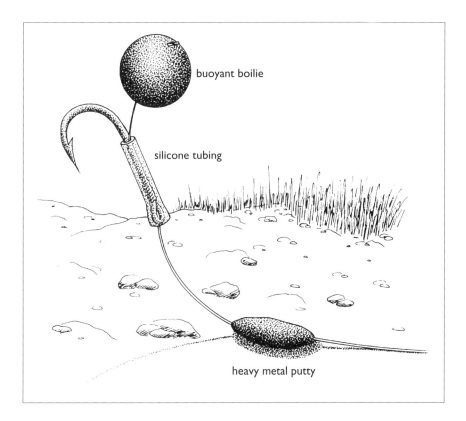

used for the maggot/caster application mentioned previously.

I take eight inches or so of fine monofilament, of about one pound breaking strain, and thread it through a normal leger stop and silicon rubber hook shank sleeve. Then I superglue my chosen particles to the end of the hair. The best way to do this is to apply a drop of glue to one face of the chosen particle, and then trap the line in place with another particle. Using two grains of corn mounted this way is a brilliant presentation and one of my favourite summer rigs. After a few seconds, pull the line back through the leger stop and silicon tubing until the hair is the required length, and then tighten the leger stop, which holds the hair firmly in place. When you need to change the bait, it is a simple matter to snip off the remains of the old bait, pull a little more of the hair through, and you are back in business once again. This is a far quicker and easier method than fumbling around tying up fresh hair rigs between each cast.

POP-UP RIGS

Boilies and Mini-Boilies

These rigs are exactly as before, but using buoyant boilies. The only amendment to the rig itself is the small blob of heavy metal, the positioning of which determines the distance from the bottom at which the bait will be presented.

Paste Baits

For buoyant paste offerings, tie up the hair rig with a small cork ball or polyball in place of the leger stop. Then mould your paste round the ball, place heavy metal again in the appropriate place, and you have your finished rig. In both of these rigs, the heavy metal stays in place better if it has something to key on to. For adjustability, a movable float stop knot is ideal.

Particle Baits

All particles can be presented as buoyant offerings by mounting them in conjunction with

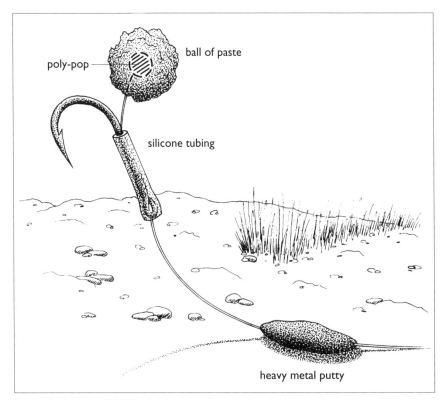

Pop-up paste rig.

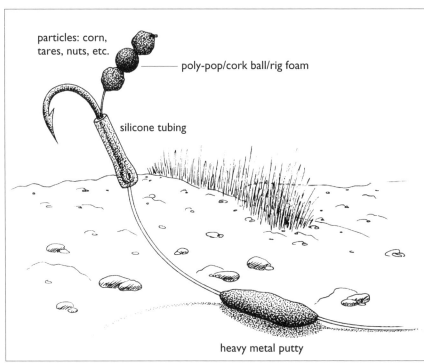

Pop-up particle rig.

Just add maggots for one Medusa rig.

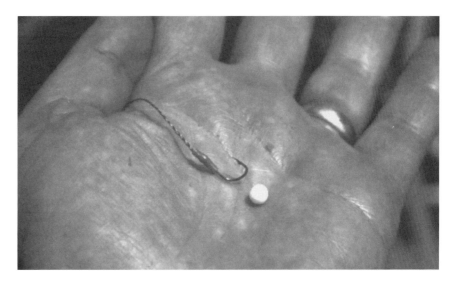

either a small polyball or a small piece of rig foam. If you are using a polyball, you can go to the trouble of colouring it to match the bait with a marker pen. I am not sure how much difference this makes, but it is aesthetically pleasing. When using sweetcorn, I cut a flat section from the middle of a polyball, and superglue corn grains either side to make a sandwich, and this has worked very well.

The Medusa Rig

One of the most lethal presentations for maggots is on this rig. A polyball is mounted on a short hair and then maggots are superglued by their fat ends to the ball, until it is a writhing mass of live maggots. This living, wriggling ball, presented just off bottom, is totally irresistible to fish.

Exactly the same as the Medusa are two variants I have christened the pinhead rig and the zit rig. In the pinhead, casters are glued upright on the polyball and in the zit the polyball is covered in hemp grains. Both of these rigs are quite fiddly to create, especially with the casters, but both have produced fish. They are also lots of fun to play about with, and as I go fishing primarily for fun I need no other justification.

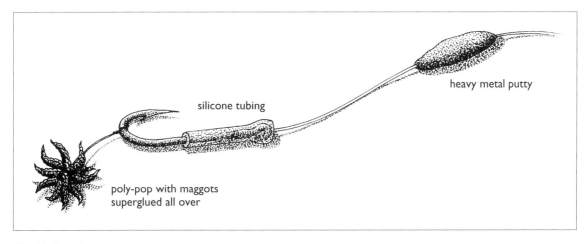

The Medusa rig.

6 FREELINING AND STALKING

OBSERVATION AND CAUTION

Fishing for chub in the heat of summer, with the foliage at its lushest and the water low and clear, demands stealth, quiet and concealment on the part of the angler, otherwise this wariest of creatures takes fright and flees.

Such stalking appeals to that latent hunting instinct which is part of the reason that we anglers go fishing in the first place. If your heart does not start pounding as a big chub launches itself at that slug you have just presented, with its mouth agape and its gills flaring, then you have no right to be an angler.

Location of summer chub in many rivers is visual, as the fish very obligingly show themselves readily. When a river is low and clear it is a good idea to walk the banks with a little notepad, jotting down the exact locations of every chub you spot. This information will prove invaluable later in the season. The same book should be used for noting the positions of riverbed depressions, the extent of weed beds and lilies, and so on. One of my more valuable purchases in recent seasons is

Chub are easily spooked in low, clear, summer conditions.

a pair of breast waders and every summer, when my fisheries are low and clear, I walk along miles of riverbed, noting down every interesting feature I find. I have lost count of the productive swims I have found in this manner, many of which would have been completely overlooked by more orthodox bankside searching techniques. I am thinking here particularly of depressions in the bed that are masked from the casual observer by either lilies or streamer weed. Knowing the location of such depressions in the winter, when the levels are much higher, gives you an invaluable edge over other anglers who lack that specific knowledge.

Where summer chub cannot be located visually, because of depth or very heavy weed cover, always search for them under cover or in the vicinity of good oxygenation. Just downstream of gravelly rapids and the runs out from weirs are reliable, as are areas where sidestreams or other flows join the main river.

In weedy rivers, chub have a habit of pushing their snouts under the root formations of streamer or lilies, at the downstream extremity, or of sheltering among the downstream stems of bulrushes. This often leads to the characteristic clue for the summer chub hunter, that of an occasional glimpse of a big black tail protruding from the foliage. When you are searching for summer chub in situations like this, walk slowly and carefully, wear a wide-brimmed hat and glasses with polaroid lenses, and spend several minutes studying each likely spot. Chub are rarely still for long and if there is a chub under that inviting clump of streamer, he will eventually betray his presence to the patient observer.

A well-known facet of chub behaviour is their fondness for overhanging foliage. Any line of bushes or trees, or rubbish raft around trailing branches, is almost certain to harbour chub at some time, as is an area where fallen timber litters the riverbed.

Keen observation.

RUSH BEDS

In high summer, many good chub will be found lying in tiny gaps in rushes, and most of these swims will demand the use of totally static baits to prevent constant snagging. This is where baits such as slugs are nowhere near as effective. They are certainly better fished on the move, slug spinning, as I fondly refer to it. For true static ambush baits, lobs are my favourite, perhaps with a little air in the tail to make them waver attractively, although if lobs are not available, offerings such as cheesepaste, luncheon meat or boilies can be just as effective.

Many years ago, there was a thirty-yard length of an Ouse sidestream that ran between heavily wooded high banks, a stretch that was almost solid with weed and looked no more than knee-deep anywhere. The central channel in summer was a complete mass of head high reeds, the only clear water being the marginal fringes, where the water was ankle-deep over gravel.

Twice in one day I arrived on that high bank to disturb a big chub basking in those marginal shallows, and each time it shot into the central rushes. Obviously, there was a bolt hole of some description there. These days, it would be time for the chest waders, but then such luxury was undreamed of. So it was down to underpants for an exploratory trip into the river.

After two full seasons of fishing that stretch, I was amazed at what I found. Right at the centre of the rush bed was a short length where the individual stems bent over to form a kind of tunnel, and this coincided with a sudden depth increase to about three feet. The deeper water was in the form of a narrow trench for about six paces, when it opened out into a pool about seven feet wide. Only by wading slowly downstream, and forcing my way through the dense rushes, did I find this pool, which was totally hidden by the way the reed stems had arched over in a kind of protective canopy. I defy anyone to have seen that swim from the bank.

Top angler Matt Hayes plays a good chub through rushes.

The chub that caused the excitement. Matt's three-and-a-half-pounder that took a slug in dense rushes.

Jungle warfare in high summer.

On that occasion, opening the swim out would have been highly inappropriate as its seclusion was the reason I felt it may harbour the big chub.

In the end, I decided to fish for that chub from in the river itself. Tucking a bag of cheesepaste down the waist band of my underpants, I carefully positioned a small fishing stool in the middle of the dense rushes at the head of the narrow trench, so that my rod tip just protruded over the trench when I was seated. My landing net was also placed to hand and then I baited my hook with a large piece of cheesepaste and waded down to the pool, where I deposited the bait in the centre of the little clearing. Keeping the rod tip submerged, so that I did not foul any of the closely growing rush stems, I then slowly backed down the trench, paying out line as I went. Once seated on my stool, I gingerly took in the slack, and waited on events. I knew it would be a long wait after that disturbance, but it was a hot day, pleasantly cool in the river and there was certainly nothing better to do!

About an hour later, there was a sudden twitch on the rod tip, followed by a full-blooded wrench, and seconds later I was on my feet playing my big chub; 4lb 14oz it weighed, a fish that gave me immense satisfaction.

CABBAGE PATCHES

For the purpose of definition, I have always referred to lily beds as those areas where the bulk of the leaves are on the surface and cabbage patches as those river swims where the current is such that most of the leaves are submerged, even in summer. Some swims, obviously, in the low water of summer, will exhibit both sunken and surface leaves. A proportion of a river's chub population will spend much of the midday period basking under lily pads, showing general disinterest in things going on around them. Or so it seems. One approach I can recommend is the use of the induced take around the fringes of the weed bed with moving naturals, especially big, black slugs. Cast the bait, freelined, to land as close to the extremities of the pads as possible. Allow it to sink and leave it for a minute or so. Give the bait a little jerk by a sharp tug on the line, and let it sink again. Then repeat the manoeuvre, this time retrieving a few inches of line, perhaps pulling the bait to just under the surface, before allowing it back in free fall. Chub find these teasing little movements irresistible, and some of the bites you can get have to be seen to be believed.

This four-pounder accepted a slug amidst dense cabbages.

Fishing for chub over dense lily pads with floating crust is another heart-stopping activity. I use heavily greased line for this game, and manoeuvre a big chunk of crust into the tiniest gaps of clear water imaginable. It is difficult to describe on paper the excitement when you first see the lily pads shaking as chub approach the bait, and as a great pair of white lips materialize under the bread, and silently suck it into the depths.

One presentation I love to use in dense cabbages is to arrange for a lobworm to lie on top of a surface pad and then carefully inch it over the edge, so that it topples into the water naturally. This presentation promotes some very savage reactions indeed.

STREAMER BEDS

At first glance, a stretch of summer river apparently completely choked with ranunculus looks totally daunting, if not impossible. Most anglers take the easy option and walk straight past such lengths, preferring more easily fished areas.

By taking this decision, some of the most heavily populated areas of a summer river are being utterly ignored and in this section I want to explain my method of getting the best out of dense ranunculus.

It can be difficult to spot chub in streamer, even in shallows, as they are extremely adept at concealing themselves under the wafting fronds. In an area of dense streamer, there may only be narrow channels of clear water between the beds, and it is these areas of clear water that you have to aim for.

Thirty or forty yards of streamer can contain dozens of such little clear runs, and each one can harbour chub. The way to fish is to be methodical and cast to each in turn, unless you are lucky enough to locate a chub by catching a glimpse of a big, black tail under trailing tresses.

Naturally, accurate casting is an essential ingredient for successful freelining in streamer. The bait has to land in the clear water and sink naturally. Generally, if it alights on top of the weed itself and drags, you have blown your

chances in that swim for a while, as the chub spook badly to this type of disturbance. Casting accuracy is obviously enhanced with a heavier bait, and as it is important to do without lead in these situations, the ideal choices are the dense offerings of big slugs or bunches of lobs.

Chub lying under streamer take baits with supreme confidence provided they arrive in a natural fashion, and large catches of summer fish are possible if you know what you are doing and can cast accurately. So take plenty of bait!

The alternative approach to fishing streamer beds is to locate or create feeding hot spots, and then fish each in turn. Let us have a look at the technique for doing this.

The first thing we have to realize is that what at first appears a totally uniform glide solid with streamer is usually anything but, the streamer tresses normally hiding river bed variations in the form of depressions, obstructions and so on. It is these underwater features that will often dictate the whereabouts of the fish, although the shelter afforded by the flowing tresses is often sufficient by itself, without variable bottom contours. This however, is usually only true in summer, when flows are gentle. In winter, when higher current speed leads to increased turbulence, the underwater depressions take on far greater significance. It is therefore vital to locate these features if you intend fishing the same stretch in winter.

The obvious method would be to plumb progressively down the weedbed. Using a heavy lead ensures a true reading as it will not tend to be washed away by swift flow and the lead will plunge through the tresses easily. In deep stretches, this is the only viable method and I recommend taking as many soundings as possible to build up the most complete mental image of the riverbed.

In shallower stretches however, and many stretches thick with streamer will be shallow, a far more efficient and infinitely quicker method of mapping the river bed is by wading it, either in swimming trunks or chest waders. The way I do it is to start at the upstream extremity and slowly move downstream, feeling ahead of me with an extendable landing net handle. I have found many unexpected depressions of two feet or more by

Sometimes you have to go in after them.

wading in this manner. The handle prevents me from stepping into deep water without warning.

Having located the hot spot in the swim, and most streamer beds will have one, even if it is only a depression of a few inches, you now have to decide how to prepare and fish it.

Where you find a generally shallow run containing a substantial depression, a very common feature, it is almost certain that the depression will act as a holding spot for many species, particularly chub and barbel, both of which have great affinity for streamer. Until a few years ago, having found such a depression, I would bait it, after having cleared perhaps a few streamer fronds to allow access to the swim. And I caught plenty of fish. Now, however, I do not bait the holding spot, but an area perhaps five yards away. The reason for this is that, once a fish gets nervous, it will bolt for home. By fishing the holding spot, we are fishing its home, raising the possibility of the chub vacating the area altogether. This technique was first perfected in my

barbel fishing, but it is just as relevant for chub, as my catches of big chub from prepared barbel swims will testify. By fishing a few yards from its holding spot, we know exactly where a spooked fish will go. It is then a simple matter of topping up the bait in the fishing area and leaving the fish in peace long enough to get over its fright, when it will emerge from its front door again and recommence feeding.

Having discovered the holding spots in a long stretch of streamer, let me now make two points about the actual swim or swims to be fished. First, do not make the swims too remote from the holding spot; a few yards is ample. You need the fish to feel secure in the knowledge that they are not too far from home should danger threaten. Second, and this is most important, remember that you dictate where the fish will feed by your baiting technique. For example, say you have found a depression in mid-river, two rods' lengths from the near bank. There is nothing to stop you making the fishing area one rod's length from the

Trefor West plays a good fish through Avon streamer.

bank. Your bait will create the feeding hot spot. The advantages of this are obvious. At one rod length, control of baiting and fishing accuracy is simple, and you can more easily observe what is going on in the low water of summer.

Having decided on the swims to be fished, I now remove the minimum number of streamer tresses to be able to fish without getting hung up. A gap in the streamer of a few inches wide is ample, so long as you can locate it accurately. This is where my extending landing net handle is pressed into service again. Equipped with a screw-in scythe blade, it is capable of very precise and delicate streamer frond surgery.

Let us hold a mental image of fifty yards of unbroken streamer. Having waded it, we have isolated five areas of interest we think might be holding spots and have chosen nearby fishing areas accordingly. A few minutes' work in each area has opened up five little swims, all one rod length from the bank, which can be baited with pin-point accuracy. Those tasks completed, taking perhaps an hour or less, we have transformed a stretch of river on which we have not a clue where to start into one where we can fish five precise swims, with confidence sky high. I recommend the technique to you; I have taken countless good chub and barbel using it.

HEAVILY OVERGROWN AREAS

It is an undeniable fact that big chub and dense snags go together, and in summer and autumn particularly, many rivers holding specimen chub contain many areas of this type. Especially interesting are smaller, neglected rivers and streams, where fallen timber abounds, there are dense, overhanging bramble beds, or a maze of low growing and criss-crossing branches, and so on.

Unlike other defined swim types, such as streamer beds, for presenting natural baits, or fast shallows for floating crust, it is impossible to give any hard and fast rules for fishing jungle swims, because they are so incredibly diverse. What I would like to do, therefore, is tell you about some of the situations I have been faced with, and how the problems were overcome. Hopefully, you will be able to adapt my experiences to situations in your own fishing.

For jungle chubbing, apart from the normal tackle, it is wise to have with you equipment necessary to make a swim fishable, or create sufficient access to be able to present a bait in the first place. A small cupboard in my van contains the following items:
1. A pair of secateurs
2. Heavy gardening gloves

That debris-strewn far bank is home to many big chub.

3. Small tree saw
4. Small portable spade
5. Weed drag
6. Scythe blade for screwing into extendable landing net handle
7. Chest waders, old beach towels and change of clothes
8. Length of rope for temporarily tying back larger branches
9. Elastoplast, bandage and antiseptic cream

Swim Preparation

I cannot emphasize enough that under no circumstances should you undertake mass pruning or swim clearance operations. I myself am a great believer in leaving a river in as natural a state as when I found it.

Swim preparation in this context means simply undertaking the minimum work necessary to make the area fishable. This could mean creating a tiny access through brambles, or removing a couple of dead branches that would otherwise make bait introduction impossible. The drag could be used for removing a pile of fallen timber from the margins, the scythe blade for removing the annoying trailing blackthorn branch or cutting out the fallen reedmace stem that continually fouls the line. The possibilities are endless.

The elastoplast and bandage are obviously a precaution against the inevitable cuts and scratches you will get, while the towel and spare clothes provide for the day when you climb that old tree for a better look and fall in. Trefor and I have done that many times!

Tackle

In jungle swims, rarely will you have the luxury of playing a chub in the accepted sense of the word. Usually, allowing the fish two yards of line after hooking is inviting irretrievable snagging. The name of the game is therefore one of hook and hold, for which adequate tackle is absolutely essential. My minimum gear for big chub in these circumstances would be a barbel rod and 6lb or 8lb line, although I would have little hesitation in coupling a carp rod with 10lb line if conditions warranted it.

Strong hooks are a must: ones that will not pull out under extreme pressure. I have always used Au Lion d'Or in the larger sizes, but I can also highly recommend Drennan boilie hooks, which are very tough. At the time of writing I have just obtained some of the new Terry Eustace Penetrator hooks, and those also look ideally suited. I do not recommend the chemically sharpened patterns, which, although very much in vogue at the moment for general angling, are not suitable for hold and heave tactics, as they tend to cut out.

Another essential in the tackle box is line grease, or silicon spray floatant. Allowing surplus line to sink into snags is inviting problems.

Long-handled landing nets can be awkward to manoeuvre in tight situations, and I prefer one of those very light, extendible patterns used by matchmen. Under full compression, the handle is only about four feet in length, but it extends to eleven. Although I have used triangular nets all my life, they really can be a pain in thick undergrowth. I have just started to use one of the Keenets spoon patterns, the 31in Mega Spoon, and I have to say that it is brilliant for chub and barbel on overgrown rivers. With no sharp corners, snagging on the undergrowth is far less of a problem. It is important to keep the gear to a minimum in a thicket, and I therefore dispense with seats and boxes, all the bits I need being kept in a small bag over my shoulder. What I have seen a friend using, which is a brilliant idea, is one of those 'bum bags', so popular with holiday makers for keeping valuables in when wearing just shorts or swimming gear. The better ones are split into compartments, which could house leads, hook boxes, spare bait samples and so on.

Last but not least, even in hot weather, keep as much of your flesh covered as possible. As well as avoidance of obvious scratches and nettle stings, overgrown areas are home to myriads of mosquitoes and other biting insects. To a family of mosquitoes, the bare legs and arms of a sweaty chub angler must be better than a barbecue!

Jungle Warfare
The first example of this concerns chub that live under dense thickets of impenetrable bankside foliage, of either brambles, alders or the like. This particular swim was where there was a twenty yard stretch of dense blackthorns lining quite a high bank, their roots protruding into the water through the bank wall. The blackthorn bushes extended over the water for several feet, their outer branches draping down into and below the surface. As the main flow went under those blackthorns, the swim was a screamer for chub.

Dense midriver cabbages and head-high reedmace made casting across from the far bank impossible in the two tiny spots where there were gaps in the draping branches, and the blackthorn main stems were far too close together to make cutting through from the near bank a viable option without causing major environmental damage.

Presenting a bait from upstream on the same bank was the only sensible access, but here there were also problems. About five yards down from the start of the foliage there was a large branch level with the surface, which prevented floating baits such as breadcrust from further progress in the centre of the run. The turbulence created by that branch inevitably threw floating offerings into the very snaggy near bank, and out of sight under those protruding roots. I did have a few bites on floating crust that way, but as the bait was not visible, therefore making timing the strike hit and miss, the success was extremely limited. And snagging and tackle losses were high. The very low-growing foliage at the head of the run also made it impossible to cast a bottom bait to land just up from that offending branch, and drifting a bottom bait far enough under the cover was also out because of the thick bed of cabbages that acted as a kind of closed front door to the swim. Quite a dilemma.

In the end, the key to unlocking that swim proved nothing more complicated than a loaf of ordinary medium sliced bread. It was obvious that the presentation required was a slow sinking offering introduced just above that surface branch, one that would then come to rest at the centre of the blackthorn canopy. So what I did was use a couple of air-injected lobs on a size 6, and no weight on the line, and manoeuvre the bait on to a slice of bread. That was a bit of a game in itself, taking about three slices per successful 'landing' of the lobs. With the pick-up disengaged, the bread then carried the hook bait under those low branches until it reached the large obstruction, at which point a little tension on the line from me pulled the bait off the bread. Releasing the line again allowed the bait to drift under the branch, to settle on the bottom a further five yards or so down the run.

This early Claydon Brook five-pounder was extracted from a tremendous tangle of fallen timber.

The first time I fished the swim in that way, I had several nice perch and chub on lobs, and a big chub on a chunk of cheese. After a lot of head scratching, the solution in that swim was simple and yet so deadly.

My good friend and great barbel angler Trefor West is no slouch when it comes to chub either, and one of his jungle warfare exploits is well worth recounting, as much of this type of chubbing is definitely mind over matter.

Trefor was natural bait chubbing with crayfish, and he came upon an area with an impenetrably wooded opposite bank. At one point a large willow had toppled in the river, its branches forming a criss-crossing maze at about midstream. The two larger branches, although not actually touching the water, were only a foot or so above the surface. Had it not been for the big chub lying the other side of the tree under the far bank, Tre-

for would have walked straight by. But having seen it, he had to catch it.

There seemed no way of presenting a bait to that fish without casting over the tree branches, but Trefor hit on a plan. The swim required a bit of deliberate chub scaring. Lying his rod on the bank with the pick-up disengaged, he baited the hook with a dead crayfish and then waded across to where he had seen the chub. Coming to the branches, he ducked under them, and eventually stood in the spot where the fish had been lying. Right on the edge of the far bank, Trefor arranged a little nest of twigs and grass, on which he lay the crayfish, and then he re-crossed the river to his tackle. Very carefully, so as not to dislodge the bait, he took in the slack and then sat back to wait for a while. In this case, there was no point using the bait on the bottom as crayfish are best fished on the move and he had with him nothing like meat or cheese, both of which are good when fished statically.

For half an hour he sat there patiently, until he caught sight of the chub returning to his normal position, under the far bank. Taking the line in his left hand, Trefor gave it a sharp, six-inch tug, which dislodged the cray and made it give a little jump into the river, where it landed with an audible plop. Seconds later, there was an almighty swirl, and the chub was on, a fish that ultimately proved to weigh around four pounds. As I said, mind over matter.

After taking seventy-six five-pound chub and three sixes in my career to date, it is perhaps strange that one of my fondest chub memories is a fish of 4lb 14oz, which I took from a real jungle of a swim on the Leam. As well as the manner of its capture, the unusual pigmentation of the fish, with its golden flanks and rich navy fins, make it one of the most memorable specimen fish I have ever taken.

The fish lived in a tangled maze of far bank alders and draping hawthorns, all of them knitted together in a dense thicket of brambles. At the centre of this thicket, a dwarf willow threw its branches to around midstream, where they hung to the water surface. This was another area impossible to fish from the far bank. It was also impossible to fish from either up- or downstream because of large trees and any fish under those alders was entitled to feel secure. Twice one early winter, I saw a very big fish at the edge of those willow branches and determined to catch it.

After weighing up the options, the only way seemed to be to go through the bramble thicket itself. Because of my paranoia about not creating environmental damage, I used my secateurs to cut a hole just large enough for me to squeeze into and then a little pathway through the thicket until I could lie by the steep bank. It was about four feet down to the water's surface.

The exact spot where I wanted to place my hook bait was masked by two crossing alder branches, so these were lassoed and carefully tied back out of the way. Lastly, a large protruding branch at the waterline, which would inevitably have cost me any chub I hooked, was sawn away

and removed. After snipping away a few thorny twigs at eye level, to protect my face, I backed out of my uncomfortable little swim and gave it a couple of hours to settle. But not before introducing a few free flake offerings.

Two hours later, the fun began. I got myself and the rod into position without too much aggravation, but the net was a nightmare. Having lowered a generous chunk of crust into the swim, I had, mercifully, a very short time to wait. Following a terrific lunge on the rod, my big chub shot upstream with great power.

The limitations of my cramped little swim soon became obvious, as the lack of head room meant I had to hold the rod in the middle to exert any kind of pressure. Basically, the fish went where it liked. Netting it was hilarious, the mesh being tangled, it appeared, in a thousand separate places. But eventually I managed it, and emerged from the torture chamber of brambles covered in cuts and carrying the most magnificent chub I have ever seen. After I returned that fish to its home under the alders, I refilled my hole with all the cut brambles and branches I had removed so that no-one would ever know it had been disturbed. I vowed that I would never re-open that swim again. I never have.

The ultimate in jungle warfare, of course, are those areas where there are literally tiny areas of clear water amongst masses of fallen timber. Where a fallen tree is right across a stream, some of the clearings cannot even be seen without climbing into the branches. The only option here is surface fishing with floating baits on very strong tackle. Brute force and ignorance aptly sums up the approach once a fish is hooked.

My last example is from a cold winter's day when the temperature hovered around zero all day and snow flurries made it feel arctic.

Surprising conditions, therefore, to take a few chub on floating crust, as Trefor and I did that day. That had not been a deliberate decision. A few chub had taken floating bits of our bread mash, and we had not been slow to take advantage of the fact.

Just before dusk, I was fishing immediately upstream of a huge fallen willow and threw the remains of a sandwich into the branches for the birds. Some of the bread tumbled through the tangle of branches and seconds later there was a loud slurp as something sucked it down. This was intriguing and I clambered into the branches to see the residue of a swirl where there was about a foot square of clear water between the woodwork.

For the hell of it, I impaled a chunk of crust on my hook, climbed back into the branches and then lowered the bait into the little clearing. As snow began falling again, great white lips engulfed the bread. There was the most incredible upheaval as the chub thrashed the surface and I yelled Trefor to bring the net. He was soon on the scene, and a sight I shall never forget is of his swaying over a freezing cold Cherwell on the flimsiest branch imaginable, as he at last successfully extricated the fish for me. It wasn't even four pounds, but it was a lot of fun.

Jungle fishing requires a certain attitude, and an open mind to boot. As I said at the beginning, there is no one single approach. But in many ways, it typifies true angling. There are those who see the obscenity of stocking big barbel into little, overstocked holes in the ground as angling. Give me the purity of overgrown little chub rivers any time.

INDUCED BITE TECHNIQUES

It is always preferable to work along a small chub river in an upstream direction, so that you approach any basking fish from behind, making your own concealment that much easier. Let me assume for a minute that I have spotted half a dozen good chub basking idly in a mid-river clearing in a rush bed, and have managed to insinuate myself low in the undergrowth just downstream of their position, without their becoming aware of my presence. I know that a bait should be taken instantly, providing I make no silly mistakes. Having greased the line, I cast a slug to land a good three yards above the shoal, from where it starts to sink and bump down with the current.

Instantly, there is a grand prix-style race for the bait, one of the fish engulfing it at top speed. So often have I experienced this initially violent reaction that I am now prepared for it by not having the line too tight, either inviting a stolen bait or a badly spooked fish. It is vitally important to allow a foot or two of slack to give the chub that vital couple of seconds to turn down with the bait before striking. I remember on the Upper Ouse actually being smashed on the bite using crayfish, by having too tight a line!

On another day, the reaction to the slug might be very different. All the fish could totally ignore the bait at first, until it starts to drift past them, when one of the fish might take it very lazily, by intercepting it with a barely perceptible flick of that big black tail.

Twitched crayfish across the gravel proved to be this chub's undoing.

Bouncing cheesepaste down a run was the successful method used to take this specimen.

Where chub have seen the presentation often, and are starting to get wary, they may consistently ignore this straightforward presentation, and need inducing into a take. There are two ways of doing this. First, you can try dropping a bait with a good loud plop on the tail of a fish. This is an 'all or nothing' approach. Sometimes, the fish will whirl round without thinking and snap up the bait in an instant. At other times, it will take off in a panic. From my experience, there is no way of knowing which to expect and so I will always try the following induced take technique first.

If I have tried the usual presentation without response, but the fish do not appear unduly alarmed, I will arrange for the bait to come to rest not too far from one of the chub. With the fish in the mood I have in mind, it will lie there looking at the bait, neither moving forward to take it nor retreating. After about thirty seconds, I will take in just a few inches of line quite sharply, making the bait twitch and hopefully disturb a small puff of silt. If there is still no reaction, my next movement will be more exaggerated, perhaps making the bait jump six inches. Like a kitten watching you move a ball of wool, chub cannot resist the bait making these movements, especially if the bait is slowly 'escaping', and will pounce on it whether they are hungry or not. The reaction is purely instinctive and completely involuntary, inbuilt for the fish to take advantage of opportunities for feeding that can be very fleeting.

In the summer, surprisingly large numbers of chub can congregate under small rafts of floating algae and rubbish accumulated around tree branches, and these swims are also fished effectively with the induced take technique. What I do is drop a slug at the upstream extremity of the raft and let it sink naturally, allowing plenty of slack line so that the bait drifts downstream as far as possible. Assuming there is no bite while the bait is sinking, I allow the bait to remain static on the bottom for perhaps a minute, before starting a retrieve in a series of staccato six-inch jerks. Many is the time I have had the slug just under the surface at the end of such a retrieve when a great pair of white lips have appeared from the depths and engulfed it. A good bait to use for this upstream twitching technique is lobworm injected with sufficient air so that it only just sinks. By the time this bait touches bottom it can have drifted right to the downstream extremity of the swim.

7 WINTER LEGERING TECHNIQUES

FISHING THE LINK LEGER

Winter chubbing is undoubtedly when the fish are at their fighting best, and this is when legering comes into its own. Most of my winter chubbing is carried out with a straightforward link leger. These days, the lead is attached via a link swivel, for ease of weight adjustment for varying swims or techniques. For fishing a glide or crease for example, I will search first of all on the edge of the fastest water. This may require, say, ⅝oz of lead. I will fish progressively further down the swim on this lead and then, depending on results, may select a lighter lead and repeat the procedure. This has the effect of making the bait swing in closer to the near bank, where the flow is more gentle. This approach can be varied *ad infinitum*, until the feeding zone is located.

Alternatively, I may be fishing a large raft and wish to place a bait as far under the rubbish as possible. A good ploy is to use a large buoyant bait, such as a chunk of crust, and a minimum of lead, so that the bait only just sinks. If it takes several yards to sink to the bottom you can easily calculate how long it will take to settle in your chosen swim.

Where you wish to fish a swim behind obstacles such as mid-river rushes or fallen timber, or search the slacks behind dead cabbage root systems, upstream legering can be the most effective presentation. For this it is more important than ever to allow fast and simple amendments to link weight, as the presentation has to be just right. You want to be able to put a good upstream deflection into your rod top or quivertip without pulling the bait out of position. On the other hand, you do not want to anchor the bait to the bottom or it will take too great a pull to move it. The sensitivity of upstreaming is that when a fish pulls the bait, the terminal rig dislodges and drops downstream, creating slack and leading to zero resistance to the biting fish, such that its suspicions are not aroused. Too heavy a lead will

The simple swan shot link leger.

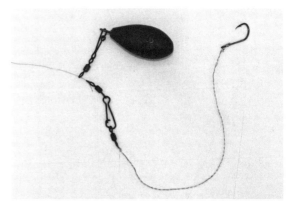

My normal snap link leger. Note that when this rig was tied for the photograph a bead between the two swivels was accidentally omitted.

Straightforward snap link leger rig.

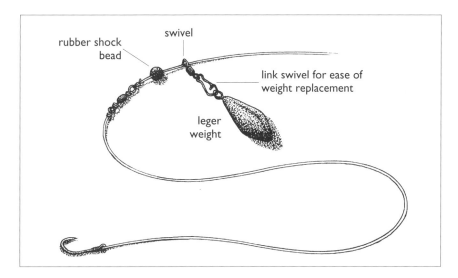

destroy that presentation, and upstream bites will be transformed into savage pulls that are continually missed. There is a detailed explanation of upstream legering techniques later in this chapter. Let me now take a more detailed look at link legering various winter chub swim types.

Fishing in Streamer Weed

In the chapter on watercraft, I have described in some detail what to look for in determining the swims to fish in winter in stretches of water adorned with ranunculus. To recap, we are looking for the consistently smooth flows between the boils and vortices.

One of the features of fishing amid streamer is that the link weight can be reduced from what would normally be required for an equivalent current speed in more open water. This is because the tresses act as a brake on the line and hold the terminal rig in position. The advantage

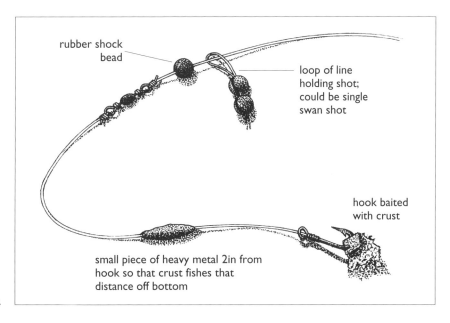

Simple swan shot link leger.

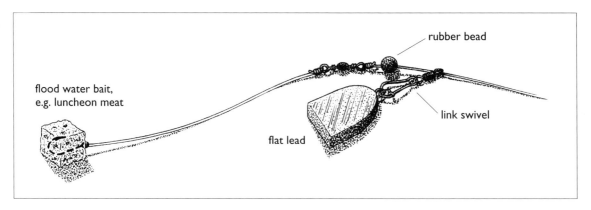

Snap link leger rig for flood water.

of this method also is that you are less likely to become snagged.

My technique with these swims is to sit a few yards upstream of the flat, and cast the bait to alight a yard or two upstream of the required position and slightly further across river. Exactly how much further upstream and across river will depend on both current speed and depth, and can only be found by trial and error on the day. The object is to land the bait on clean gravel, and not in the middle of the weed. Having settled on the gravel, the terminal rig will then slowly roll round to fish under the trailing tresses, if the link weight is correct.

In powerful currents or in flood conditions, a very effective approach to streamer bed flats is to fish them from a considerable distance upstream with a heavy link leger incorporating a flat lead. With the line at the shallowest angle possible to the direction of flow, the pressure on the line is minimized. This presentation is ideal for touch legering, as the rod is pointing directly at the bait, and some very impressive pulls can be experienced.

Fishing Riverbed Depressions

Most rivers contain stretches of shallow and apparently featureless water, of uniform flow from bank to bank, these areas often look barren and hardly worth the effort of fishing them. In some cases that may be true, but such areas often harbour exciting swims in small depressions in the riverbed. Often, these depressions are impossible to locate at winter level, unless the surrounding river is so shallow normally that it is running ripply, with a smooth flat betraying the depression. Generally, therefore, any prior knowledge of the river bed from a summer reconnaissance will be extremely valuable.

I fish these swims aiming to present the bait at the downstream extremity of the depression, where the river bed begins to rise, and the link weight is selected so that the bait stays in that position. Unlike deeper, uniform glides, where moving baits down the glide will be accepted, the water surrounding a depression may be totally devoid of fish, so the bait must stay put. As many of these swims will be found in midriver, it is frequently necessary to fish across faster flows, and flattened leads are useful for presenting static baits in the hot spot. The term 'hot spot' has not been used accidentally, because such a depression can often be the only holding spot for quite a long length of river, and as such attract surprisingly large numbers of fish. This phenomenon is even more pronounced in high water, where the depression provides a useful haven from the more turbulent flows surrounding it.

Fishing Uniform Glides

The bulk of winter chub swims will be suited to the mobile approach, each one being given a relatively short time before moving on. In good winter conditions, chub will take a bait immediately it is introduced and, in a restricted swim, there is

A uniform glide at Throop produced this 5lb 6oz specimen.

often little to be gained from staying biteless for more than about ten minutes. As often as not, that indicates that no chub are present.

Long, uniform glides, with steady flow and smooth surface, indicating both an even riverbed and reasonable depth, are the exceptions, and such swims can be fished all day, gradually being built up by progressive baiting, with large numbers of fish eventually being attracted into the swim.

Unlike many smaller features, long glides of this type are rarely chub-holding areas. It is more likely that separate shoals of fish use them as occasional grazing pastures, as food availability dictates. Careful baiting, therefore, can continually attract new fish into the area, often from a considerable distance downstream, and large catches of fish are possible.

I like to fish such a swim progressively, following a pre-set pattern, so that every inch is searched. After the initial introduction of feed, I make my first cast about five yards down the glide in mid-river, selecting a link weight appropriate for holding in that position. Keeping the loose feed trickling through along that line, each subsequent cast will be fractionally longer, until the entire mid-river line has been thoroughly examined.

Depending on results, I might then amend the line of attack by increasing the terminal weight, to hold further across the flow, and then progressively search that new line. The next ploy could be to lighten the link to make the terminal link swing further inshore. By constant amendment of terminal rig in this fashion, a few hours' fishing will have seen the swim thoroughly searched.

A bonus with such a swim is if it terminates in cover of some description, such as a large tree or line of bushes for instance. If this is the case, very big chub could have taken up station right under the cover, mopping up the constant trickle of free feed. A good method of getting a bait to them very naturally is to reduce the link weight right down and fish it in conjunction with a buoyant bait only just heavy enough to sink. Obviously, a big chunk of crust is ideal. Dropping this bait a few yards upstream will see it sink very slowly, and drift right into the hot spot as naturally as if it were unfettered.

Believe me, that is a deadly presentation.

Inducing Bites

Inducing a bite simply means persuading a chub to take a bait by moving that bait in such a way that it provokes the fish into attacking it, even though it might not be hungry. I have always tried to draw the analogy of the kitten with a ball of wool. If the ball of wool is lying undisturbed, the kitten may have no interest in it. But pull the wool away and see what happens. As often as not, the kitten will pounce on it.

With chub, especially in a reasonable current, much of their food is moving with the flow or has a life of its own. The fish therefore often have to make an instant decision whether to take a food item or not, before it has passed them by. Many of our angling baits do not behave in that way. A piece of legered crust, for example, may arouse the same interest as the static ball of wool does in the kitten. But suddenly pull the crust away, or make it bump downstream, and the chub's instinct will come to the fore. The time for indecision is over and, like our kitten, he often pounces on the bait before it can escape. So effective is this ploy for winter chubbing that my baits are rarely still for long in reasonable water temperatures. Only when it is very cold do I let baits remain static for extended periods. Normally, having cast a bait into position, it will only be allowed to remain where it settles for a couple of minutes before I either raise the rod point, at the same time letting a little line out, to drop the bait downstream or wind in a few inches, to draw the bait upstream. It does not seem to matter that some of these movements must appear unnatural. The mere fact that, in the chub's eyes, the prey is trying to escape, is sufficient to provoke an attack.

THE BOLT RIG

In my winter chubbing, I have two uses for a heavy bolt rig, which are for dealing with finicky bites, and in conjunction with fishing hard boilies. Let us consider the bite problem first of all.

As you will read elsewhere in this chapter, my normal response to nervous, unhittable chub bites would be to revert to an upstream presentation. In 95 percent of situations, that easily solves the problem. However, on the other 5 percent of occasions, an upstream presentation may not be possible because of the bankside geography, and I am forced to persevere with the traditional downstream approach. In this situation, the bolt rig usually provides the answer. Just as with carp fishing, the idea is that a bait is fished with the hook point proud, using a heavy, fixed lead of at least two ounces in conjunction with a short hook link of no more than 6in (15cm). For crust, I drop to a 1in (2.5cm) link. The theory is that even a tentative pluck will make the chub aware of the heavy resistance, causing it to bolt in alarm. The exposed hook point catches the lip and self hooking occurs.

In-line bolt rig, with hair.

By its very nature, this approach is static, and the rig is not one suited for searching techniques, or even for inducing bites. Because of that, I use it very rarely indeed. It is, however, a useful weapon in the armoury, especially where you might have located an extra big and suspicious chub. The 'sit and wait' approach behind a bolt rig could provide the answer.

As an extension to that, the approach can be useful when you are fishing sluggish stretches containing a few big fish, and you would like to fish two rods, presenting baits in two different areas. This approach is becoming more popular with anglers seeking big barbel. The self hooking qualities of bolt rigs allow a slower response time to a bite, useful when there are two rods to watch, and the fishing can be very relaxed. On a stretch of river where you might be expecting a bite once in a blue moon, this approach has distinct merits. I consider chub and barbel fishing in this style to be carp fishing in running water.

Which leads me on neatly to fishing with boilies, the ultimate expression of the exposed hook point principle, utilising the hair rig. This applies to full sized boilies as well as mini- and midi-versions. Over the last couple of seasons, I have been experimenting a great deal with boilies

Short link bolt rig.

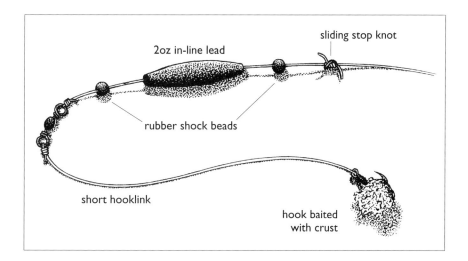

for barbel, and the large number of good chub that have succumbed has been a real eye opener, as are the tremendous bites they give on bolt rigs. Although boilie fishing for me will never replace my traditional mobile approach for chub, which is a great love, it would be churlish to deny that the technique is lethally effective. If you are an angler who prefers to fish statically behind two rods, bolt rigging with boilies will catch you plenty of chub. It is, however, a method not really suited to the smaller, more intimate waters, where the more mobile methods will still have the edge.

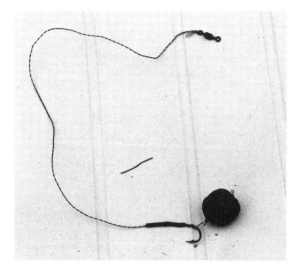

Bolt rig hooklink baited with boilie.

LEGERING UPSTREAM

Mobile Fishing in Long Glides

Over the years, the one single aspect of my writing that has prompted the most questions and request for further information is upstream legering. It is obvious that many experienced anglers have not been able to get their minds round the principles involved in the method, its mechanics and why it is often so immensely superior to the traditional downstream approach.

What I would like to do, therefore, is take a detailed look at the method, first examining why it is so efficient and then explaining how I go about it. Let us examine first two of the major advantages of upstreaming.

The most obvious, of course, is in dealing with fast, nervous bites, when a downstream presentation will see jabs on the rod top which prove difficult or impossible to hit. This kind of indication is common with chub that are pursued intently, such as at Throop on the Dorset Stour. When Trefor and I spent a lot of time at that venue the chub had the reputation of being very finicky and giving only microscopic bites. Most anglers attempted to overcome the problem by scaling down bait and hook sizes, whereas we kept faith with big baits, simply amending our presentation to fish baits upstream instead of down. I remember well one trip when I spent the whole of a two-day session legering crust on size 6 hooks

Trefor upstreaming a long glide on the Bristol Avon.

upstream in several swims. Without exception, the bites were unmissable, an initial pluck being followed by a total collapse of the line downstream as the lead shifted, giving me all the time in the world to strike. Nine chub to 4lb 14oz were landed, when other anglers, legering downstream, were getting more and more exasperated at striking at and missing fast plucks from nervous fish. When chub tentatively mouthed my baits, the fine balance in the tackle meant that the fish felt no resistance, ensuring that it suspected nothing amiss and held on to the bait with confidence.

The second advantage of upstream legering is that it is a method that can automatically locate a hot spot in a swim, when that would not be possible by downstreaming, unless you have a really intimate knowledge of the riverbed. I will be going into the actual mechanics of the method shortly, but just suffice it to say that searching a section of river by upstreaming relies strongly on

periodically shifting the lead so that it bumps down the flow. It can easily be seen that natural obstructions will halt the progress of the lead, and here I am thinking of sudden rises in the bed, weed roots, bits of old timber and so on. In other words, exactly the kind of features that can be attractive to fish!

During the actual fishing, the intention is to present baits in each likely area or in pre-baited swims, and most anglers position themselves at the upstream extremity of the swim and fish each area in turn by casting across and down to it. This simple method catches chub regularly. In some swims, however, there are inherent weaknesses associated with searching a long glide by a succession of down and across presentations. First, as we cast to each area in turn, there is the initially alarming effect of a lead plummeting into the swim. The fish recover their composure in time, sometimes very quickly if they are feeding hard, but it is nevertheless a frightening effect which we could do without.

Second, we may decide to cut down the amount of casting by arranging for certain swims to be fished by rolling the bait into position rather than casting directly to the swim. We could do this by casting to a far bank swim, fishing that for a while and then, by lifting the rod point, encourage the terminal rig to roll into mid-stream to search another baited area. If nothing resulted from that, the procedure could be repeated to search a near bank swim. The amount of disturbance to feeding fish could be further minimized by, instead of casting directly to the far bank swim, casting beyond it and rolling the initial bait into position.

So, what is wrong with that approach? The answer is threefold. First, we still require several casts to cover a long glide fully , and at least some of these will be directly into prepared swims. Second, because the presentation is across and downstream, the tautness in the tackle will mean that, when the bait is rolled into mid-stream and then into the near bank, it will move in an arc across the flow. This is highly unnatural and could be enough to dissuade a suspicious chub from intercepting the bait. Third, the method means that the bait will only ever fish on the line of each arc, and in a big swim this can mean that a lot of water is left unfished. This can be vitally important for winter chub fishing. Although hot spots may have been created by baiting, there are still plenty of bites to be had by fishing areas outside the baited areas, as fish commute from one to the other.

Let us now examine how a different approach by legering upstream overcomes these objections. If I sit at the furthest downstream extremity of the swim, my initial cast would be a couple of yards above the most upstream point of the swim on the far bank. After the lead has settled, the intention is to work the bait progressively down the flow, allowing it to settle, and fish statically along the run at intervals or where a natural feature halts the lead's progress. To do this, the rod point is lifted, and a little line is drawn which dislodges the lead so that it bumps down-

stream into the required position. That is the first difference to note. The lead bumps downstream in a straight line, rather than moving in an arc, because the upstream presentation has allowed the creation of slack line when the lead is disturbed. There is therefore nothing preventing the terminal rig progressing naturally downstream with the current.

After a while in the first area without a bite, I shift the lead into the second far bank swim. Again, the lead is lifted and line drawn so that the bait steadily bumps downstream to settle in the second designated spot. Note, however, another vital difference. In this presentation, the entire length of riverbed between the two swims has been searched by the bait as it slowly moved through. We have had many chub which have intercepted baits between swims to this approach. In fact, moving baits are deadly for winter chub on occasions. I have known days when a static bait would remain totally untouched, but as soon as it was moved, it would be taken with a bang; another example of the induced take, of course.

You can now see that the entire far bank run could be searched in this progressive manner, every inch of bottom having being covered perfectly naturally and without once having to cast directly at a feeding fish. Obviously, the next moves would be to cover the mid-stream run and near bank run in the same way.

Now that I have, I hope, convinced you to give the upstreaming technique a fair trial, let us have a look at how we go about it in practice.

The first thing to get right is the terminal rig, and the standard link leger, incorporating a snap link, gives the ability to change leads quickly. This is vitally important as a single swim may often require a different lead at different points along its length to fish upstream efficiently. The lead must be such that it holds steadily against the flow, but only requires a gentle pull to be dislodged. Once disturbed, it should quickly settle again and not wash downstream too easily. Generally speaking, if the lead moves a couple of feet downstream and then re-settles, you have it about right.

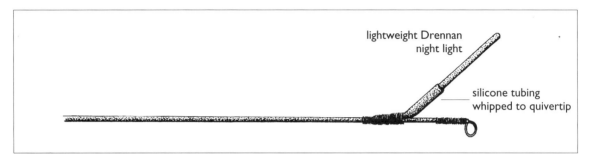

lightweight Drennan
night light

silicone tubing
whipped to quivertip

Quivertip Drennan night light adaptor.

The quivertip is essential equipment for efficient upstreaming, and I now use my Sharpe's Barbel Quiver Supreme, incorporating a built-in medium-strength quivertip. The quivertip is an invaluable aid in assessing when the terminal weight is about right. I always work on the principle that I need a four-inch upstream deflection in the tip to be maintainable before the lead yields to the pressure and bumps downstream. This assumes a fairly brisk winter flow, when upstream legering will be at its most efficient. Upstreaming is effective in more sluggish flows, but it is considerably more difficult to maintain a substantial tip deflection without using too much lead. In these circumstances, it is often worth deliberately fishing too heavy and then

fishing with a far greater than average tip deflection to counteract the excess weight. Alternatively, if you use screw-in quivers, select a much finer tip than normal, allowing a far greater deflection for the lighter lead required.

For mobile fishing of a glide, once the first cast has settled, take in the slack and tension the line by imparting the required upstream deflection in the quivertip. After a few minutes with no response, lift the rod point, and at the same time gently pull a little line with the left hand. This will dislodge the lead and it will move down the current. Once it has settled again, repeat the procedure, and continue this process until the whole swim has been searched.

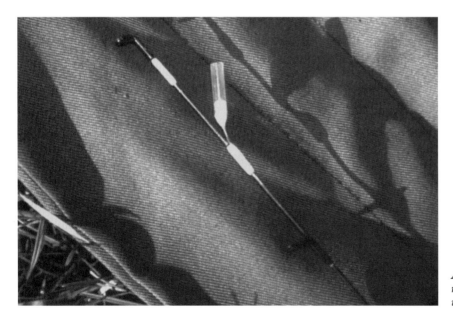

A flexible quivertip is required for efficient upstreaming.

When the lead is repositioning itself, the movement on the quivertip is quite characteristic, gently moving backwards and forwards before the terminal rig settles. As I said earlier, there is a high expectation of a bite as the bait is moving.

Bites to the upstream presentation are unmistakable. If the lead is correct, the usual bite to a static bait is an initial bump as the bait is lifted, followed by a kick back of the quivertip as the line tension relaxes. It is slightly more tricky when the bait is moving, and the bites usually take one of two forms. Firstly, you often get a savage lunge on the tip, caused I believe by the chub having eyed up the bait and then suddenly pouncing on it as it appears to be escaping. Secondly, the lead refuses to settle after being dislodged, for the simple reason that the chub has intercepted the bait and is casually dropping downstream with it. This may sound difficult to interpret on paper, but once you have become used to the time it takes for the lead to re-settle, it is very obvious when the terminal rig behaves differently. It pays to strike at any unexpected movements.

Static Situations

In my chubbing, I use the above upstream mobile technique in long glides usually when I wish to search the far bank run, which is impossible to do properly when legering downstream. For mid-river or near bank glides, however, especially when using mashed bread feed, most of my glide fishing is with the downstream presentation. It would be fair to say that only a small percentage of this type of mobile chubbing would be done by upstream legering.

However, the reverse is true with static situations. These would include the slacks behind obstructions such as rush beds or rafts, or for fishing the downstream areas of a line of bushes or trees. Often, the only efficient approach is from downstream of the swim. One of the most reliable winter chub swims is the 'V' of quiet water created by a mid-river bed of dead rushes. This area can be tiny, but will invariably attract chub. I aim for the bait to fish at the point of the 'V' in normal flow conditions, or tighter behind the obstruction at higher than normal flow rates.

This is a situation when you do not want the bait to move once it is in position, and it pays to use a rest once the tackle is balanced. The same mechanics apply as previously explained, but it is often necessary to use a little more lead than with the steady glide. The reason for this is that the bait is fishing an area of quieter water, often in mid-river, which would normally require modest lead, but the intervening faster flow has to be taken into account. For swims of this type, the bait must stay in the correct position and you must not be afraid to pile on the lead in order to achieve that objective. Even if two ounces is required to achieve a balance, a modest pull from a chub will easily shift it.

Where exceptionally fast flows are being fished over, it is a good idea to fish the rod high to keep as much of the line off the water as possible. If you are fishing in this manner without response, an excellent way of inducing a bite is to drop the rod point so that the line falls into the fast flow. The increase in line tension thus created will drag the lead out of position, ensuring that a hesitant chub has to make a decision quickly, before that tempting morsel escapes!

Let me make one last general observation about upstream legering. As a method requiring fine tackle balance to be at its most efficient, it is extremely vulnerable to false bites if there is much flotsam in the river. It takes very little drifting weed to dislodge a critically balanced terminal rig, and in those circumstances the method can become very trying. By implication, it therefore becomes inefficient. These days, where drifting debris is a problem, I content myself with orthodox downstream fishing and wait for a good pull.

TOUCH LEGERING

For many years, all my winter chub fishing bite detection in streamy water was via touch legering, but I have to admit that these days, the quivertip has superseded my fingers in daylight. However, after dark, I still revert to touch legering, as I believe that there is no method of bite

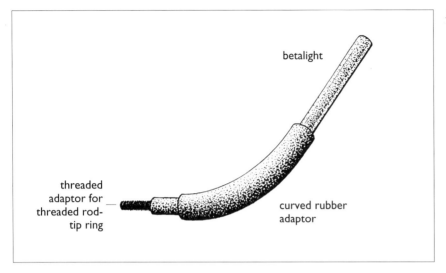

betalight

threaded
adaptor for
threaded rod-
tip ring

curved rubber
adaptor

Rod-tip betalight adaptor.

detection that can match its sensitivity in flowing water. For this night fishing, I usually dispense with the quivertip and rely entirely on my fingers, although I will use a rod-tip betalight to assess direction when playing a chub.

To get the best from touch legering, it should be realized that it is a method requiring a good flow to tension the line over the fingers. Where the water is so sluggish that it is difficult to maintain a tight line, other bite detection methods have the edge.

Touch legering requires practice to perfect, as does anything worthwhile, but once mastered you will find that no other method of bite detection gives such an obvious early warning of a chub's interest in your bait. This applies equally upstream or down. For normal downstreaming, the urgent tightening of the line acts like an electric shock, while in the upstreaming situation, the sudden removal of tension from line that was as taut as a banjo string is equally unmistakable.

When you are learning the technique, I recommend a few trips to an easy river, perhaps containing a good head of medium chub. With bites in plentiful supply, you will soon experience the range of bite variations. It is a good idea to touch leger without a quivertip in daylight to start with, which will be a good grounding for those after-dark trips when your fingers will provide the only early warning system.

There are two methods of touch legering, both equally efficient, and which one you use depends on personal preference. I always crook a little line over the index finger of my right hand(the hand holding the rod) whereas others prefer to take a loop of line in the left hand. Chub bites on your fingers are generally unmistakable, an initial pluck being followed by a slow draw. This is almost impossible to miss, providing you wait for the drawing of the line. Occasionally, however, you will experience the succession of small plucks and often these will be so delicate that no indication is seen on the rod tip. These are sometimes caused by confident chub rolling the bait in the mouth and a strike can provide a bonus fish. More often, however, small bites take the form of fast jabs, and these are from suspicious fish, or chub that live in hard-fished stretches. There is a high percentage of missed bites when striking at these indications. In these circumstances, a switch to upstreaming often works, and now you are waiting for the collapse of line tension over your fingers.

Another approach to nervous, jabbing bites is to give a little slack immediately the bite is felt, or, alternatively, take in a few inches of line. Both of these manoeuvres impart a little bait movement and they can induce a hesitant chub into giving a firm pull.

For the most efficient touch legering, arrange for the rod tip to be pointing at the bait as much

*Touch legering provided the early warning of the arrival of this
5lb 10oz Leam beauty (above).*

*A slack line bite across my fingers to legered cheesepaste was the signal
to strike into this Cherwell four-pounder (below).*

as possible, although modern frictionless rod rings make this less vital than it used to be. The shallower the line angle, the more direct contact you have with your quarry. Touch legering, especially in the dark, provides fascinating fishing. It has given me many years of enjoyment and I can heartily recommend it.

BITE DETECTION AND METHODS FOR SLUGGISH STRETCHES

Most chub give good, positive bites in streamy water, and I have often stated that I do not seem to experience the tentative chub bites that other anglers write about, other than on very hard-fished waters where the chub are becoming excessively spooky. However, the exception to this is the stretch of uniform slowness and featurelessness. Because of the lack of flow, chub have all the time in the world to examine a food offering before taking it, and therefore become far more circumspect. The lack of flow makes bait presentation less natural, and it also makes inducing bites far more difficult. On a streamy stretch, if a bait has come to rest unmolested, a bite can be encouraged by lifting the bait from the riverbed, such that the current catches it and propels it downstream very naturally. Nervous fish are often fooled by inducing bites in this way.

With no flow, the only way the bait can be moved is by drawing it manually and, although

A deep, slow section of the Leam concealed this chunky specimen.

5lb 14oz: easily my best from the Cherwell (above).

Four clonking chub for Westy from a wet, windy Wensum.

Stalking chub on the Upper Ouse.

Red corn mounted on an adjustable hair rig (above).

An Avon weir at sunset.

A 5lb 5oz fish on feeder fished maggots from Ibsley (above).

A lovely stretch of the middle Ouse in midsummer.

Landing Hampshire Avon chub for Bob James (above).

A severe frost was forming when this 5lb 6oz Wensum cracker engulfed a huge chunk of meat (left).

Quivertipping the Cherwell (above).

A magnificent 5lb 5oz Leam specimen.

Aldermaston Mill, home of gigantic chub (above).

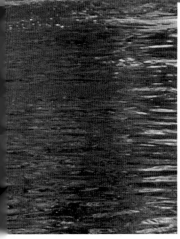

Look at the superb condition of this 5lb 10oz Upper Ouse specimen.

5lb 7oz from the Wensum. The larger fish of a brace of five-pounders.

Returning a five-pound Middle Ouse specimen.

The Cherwell in winter (below).

this certainly works, it is by no means as natural as persuading a current to do the work.

These days, most of my daylight chubbing is carried out using the quivertip, reverting to touch legering after dark. In these slow stretches, however, I will often use either a swingtip or butt indicator. These are especially useful when there is a very slow flow, and the bait is presented upstream. In these circumstances I recommend using an overloaded swingtip or butt indicator, with the indicator being set at about 45 degrees. The correct loading on the tip is easy to establish, using lead wire. Having cast out, tighten as much as possible to the bait without dislodging it. Then add lead wire to the tip a little at a time until you have the correct deflection. Using an upstream presentation, any bite will see the tip drop like a stone, as it takes in created slack, and this is a method of converting what would be a tiny bite into a very obvious indication. Fishing upstream with a dropping swingtip arrangement gives close on 100 percent conversion of bites to hooked fish.

The same effect can also be obtained with a quivertip, but when the flow is sluggish a very flexible tip is required to give a substantial upstream deflection, unless an inordinate amount of lead is employed. As most quivertip rods are equipped with a medium, middle of the road tip, you will fish more efficiently with the swingtip.

For readers who do not possess a quivertip, swingtip or butt indicator, efficient upstream legering can be achieved on sluggish stretches by utilizing a simple bobbin between the butt ring and reel. The bobbin should be such that the weight can be varied, by addition or subtraction of shot or lead wire. If the bobbin body can take a betalight or starlight for fishing after dark, so much the better.

After casting and taking in as much of the slack as possible, place the bobbin on the line. Gradually increase the weight until the indicator drops a fraction, when you have a perfect balance between the terminal rig and the weight of the indicator. Once again, the slightest bite will see the indicator drop sharply.

There are a few elementary precautions to make the set up as sensitive as possible. First of all,

My simple glow bobbin indicator.

arrange for the rod to be pointing directly at the bait, if possible. Second, in rough conditions, sink the rod tip by as much as a foot or more if needs be, to avoid wind action catching the line from the rod-tip or blowing debris on to it. Third, use the minimum amount of lead necessary to enable casting to the desired spot, and matched to the bait used. A piece of cheesepaste would obviously require less casting weight than breadcrust, which is more buoyant.

The whole point of the presentation is that the bait should be on the brink of being shifted downstream for the method to be at its most efficient. In normal upstreaming in flowing water, the balance is largely between terminal weight of lead and current speed. In slow or nearly static stretches, where the effect of current is negligible, the balance has to switch to being between terminal lead and the drag of a heavy or tensioned indicator. It is a simple matter of balancing all the forces at work.

Simple as it is, in very rough conditions the bobbin has one obvious advantage over the swingtip. There is little to be gained from sinking the rod tip when using a swingtip for bite indication.

An early Cherwell specimen taken from under the far bank on the drop bobbin approach.

Invariably, when the decision has been taken to fish such a stretch of river, the whole tempo of the fishing slows down. Coupled with what is generally a higher average size is a smaller head of fish. There is no mystery about why this should be. Just like all animals, the older and fatter they get, the more they like a quieter, lazier existence. Chub fishing becomes much more of a sit and wait game than in streamy water, when I can be on the move constantly, with the hookbait rarely still. The lack of flow means that you have no current assistance in searching likely areas and you therefore are forced to cast directly to where you judge the chub to be. There is no other choice, but the bait presentation is far from ideal. For this reason, you have to be more patient than with more orthodox chubbing, to allow the fish to recover from their alarm.

Earlier, I mentioned creating artificial hot spots by baiting and this is, in fact, one of the best methods to employ when investigating a new, sluggish stretch. What I do is keep six areas permanently baited, the areas possibly having been selected at random initially if no features presented themselves. On the first trip to the stretch, I will just fish those six areas, constantly keeping the feed topped up and alternating between them. On the next trip, I will pick six different swims, and so on. Perhaps after a few trips, a pattern may begin to emerge, and I may well now be baiting six swims, all of which have given bites in the past; that is when I can begin to fish with ever increasing confidence.

An alternative approach, especially on a day when I know conditions are perfect, is to fish as many swims as possible until my hookbait collides with a chub! For this technique, I spend a lot less time in each swim, reasoning that if a chub is anywhere near where my bait is cast, it will not be too long before he takes it. I start the day by baiting the first six swims, then fishing each in turn, perhaps for fifteen minutes. Before beginning to fish the last swim I will first bait another six and so on, continuing that process all day. This technique allows a lot of water to be covered, casting into up to as many as forty different swims over the course of an average winter's day. For the productive dusk and after-dark fishing, any swim that has produced a chub, missed bite or any other sign of chub being present, will be given a more extensive examination.

It is often difficult to see why a particular spot should contain fish constantly, when it has absolutely no features to distinguish it from a hundred identical areas. But it is a fact that this phenomenon is very common. Obviously, as soon as it has been found, regular baiting ensures that it remains a hot spot.

Having said that, it is a mistake on these stretches always to fish swims where you have caught before and ignore all other areas. In the type of water under discussion, the fish can be very nomadic and there is the chance of a big one turning up anywhere. I have long since stopped counting the times when I have caught a big fish from a swim which has been fished umpteen times previously without a bite. Because fishing these sluggish, more featureless stretches is generally a much slower game than in areas with more character, it is important that you have weather and water conditions on your side as much as possible. When conditions are likely to be unfavourable, say in a high flood or after a sudden cold snap, you are better off fishing an area where location of the odd fish that may be willing to feed is much easier.

The very best conditions on the slow stretches are when the river is fining down after a flood but is still a little above normal level, with a tinge of colour and a water temperature in the mid-forties Fahrenheit and rising. In these circumstances, we can even have the luxury of a reasonable flow, and I would use my traditional chubbing technique of quivertipping, keeping very mobile during the day, and pre-baiting several swims for the after-dark period.

Conditions can still be classed as good when the river is at its normal height, flow and clarity, providing that the external conditions are settled. This is even true in settled, frosty weather although there is a greater expectation of sport with settled mild conditions than there is with settled cold conditions.

Water temperature is an important considera- tion in all winter fishing, but even more impor- tant is the direction in which it is moving, and how quickly. If conditions are becoming unset- tled, it could be beneficial or detrimental depending on whether the temperature rises or falls. Use of a thermometer every couple of hours gives valuable information. If you do not possess a thermometer, commonsense appraisal of the weather conditions is a good stand by. For instance, in settled, cold conditions, the arrival of strong, warm, south-westerly winds would be very beneficial for sport, whereas a strong, cold, easterly airstream would do settled, mild condi- tions no favours whatever.

Devoting time to a sluggish, featureless stretch of river, where the action is very slow, demands an attitude of mind and a belief in what you are doing. As bites are often few and far between, and frequently confined to the hours around dusk in less-than-ideal conditions, the fishing is unlikely to appeal to the angler who wants a bite every five minutes. If you are prepared to put in the time for bigger-than-average specimens, however, it comes highly recommended.

There is, of course, a middle-of-the-road option, which I am using more and more these days. Most of my sluggish stretches abut streami- er areas and I spend the daylight hours enjoying traditional chubbing, while preparing swims in the slower stretch for dusk and after dark. It entails a lot of walking but, with my figure, the exercise does me nothing but good! This approach gives the best of both worlds: the pos- sibility of plenty of daylight action, coupled with a real chance of an extra big fish after dark.

PLAYING BIG CHUB

Having done everything else right, many anglers, when finally connected to the chub of their dreams in a tight, snaggy swim, suffer the morti- fication of finally losing the fish. This happens to us all at times, but I have to say that most of the losses I have seen are on account of poor tech- nique, coupled with a reluctance to use the

tackle to its full potential. This is a natural lead in to discussing the relative merits of backwind- ing and fishing off the clutch.

Let me make it clear from the outset that I use both methods of playing fish, depending on the circumstances. My main use for backwinding is where a hooklink is being employed of substan- tially lower breaking strain than the main line. A good example of this would be in reservoir roach- ing, where I often use 6lb main line to take the casting shock of heavy feeders, but where hook- links as low as 2lb can be employed. It is impos- sible to set a clutch correctly for a light hooklink. The inertia in even the best clutches can see the breaking strain of light lines temporarily exceeded, leading to breakage.

In contrast, if I am using strong gear through to the hook, say 8lb line for barbel or 6lb for chub, then I definitely prefer the properly set clutch every time.

Heavy lines ensure that the inertia factor of a fixed spool clutch is relatively insignificant, and it is therefore straightforward to set the mecha- nism at a level where you are able to use the full line power available. A similar argument can be applied to rods. What is the point in buying an expensive, powerful carbon rod for chub fishing, and then refusing to allow it to do its job because you give the fish line as soon as it bends a little past the vertical. And this is the greatest draw- back of backwinding on a powerful fish in a tight situation. I do not believe the angler exists who will allow the tackle to exert its maximum pres- sure before yielding line manually. Uncon- sciously, we all allow a greater safety margin than a properly set clutch would, and that is one of the prime reasons for many of those unfortunate fish losses in snaggy swims.

The clutch should be set so that a big chub has to battle for every inch of line, and the rod should be bent round to its full fighting curve before the clutch yields. If that is the case, the tackle is well balanced for the strength of line in use. If you are worried about hooks pulling out under that pres- sure, you are using the wrong hooks.

Another danger with backwinding is during an irresistible run by a big fish, when even the clutch

Matt Hayes was very glad of a reliable clutch when this chub made a late bid for freedom.

has to yield. With the clutch, progressively increasing pressure can be brought to bear on the fish by finger spool power. With backwinding, I have seen anglers release the reel handle during a strong surge by the fish, at which point the chub is now in control of the fight and not the angler. It is then difficult for the angler to regain control without grabbing the handle again, which can tend to bring the fish up with a jerk, often with catastrophic results.

8 FISHING THE SWIMFEEDER

It was not so many years ago that I rarely utilized the swimfeeder as a tool for chub fishing, preferring individual large baits under all conditions. However, largely as a result of my barbel fishing activities, I have come to appreciate what a devastating technique the use of the feeder can be for chubbing, summer or winter. It is fair to say that for my fishing on the smaller, upper stretches of our chub rivers, where I am more likely to be searching for just the odd bite from a big fish, I still mostly apply the freelined or light legered individual large bait approach, especially in summer. Even then, however, one particular feeder approach first applied to barbel fishing has also proved so efficient for chub that I now consider it to be one of my premier methods. Let us have a look at it now.

SUMMER TECHNIQUES

Tight, Snaggy Swim in Sluggish Flow

Anyone who has read *Quest for Barbel*, by myself and Trefor West, will be familiar with the progressive baiting technique we outlined, as it applied to small swims in summer which were no more than little holes in cabbages or streamer, or small clearings by overhanging foliage. That baiting technique would usually involve introducing hempseed over a period of several hours via the bait dropper, and eventually fishing a single bait over the bed of feed.

When I first took the technique to the Cherwell, I soon found that the method was at its most lethal when combined with maggot feed, apart from the fact that it was mighty attractive to chub.

Playing a Kennet chub on feeder-fished maggots in summer.

Heavy feeder bolt rig.

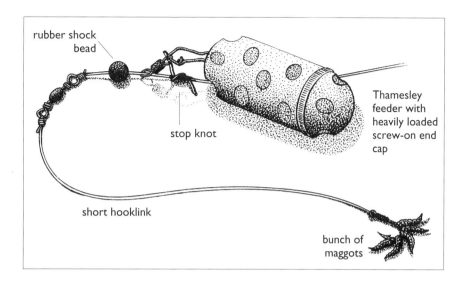

rubber shock bead

stop knot

Thamesley feeder with heavily loaded screw-on end cap

short hooklink

bunch of maggots

The method was essentially the same as before, but as well as the hemp, I also pre-baited with two or three droppers of maggots at each visit.

For the actual fishing, I found it most effective to lower a large blockend feeder on to the loose feed, fishing a bunch of maggots on a size 6 hook. Because the swims where this technique was used were invariably tight, often no more than a couple of feet of clean gravel in a jungle of aquatic vegetation, I was forced to use short hooklinks to avoid becoming hung up. Having carefully placed a bait in position, it was important to avoid further disturbance, and so I needed to be sure that I was fishing effectively and that bait was available for more than a few minutes.

One of the problems in addressing the first requirement was the large number of tiny taps and bumps on the rod tip from small fish. Using a light feeder, which was my first approach, I was often tempted into premature striking as smaller fish could and did move the feeder, giving quite fair indications. Realizing that this was defeating the object, I elected the bolt rig principle, using a large Thamesley feeder in conjunction with a loaded end cap of about 2oz. A chub or barbel picking up the bait on a short link to this rig gave unmistakable wrenches on the rod tip.

To ensure that there was free feed in the swim for as long as possible, it was necessary to reduce the leakage rate of maggots from the feeder in the warm water. A steady trickle of maggots from the feeder was ideal and this was achieved by the simple expedient of blocking two thirds of the feeder holes with insulating tape. Although this would be contrary to my normal approach in summer, where I like to use a heavy throughput of maggots, remember that this technique is being used where the feeder is held in a very tight swim, and a swim which has been steadily pre-baited with maggots for hours.

One important point to make about this technique, and something I learned through bitter experience, is that it is a bad mistake to fish the feeder fixed. The reason is simple. If you hook an extra big chub, or a barbel in a snaggy swim and the fish takes off through the foliage, a fixed feeder will get tangled immediately, leading to an enormous increase in tension on the hooklink which will either break or result in the hook pulling out. I always fish a sliding feeder, so that the line will pull through it in the event of snagging. I have landed several chub and barbel where twenty or more yards of line had been taken off the clutch, but where the feeder was wedged on a cabbage root almost at my feet.

In a bolt rig situation, of course, the sliding feeder can dilute the bites somewhat, but this is easily overcome by loosely tying a powergum stop knot above the feeder, giving a semi-fixed bolt arrangement.

Streamy Water

The more orthodox use of the swimfeeder is in streamy water, where its use is in ensuring a constant flow of bait down the current. In direct contrast to the method just outlined, streamy water feeder fishing is more effective in summer the more often you cast and the more bait you use. This is particularly true when using maggots, which I will look at first.

For a summer feeder session, the minimum bait I want is half a gallon, and a gallon is better. Cost is obviously the limiting factor here, but there is no doubt that this is one technique where you can literally buy your fish. Elsewhere in this book, I have made mention of the feeder fishing on the Royalty of years ago, when many gallons of maggots would be used in a day, and catches of chub were phenomenal.

The end rig used will depend on the presence or otherwise of weedbeds and the strength of the flow. Streamer beds are particularly good feeder swims, as careful positioning of each cast between streamer tresses, which act as brakes on the line and help to prevent the bait rolling in to the near bank, ensures that the loose feed continually follows the same narrow band. Accuracy of casting with a feeder, and then ensuring it remains put after settling, gives us the most efficient application possible.

As an extra precaution against rolling, I like to use those oval Drennan blockend feeders for streamer bed applications. Whichever blockend you prefer, either carry them in a variety of weights or keep a selection of clip-on weights to adapt your standard pattern, for coping with brisker than normal flows. Most good tackle shops carry a variety of such leads.

In streamer bed applications, I like to use as long a tail as possible, so that the maggot hookbait is free to follow the same undulating path as

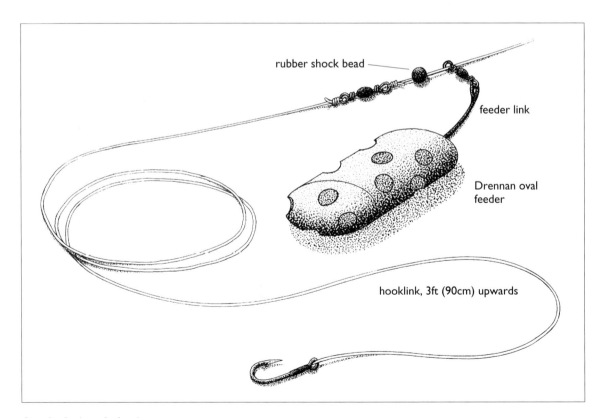

rubber shock bead

feeder link

Drennan oval feeder

hooklink, 3ft (90cm) upwards

Standard winter feeder rig.

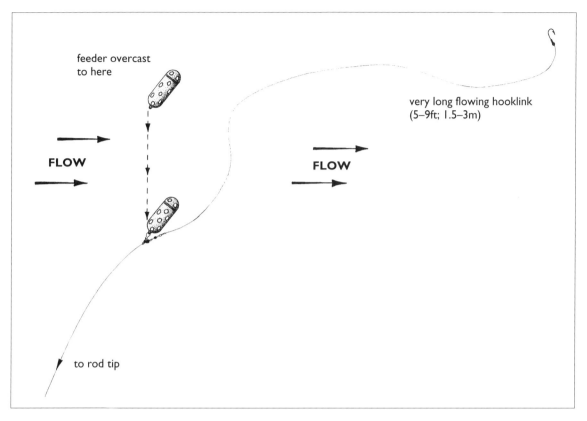

Streamy water, flowing-hooklink feeder rig.

the streamer tresses themselves. Obviously, the density of the vegetation will be the factor limiting the length the link can be before it becomes a handicap. I like it to be at least 3ft (90cm).

As before, resist the temptation to fish the feeder fixed; heavy blockends do not travel easily through streamer roots.

Another difference in my feeder approach in streamy water from the bolt rig method mentioned earlier is in the delicacy of terminal rig. In the bolt arrangement, the use of a big hook and a large bunch of maggots was deliberately designed to make it difficult for small fish to engulf the bait. With the constant casting of the streamy water method, however, the attentions of small fish can be taken more philosophically, allowing much more delicacy of bait presentation. In order for the maggots to behave in the same way as the loose offerings, I use terminal rigs, usually

of ready-tied size 16 Drennan Super Spades to 3.2lb nylon, baited with two maggots.

Where I am feeder fishing a summer glide with no weed problems, a very efficient presentation for the bigger chub in a shoal is with an ultra long hooklink. I often use a link as long as can be comfortably cast. This could be as much as 9ft (2.7m). Just as with barbel, the bigger, more cautious fish in a group of chub will often hang around at the rear, mopping up those food items missed by the more eager youngsters milling around up front. If you cast the feeder armed with a very long link further across current than the feeding line, and then pull the feeder back on line, the long hooklink is left to swing around in a wide arc, eventually to settle well downstream of the feeder. This means that the hook bait in effect bypasses the smaller chub at the head of the swim and comes into sight of the bigger fish first.

Marsh Pratley feeder fishing for Thames chub.

As a swim is gradually built up during the session, and the fish gain increasing feeding confidence, we find that the greedier and bigger chub gradually move upstream, exerting their dominance. This is when we may see bites dropping off to the long tail approach, and it will pay dividends progressively to reduce tail length. It can reach a stage where chub are taking maggots immediately they leave the feeder holes, and a very short tail length is necessary. This, however, can lead to its own problems, with chub taking the hookbait, immediately feeling the feeder and giving rattly jerks on the rod that are continually missed. A change to a bolt rig could be a solution, but as the fish are preoccupied with single maggots, is not ideal in this situation. It is far better to arrange for the hooklink to expand on being taken. To achieve this is simplicity itself. Tie in to the terminal arrangement a normal hooklink, of say about two

feet, and wrap an elastic band around the base of the feeder. Then loop the hooklink lightly into this band and adjust it so that the bait is lying adjacent to the feeder when it comes to rest. When a chub takes the maggots, however, the link pops out of the elastic band and expands to its full length before the chub feels any resistance. The result is a more positive bite. The principle is identical to the sliding hair rig for carp fishing.

As well as blockend fishing with maggots for summer chub, feeder fishing is extremely effective with all other baits, in conjunction with open-ended feeders loaded with suitable loose feed. Because of the largely inanimate nature of other baits, open-ended work is best utilized in the streamier flows, where the current does the important bait distribution work.

Open-ended feeder work is effective with both big hookbaits and particles, and it has to be

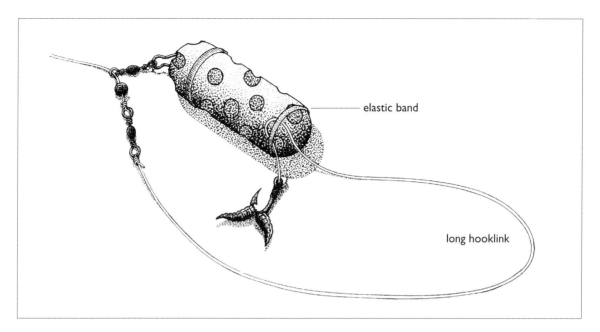

Low resistance feeder rig.

said that the hookbait is largely irrelevant. It is the feeding that is the secret. In the larger baits, bread flake is undoubtedly my favourite for summer chubbing, and I like to fish this on a longish tail, in conjunction with liquidized bread feed. As I mentioned in the earlier bait chapter, the efficiency of the liquidized bread is enhanced by all manner of additives, such as grilled hemp, sweet and savoury powders of all descriptions and powdered taste enhancers and sweeteners. Milk powder can be added to heighten the visual attraction.

For large, flavoured hookbaits such as cheesepaste, liquidized bread can be similarly flavoured. I particularly rate fish-flavoured or spicy hookbaits for this application, and a recent addition to my repertoire is the Nature's Gems range of powdered products from Rod Hutchinson, marketed by Relum Ltd. I have had one very successful chub trip using liquidized bread feed mixed with mussel extract, in combination with seafood-flavoured bread flake. I intend to try out the squid and crab extracts over the coming weeks. The other Nature's Gems powdered extract is Ultimate Spice, and this I have used

extensively in conjunction with heavily spiced luncheon meat. I can tell you that this one really is the business.

Recently, I have been using a new spicy combination with luncheon meat, which has given me crashing bites wherever I have used it. What I do is pour a teaspoon of Rod Hutchinson's Spice Sense Appeal into a bait box, put on the lid and shake the box so that the inside of it is thoroughly coated. Then I add the cubed meat, shaking again, before sprinkling a generous amount of Ultimate Spice Powdered Attractant over the meat, making sure that each chunk of bait is well coated. This certainly works better if it is prepared beforehand and frozen. Without a doubt, this bait is lethal.

The first time I used it, it produced a double-figure barbel, in the shape of a chunky 10lb 14oz fish, and a total of nine chub to over four pounds, plus two more barbel of 7lb and 8lb 2oz. Apart from the fish landed, there must have been over forty bumps and bangs from interested chub. The swim was fed with liquidized bread carrying Ultimate Spice powder, spiced hemp and small scraps of the spiced meat.

At the time of writing, I am just preparing for my next chub and barbel night session. Another secret weapon is lurking in my freezer, namely, luncheon meat soaked in Shellfish Sense Appeal, and then rolled in powdered squid extract. When I put this under the nose of Tasha, my west highland terrier, she went into a frenzy and dashed round the garden. I cannot wait to see what the fish make of it!

Open-ended feeder work with particles is carried out in conjunction with 'exploding' groundbait plugs, which blow the particles free of the feeder. This is achieved by the simple expedient of mixing the normal liquidized bread/additive combination with a quantity of dry sausage rusk. Only moments after the cast, the rusk absorbs water so quickly that it rapidly expands, causing an underwater mini bait detonation.

The particles I use most often for chubbing with the feeder are casters and sweetcorn, the corn being flavoured more and more these days. Recently, I have had spectacular results with Pescaviva corn. Most of my fish have succumbed to red Strawberry, but I have also taken a catch of seven chub, a good bream and an eight-pound barbel in an evening on the Cherwell, using orange Tutti Frutti, plus a six chub, three roach catch on the Warks Avon on yellow Banana.

There are eleven other colour/flavour combinations as well as the ones mentioned, giving plenty of opportunity for experiment. One thing I have not tried as yet is adding coloured powder dyes to my feeder contents, but this is on the agenda.

Another area of particle flavouring that I am working on at the moment is in the hemp loose feed, both for prebaiting and in feeder application. Last winter, I felt that the hemp loose feed might actually be a deterrent to nervous fish. With this in mind, I have this season tried hemp flavoured with Ultra Spice and Tutti Frutti, fishing as hook bait spicy meat and orange Tutti Frutti corn respectively. In both cases, as well as barbel and chub being caught, there was also intense activity in the swim, proving that the flavoured hemp was doing no harm and might just have been enhancing the baits' pulling power. This idea is still in its infancy.

WINTER TECHNIQUES

As a general rule, swimfeeder applications for winter chubbing will follow along very similar lines to those outlined for fishing in streamier flows already discussed for summer. Where the water temperatures are good, in the mid-forties (7°C) upwards, my winter approach is exactly the same, although I use maggots in the winter far more than I do in summer, when other particles are favoured. This is because in the winter months the attentions of small fish to maggots are far less troublesome than they are in summer.

The obvious differences in winter, apart from sparser weed growth, are enhanced height and flow speeds and lower water temperatures. Let us have a look at how these two factors affect our feeder application for winter chubbing.

Winter Feeder Fishing in Higher, Faster Flows

The approach here depends entirely on water temperature. If that is favourable, then even more bait than normal will be needed for efficient feeder work, to offset the dispersal effect of the flow. For winter fishing somewhere like, say, Throop or the Avon, a gallon of maggots would not be too much for a day's chubbing, recasting the feeder every few minutes throughout the day. The great Avon angler Mark Vials, who swears by the feeder for winter work, fishes two rods for his winter chubbing, recasting diligently about every five minutes. Mark's terrific results speak volumes for the efficiency of the technique.

Mashed bread in a feeder, with flake on the hook, will catch chub anywhere.

The other important detail is to ensure that your feeder consistently presents the stream of bait down the same line. The greater the flow, the easier it is to get this vital ingredient of successful feeder fishing wrong. Do not be afraid to pile lead on to the feeder to ensure that it remains where it is cast. Bait that is scattered all over the river because the feeder is too light, and therefore rolling all over the place, is worse than useless.

This is when flat-bottomed feeders really come into their own. Another feature of winter chubbing with the feeder, when the weed is much sparser, is that you can get away with lighter hook links, and this definitely makes a difference, especially in clearer water. More than once, I have been astounded at how the change from a 16 on 3.2lb mono to an 18 on 2.6lb has made all the difference. It took me many years to get my mind round using such tackle for chubbing, but winter feeder fishing on the southern rivers has taught me how tremendously effective it is. Stef Horak, one of the best natural anglers I know, has taken big Avon chub regularly on size 20 hooks to 1.8lb hooklinks. As with all baits, it is the presentation that is of the essence. For a big chunk of crust, I can make a natural presentation with a size 6 on six pound line. If a similarly delicate presentation with maggots requires a size 20 to a 1.8lb bottom, then anything coarser will be inferior.

In faster flows, when the use of the normal downstream feeder approach can be a problem, with the terminal rig constantly being dragged into the near bank unless you are fishing excessively heavily, a very efficient alternative is to switch to the upstream feeder. By the nature of upstream legering, any shift in the terminal rig will be in a straight line downstream, thereby still feeding the correct line. The technique for fishing the upstream feeder is exactly the same as for upstream legering generally, that of achieving a critical balance between current flow, feeder weight and tension in rod tip or quivertip.

In a situation where you wish to present a bait in or across very strong flows, it is not so much the weight but the water resistance of a big feeder that demands a variation from the normal upstream legering technique. I first saw this method outlined

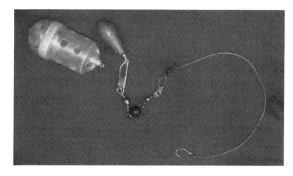

The versatile snap link leger or snap link feeder rig.

by Archie Braddock, and it works like a dream. Having cast your feeder into position upstream, allow a large amount of slack out, so that a bow in the line goes straight downstream of the feeder, and a little downstream of you. Initially, that would appear totally inefficient. In a strong flow, the quivertip will actually be deflected downstream by the pressure of the water on the bow in the line. However, when a chub pulls the bait, dislodging the feeder downstream, everything falls slack as normal, allowing the quivertip to straighten. You then have all the time in the world to strike. The essential difference in this technique from standard upstreaming is that you can get away with a far lighter feeder than would otherwise be the case.

Let me clarify, though, that this technique is not necessary for normal upstreaming with a dense lead and a bigger bait. It is only the far higher water resistance of a feeder that makes it necessary in stronger flows.

Cold Water Feeder Fishing
When the water temperature is in the low forties Fahrenheit (5°C) or below, and the water is low and clear, a small bait fished in conjunction with the feeder can be one of the most effective chubbing methods, but there are vital differences in approach from the fishing in warmer water.

First, the clarity of water demands the finest terminal rig you can safely use. Secondly, the chub will be much more lethargic, and therefore eating less, as their metabolism slows. The quantity of free feed should be cut right back, and where I may use a gallon of maggots in warmer water, I may

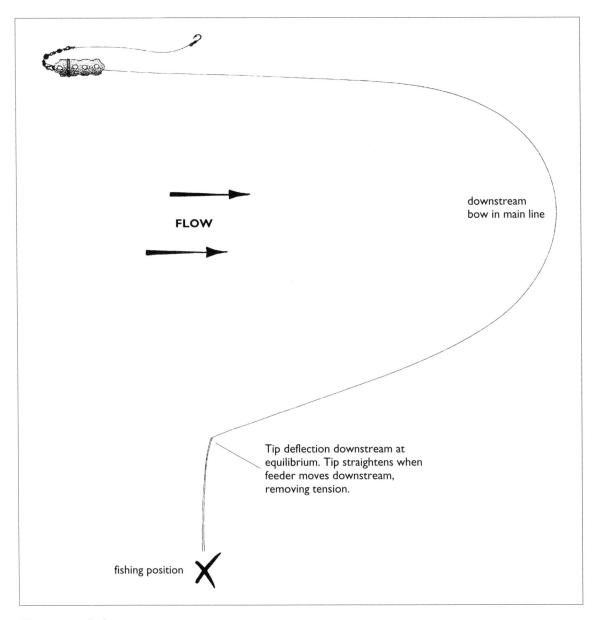

downstream
bow in main line

FLOW

Tip deflection downstream at
equilibrium. Tip straightens when
feeder moves downstream,
removing tension.

fishing position

The upstream feeder.

only use a pint on a cold day. Naturally, that goes hand in glove with far less frequent casting. This is important because the chub will be less inclined to chase bait items down the river. Better to present a small amount of feed in a fairly tight area and leave it alone for a while. This allows an idle chub the time to sidle up to it. Also, I rarely use hook links of more than 18in (45cm) in cold weather.

To limit free offerings, I often use a far smaller feeder in the winter, so that there is a modest trickle of loose maggots available at any one time. In very cold water, even the maggots become very lethargic, and it can pay to enlarge the holes in your feeder to curb the ease with which they can escape.

9 FLOAT FISHING

TROTTING

Over the last few seasons, I have done a lot more float trotting for winter chub than ever before, so much so that I can now even manage a half decent presentation! I have to say, though, that it is still a very minor part of my repertoire in my overall chubbing activities. This is because most of the swims on the Midland rivers I fish for big chub do not really lend themselves to long trotting. They are either heavily weeded, full of snags, or so heavily overgrown with bankside foliage that the use of a float would be imposing an unnecessary handicap. Even on those rivers, however, especially the Great Ouse, there are occasional nice long, uniform, gravelly glides, and it is in these that the use of the float can be the most devastatingly effective method in the right hands. In no way would I put myself in the same league as those master trotting craftsmen Bob James and John Wilson, but even I have had some satisfying bags of chub from such areas over the last two winters.

Apart from the obvious smooth, steady glide, swims I also rate highly for float work are the shelving bank of gravel that throws the flow across river, a slow, deep run under a high bank or fringing over-hanging foliage, or a run that

4lb 14oz and 4lb 13oz fish from consecutive trots with flake on the Cherwell.

Drennan Avons, ideal for chub trotting.

suddenly shelves up to much shallower water. The favourite, though, has to be the good old crease, working the float along the junction of the the two flows.

For trotting, I now use the 13ft float rod from my Supreme range, in conjunction with a Dave Swallow centrepin, truly a joyful combination. In a difficult wind, I may elect my Daiwa closed face job instead. The reel is loaded with about seventy yards of 4lb line, and for bread baits this reel line is used straight through to a size 6 or 8 Au Lion d'Or hook. For smaller baits such as casters and maggots, I use Drennan ready-tied super spades, either 14s or 16s to 3.2lb nylon. All my float fishing is carried out with Drennan floats, which have few equals, and either a loafer or Avon is my usual choice for chub, depending on conditions. As a very general rule, the lighter the stem material of the float, the closer it will have to be used for good control. The densest stem material giving good control, even in the middle of the Hampshire Avon, is wire, and Drennan wire-stemmed Avons are firm favourites with me. If, like me, your trotting is a minor part of your big fish activities and you are, therefore, by definition, unpractised, stemmed floats allow less than perfect control without easily pulling off course. It is far better to fish well with a float that is possibly a little heavy, than badly with the float that would be the choice of a top match angler.

No fancy shotting patterns are necessary for chub trotting. Quite simply, the shot are all bunched about a foot from the hook to get the bait down quickly. Rarely indeed do you need additional tell-tale shots; the bites are usually nothing if not positive.

Good trotting presentation shares many of the requirements of good presentation with floating crust, and one of the most important factors is the avoidance of drag. The foremost cause of this is sinking line between float and rod tip, and therefore it is advisable to apply line floatant before fishing. I used to use line grease quite happily, but it can become sticky and messy, especially on fine reel lines, and so I now favour silicone line floatant, which you buy in aerosol sprays. As well as being less messy, it is also considerably quicker to apply. Simply spin the reel, give the spool a ten-second spray and the job is done. It may sound obvious, but ensure that you spin the reel in the correct direction. If not, you will end up with a ball of perfectly floating line tangled round your feet!

If you have struggled up to now with float trotting, trying to compensate for sinking line, you will be amazed at quite how simple it is to mend a floating line so as to keep direct contact with the float, without pulling it wildly off course or unnaturally checking it, causing a wake, both of which are not exactly likely to endear the bait to a suspicious old chub.

Standard trotting with the Avon float.

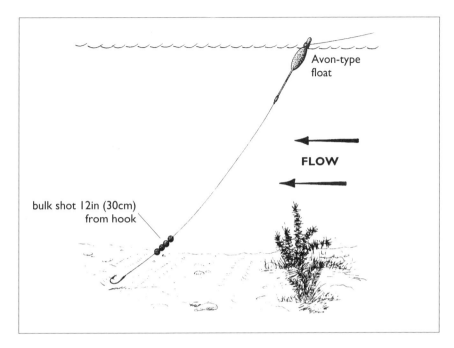

Avon-type float

FLOW

bulk shot 12in (30cm) from hook

However, gently checking the float occasionally, providing it is not pulled off line, is a good way of inducing bites, by making the hook bait swing upwards in the water with the current. Chub will rise quite a way off bottom to intercept a bait, so I set the float just to clear the bottom at the shallowest point. This is achieved by running the float through a few times to see where it drags. By inching the float up between test runs, you soon have it set.

If there are very large depth variations, of course, it means that you will be fishing much further off the bottom in some areas than in others. Generally, this will not matter, although a swim with such large variations cannot really be considered ideal for trotting in the first place. Searching the hollows with a light, rolling leger would probably be a more efficient presentation.

It is important to make sure that the line floats for efficient trotting.

The easiest type of chub swim to fish with trotting tackle is one of fairly uniform depth, brisk but smooth flow without boiling, and with a bottom consisting of fine gravel containing no irritating weed stems or tree roots. If it is under the near bank, to minimize the amount of line to be mended across the flow, so much the better. Coincidentally, such swims can be terrific for building good bags of fish, provided the loose feed is continually trickled into the run. Rarely will such glides have a permanent, resident head of chub, as there will be no feature to hold them, but new fish can constantly be encouraged to move upstream and feed over the gravel. For this reason, it pays to be patient when fishing a swim of this type, as it may take some while for the first few fish to home in on the bait trail and move into your spot. Once you have had the first bite, however, others should quickly follow. How many you catch will then depend largely on how long you can play fish without disturbing their fellows. I always try to bring them right up to me without letting the chub break surface, easier said than done, I know.

Once you have had a fish or two, and perhaps the others are becoming a little suspicious, try inducing bites in the manner mentioned earlier, by gently checking the float and making the hook bait swing upwards. Hungry chub find this absolutely irresistible. Bites are usually unmistakable, especially to large baits like breadflake, which is undoubtedly my favourite. A good Avon float will zoom under and stay under, often creating a vortex as it does so. There is none of this peering for quarter inch lifts of the float when trotting a fifty pence piece-sized chunk of flake for big chub on a size 6!

Fascinating glides for trotting, but far from easy to fish, are those of uniform depth with the exception of a pronounced depression somewhere along the length. This depression will be a natural food trap, and therefore attractive to the fish, especially where it is substantially deeper than the surrounding water. A deadly method of float fishing this kind of swim is the use of dragging trotting tactics, in which the depth is set a fraction shallower than the base of the depression. As the

Trefor lands a Cherwell four-pounder on trotted flake.

float approaches the depression from upstream, and as the depth setting is greater than the depth, the hook bait will obviously be dragging bottom. It will therefore quite simply trail behind the float. Now comes the clever bit. When the float reaches the head of the depression, which obviously presupposes you know your river well, the float is held back hard so that the dragging hook bait catches up and is then free to tumble into the depression. If the float is held back long enough, the bait will fall to the deepest setting, before starting to rise once again, thereby describing an arc under the float and very effectively searching the depression.

The major drawbacks to this technique are patently obvious. Firstly, you have to know the river intimately, and to know when to hold back

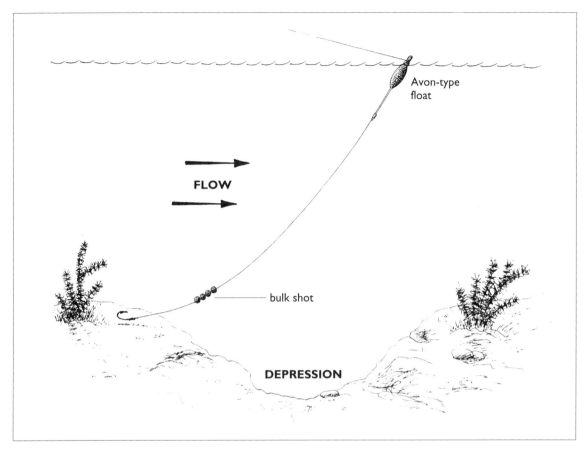

Overdepth dragging float rig for fishing depressions.

and for how long. Secondly, and most frustrating, any bottom debris makes the method a real pain, as the dragging hook continually gets fouled. This is the reason I very rarely use the technique myself. Having said that, evidence that it is deadly when used in the right circumstances came on a trip to Throop with Trefor West. He knew of a very short depression not far below barbel bend, and in three trots down, holding back in the appropriate spot, he hooked three big chub. The first came adrift, but the others were specimens of 4lb 8oz and 5lb 2oz. That was as fine a bit of angling as you could wish to see.

Another interesting trotting swim is where there is deep, steady water adjacent to dead marginal rushes, which chub love to colonize. If the rush margin is under the near bank, fishing it is simplicity itself, the tackle merely being lowered at the head of the run and being allowed to trundle along the rushes. I like the float to be hard against the rushes at all times. Loose feed is simply dropped at your feet at the head of the run.

A far bank rush margin can also be fished the same way, but this technique can be trying if there is a brisk intervening flow or a troublesome wind, or both. The method is at its best when searching the extreme edges, and any less-than-perfect conditions will see your bait pulled off-line fishing a far bank margin, no matter how good your tackle control.

I think my favourite trotting swims are those found under steep vertical banks containing undercuts, in times of high water or flood. In these conditions, chub, along with other species,

Trotting the famous Throop fishery.

Jonathan Riley trotting for chub on the Hampshire Avon.

pack into these undercuts. Again, I fish the float right along the edge of the bank, holding it back hard every few feet, so that the bait swings upwards and inwards to search under the undercut. Lobworms are brilliant for this fishing when the river is well coloured.

Some of my fondest memories of the Claydon Brook in the sixties centre round a swim of this type. This particular undercut was about four feet long, and I lost count of the chub and perch I took there. A highlight was a misty, drizzly November day when the river was carrying about a foot of extra water, with the colour just clearing, after a flood. That day, every time the float reached that magical bit of bank, it would disappear. Entered in my diary for that day are 13 perch to 2lb 8oz, roach of 1lb 8oz and 1lb 15oz, an 8lb pike and three chub of 3lb 14oz, 4lb 4oz and 4lb 14oz.

Although I thoroughly enjoy trotting, I have to admit that when big chub are the quarry I nearly always use legering techniques. There is, however, one use for the float that is useful to keep in mind: all rivers at times, especially the harder-fished ones, go through periods when bite after bite from chub will be missed. I have known days on Throop and the Ouse where two-foot pulls on the rod tip would be met by striking into fresh air time after time. A way to cure that problem almost entirely is to switch either to upstreaming or to trotting. I will never forget one weekend at Throop, where both Trefor and I missed about a dozen 'unmissable' single savage pulls. When we eventually switched to the float, the conversion of bites to hooked fish thereafter was 100 percent.

An extension to pure trotting is a method known as Stret Pegging, which I now see used very rarely. When used in conjunction with trotting tactics, this can often produce a bigger-than-average specimen, by searching those areas where perhaps some of the loose feed will have settled out of the main flow.

Bob James preparing for the Wallis cast on the Hampshire Avon.

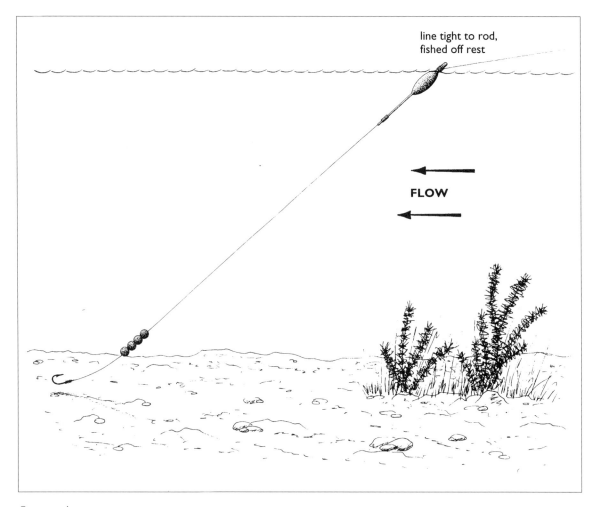

line tight to rod,
fished off rest

FLOW

Stret pegging.

When you are trotting a swim bordered by much slower water, a crease for example, it is a good idea to push up the float occasionally, cast out to the normal position and then let the float drift round on a tight line to settle in the slacker water. This laying on in streamy water is known as stret pegging. It is best if a rod rest is used for this fishing, as the float is less prone to swinging around than if the rod is being held. Also, it allows you to give your trotting arm a little respite. The float will normally be fishing at half cock when fished on a tight line in flowing water. If it continually goes under because of water pressure, keep deepening the float setting to reduce

the line angle, and eventually it will settle in a stable position. Some chub bites to this tight line float fishing can be as dramatic as they can to tight line legering, so stay alert!

I cannot leave the subject of trotting without mentioning the art of casting with the centrepin reel. I strongly recommend you master the technique of the Wallis cast. Once learned, fishing the pin becomes an absolute joy. The Wallis cast, however, is virtually impossible to describe on paper, it has to be taught in practical demonstration. That reminds me of a delightful day in Bob James, company on the Avon, where Bob first taught me the intricacy of the Wallis cast, leading to some hilarity. Let me end this section by quoting from an article I wrote at the time.

First of all, though, it was tuition time and Bob demonstrated the Wallis cast to me several times. It looked easy, and on each cast the float sailed effortlessly to the far side of the river. Now it was my turn, and my float sailed effortlessly five yards into the marginal rushes! 'Right,' said Bob, 'apart from your right hand being in the wrong place, your left hand being too high, your not having enough line from the rod tip, your not having enough line over your left thumb, your failing to spin the reel during the cast and standing wrong, everything was perfect!'

The next fifteen minutes were hilarious, both of us often helpless with laughter as I gradually eliminated the various mistakes, apparently cursed with two left hands, each equipped with five thumbs! As with fly casting, timing is of the essence. Eventually, however, I had more or less mastered the mechanics of the Wallis cast, with most casts making midstream quite easily. All it

needed now was practice. I was encouraged by Bob when he said, 'When you achieve two consecutive casts that make midstream without a tangle at the reel, you'll be a more accomplished caster than Chris Yates!'.

LAYING ON

Stret pegging, as described in the previous section, is really laying on in streamy water, so in this section I am discussing purely that laying on I do in slack or very sluggish flows. This will principally apply to summer chubbing.

I can summarize the times when I utilize a float for summer chubbing as those where I would normally freeline but wish to achieve a particular objective. The most common scenario is where I am fishing in or across dense cabbages. Here, as with summer perching, I like to manoeuvre a self-cocking float into the gaps between the pads, dropping the bait straight down, and fishing with the line above the float well greased. Obviously, the float in this situation is not primarily for bite detection, but more to minimize snagging.

The Drennan insert waggler. Ideal for laying on day or night.

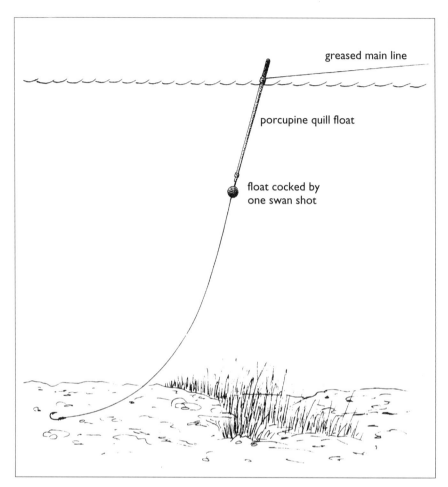

Simple laying on.

greased main line

porcupine quill float

float cocked by
one swan shot

*Laid-on lob in the cabbages
produced this five-pounder
from the Ouse.*

Laid-on lob scores again.

Fishing the nightlight float.

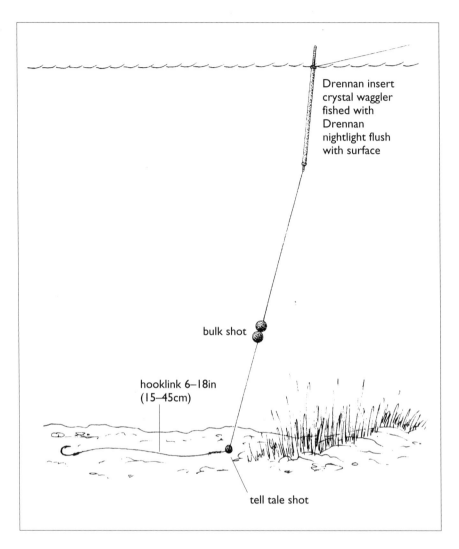

Drennan insert crystal waggler fished with Drennan nightlight flush with surface

bulk shot

hooklink 6–18in (15–45cm)

tell tale shot

The second situation, which is more common in my experience, is on a summer night, when I lay on under a betalight float, just for the fun of it. It is also a particularly efficient method. If your chub are wary, even the addition of a little lead to give a tight line to aid bite detection can lead to some very frustrating knocks and bumps from chub, with very few fish landed. The betalight float solves the problem, plus being a thoroughly fascinating method to use.

10 SURFACE FISHING

FLOATING CRUST

I have always had a soft spot for summer chubbing with floating breadcrust. It is a method I use when I fancy a break from serious big fish hunting, although I have had two five pounders on the method. A day spent wandering the banks of a small stream, insulated against the frantic pace of life of the nineties, is wonderfully therapeutic. It is also visually exciting, like catching carp on chum mixer or rudd on surface baits, or tempting trout on the dry fly.

There are certain summer swims where the use of floating breadcrust for chub is particularly appropriate. These are usually shallow, gravelly runs with a lively current, especially where the current speed starts to slow as the depth of the water increases. Such shallows often hold large numbers

The ideal feature at the end of a floating crust swim.

A big chub approaches a piece of floating breadcrust.

of chub in summer, as they are naturally highly oxygenated, and it is therefore easy to understand why the method is so productive in low water, drought-like conditions. During the middle part of the day, when oxygen content is low, most fish will be uninterested in feeding, apart from those fish that are to be found in the sharper flows. This is even more true on those days, sadly rare in this country, of hot, bright sun from a clear blue sky, and no wind to ruffle the surface.

Although the method is simple in concept, that of impaling a chunk of crust on a hook and allowing it to drift naturally with the flow, there are some important considerations to bear in mind if you are not going to become totally frustrated with the technique. Firstly, as in every other aspect of angling, bait presentation is of the essence if you are going to get the best out of it. Remember that the crust must be totally free to follow all the natural current variations, without moving unnaturally across the flow or, worse still, dragging and causing a wake. Think of floating crust fishing in the same light as trotting, where a smooth presentation down the current is also the objective. Good matchmen will confirm that dragging the float off line due to poor

tackle control is not conducive to success. There is, however, one important difference from trotting. With the float, it is quite acceptable, in fact it is a recognized bite-inducing technique, to hold the float back occasionally to cause the bait to rise in the water, perhaps to take advantage of a known feature, or to help the bait over a weedbed. With crust, however, all that will do is cause an unnatural disturbance on the surface as the crust creates drag and the chub will spook. I have seen as many as six chub crash out of the water together in alarm and bolt away when I have inadvertently checked a crust unnaturally.

With regard to the foregoing, then, it requires practice to learn how much line to let out as the crust progresses downstream. Too little line, too slowly, will result in drag, while too much will see loops of line on the surface drifting everywhere, possibly pulling the crust off course. This effect will be greatly accentuated on a windy day. Another drag creating problem is that of surplus line sinking between rod tip and crust. That last sentence gives a clue to the first rule of thumb when floating crust fishing. For maximum efficiency, the line must be heavily greased. It goes without saying, however, that it is just as important to control the rate of line release using greased line. Excessive line floating on the surface is just as detrimental to bait presentation.

As with fishing for carp with floaters, chub often have to be educated into taking floating crust by loose feeding, until they are taking confidently. It is very common to see the first few offerings ignored, or approached very nervously. As soon as one is taken confidently, without mishap, the chub rapidly increase in confidence, whereafter every loose offering is taken avidly. At that point, a properly presented hookbait will be accepted straight away. Sometimes, if the fish are particularly suspicious, which is often the case on very bright, sunny days, they will keep coming short at crusts, swirling just under the baits to break them up, for some considerable time. When they do at last take one in their lips, it will be very gingerly, and a premature strike can undo all your good work. There is no alternative but to be patient. If you are

Seven chub in seven casts to Trefor West on floating crust from the Ouse.

prepared to feed steadily for as long as it takes, the fish will eventually feed confidently.

As with all rules, there are exceptions. The above loose feeding technique is one I always use in a swim I feel may contain numbers of chub, where one nervous fish can communicate its fear to the rest. A different circumstance exists where I find a solitary specimen in a small swim and where I feel the best approach to be with floating crust. In these situations, I have often found the first crust down to be taken immediately although following offerings are refused. I have no idea why this should be, but it has happened a lot. Believe me, it can be totally frustrating when you see a great big chub take a free offering immediately and then steadfastly refuse any other morsels, no matter how good the presentation. I will never forget a five-pound-plus fish on the Ouse many years ago. He was lying in a tiny run between two rush beds, no more than a foot deep. A loose offering was gobbled up without hesitation but, when my hookbait followed, perfectly presented, it was refused. Other subsequent free offerings were also refused. Strange!

In a swim containing numbers of chub, once they are over their initial nerves, two or three fish can be taken quite quickly. Before long, the remainder of the shoal become agitated and recommence the behaviour of coming short, to knock the crusts into tiny fragments that sink and can then be taken at leisure. In these circumstances, it is a waste of time stopping fishing and recommencing loose feeding in an attempt to re-establish the chub's confidence. For that day at least, the damage has been done.

As I have said, the chub start eating the particles of bread that have sunk after being knocked off by the swirling at the surface. What this indicates is that the fish are not frightened of the bread as such. It is floating bread that has them spooked. We can take advantage of this in two ways. One way is to float a bait down with the large piece of crust an inch or so up the line, and a small hook baited with a piece of flake sunken, to simulate a particle just breaking away.

Alternatively, use a piece of legered crust or flake in the area where the chub are swirling. Bait presentation for this, however, is vitally important. Remember, we are now fishing for wary chub and a lump of lead landing on their heads is likely to be the last straw. My recommendation is to use a single swan shot leger and a piece of crust large enough to take a fair while to sink. Then cast the bait a few yards upstream of the shoal, so that, as it comes to rest, the bait appears to have arrived naturally. Once a fish or two have been taken on sunken baits, you have had the best of it and it is time to look for pastures new.

Although I rarely re-visit a swim I have given the treatment with surface crust and then sunken crust, as explained, I make an exception in a swim where a big chub has been spotted but not caught. Such a wary individual can usually be tempted by a totally different bait later in the day, if you pre-bait and then leave the swim in peace for an hour

or two. I have had several bonus specimens by introducing a dozen or more lumps of luncheon meat or cheesepaste into a crust swim as I am leaving it, and then creeping back quietly at dusk.

When fishing in shallow water, as the bulk of floating crust swims will be, it is inevitable that the shoal is going to be spooked quite quickly, by the unavoidable disturbance that results from striking and playing fish. This is an occupational hazard, and you must be prepared to be mobile. However, there are ways you can minimize the disturbance to get the most from each swim. First, the striking technique is vitally important. It is very easy to be excited into premature striking when you see the vortex where your crust was. A strike at that moment will often result in your recovering a bare hook or, even worse, momentarily feeling a pricked chub before the

There she blows.

hook pulls out. You must tell yourself to exercise restraint. When the crust vanishes, allow that second or two to elapse for the chub to turn down with the bait before striking. That way you should solidly hook every fish. Having hooked it, bring it upstream as fast as possible, with the rod held as low to the water surface as practicable. You are trying to avoid the fish splashing at the surface in the midst of all its companions. Easier said than done, I know, but if you keep your wits about you, two or three fish may result from a swim instead of just one.

As with float trotting, it is preferable to drift the crust directly downstream from your position if possible, and I always prefer to be stationed in mid-river on the shallows, well upstream of the area in which I expect bites to materialize. Once in position, I keep movement to a minimum. My normal procedure is to wade to mid-stream, in either thigh or breast waders, with a short handled landing net handy and a trout bag full of crusts over my shoulder. I am in no hurry to start fishing, first contenting myself with dropping half a dozen freebies at my feet and monitoring their progress downstream. When the first ones are taken, I know the line of drift for my hookbait.

Another good pre-baiting ploy when fishing from mid-river is to introduce the occasional handful of dampened, liquidized bread as well as loose crusts. The opaque cloud produced, which can be enhanced by the addition of a little dried milk powder, grabs the chub's attention very quickly and encourages them actively to search for the solid bread fragments.

As far as tackle is concerned, I will generally fish slightly finer than I would for legering, when 6lb main line is my normal gear for chubbing. For surface fishing, I opt for well-greased Drennan Specimen Plus or Berkley Trilene XL in 4lb breaking strain. Obviously, the finer the line, the fewer problems we have with drag and wind drift. A long rod is a help, and I will now use the thirteen foot Specimen Float rod from my Supreme range, designed for trotting for specimen fish. Although I have used a normal fixed spool reel successfully for crusting to date, there is no doubt that a smoother presentation would be achieved

with a good closed face job or, even better, a top-quality centrepin. I use one of the superb pins made by Dave Swallow, of Ibsley.

To me, the most exciting fishing with floating crust is for big individual chub in swims where the use of a surface bait offers the only possible method of enticing a bite. I am thinking of those swims where the use of a bottom bait invites almost certain snagging, or where it is simply impossible to get a bait to the bottom, because of the presence of weed, branches and so on. Small holes in dense mats of surface lilies spring immediately to mind, or tiny clearings on the top of surface streamer tresses.

In those small, neglected streams so beloved of big chub, you will often find areas where fallen timber lies on the bottom in shallow water, the branches forming a criss-crossing lattice. These areas are a major attractant for specimen chub and are simply impossible to fish with bottom baits. I have caught lots of nice chub by floating crust alongside the branches and watching fish come from under the timber and suck it in. But use strong tackle for this game. No line need be on the water, so you can use tackle as heavy as you think the snags warrant without it affecting your bait presentation.

Similar fishing can be had in small holes in extensive rubbish rafts. I have spoken often of the excellent chubbing to be had under rafts, but in the situation where the bottom is too rubbish-strewn for effective legering, fishing at the surface is a first class alternative.

The story of my biggest surface caught chub, a 5¼-pounder from a Great Ouse tributary, makes an interesting conclusion to this section.

It was a very hot August, the water being very low and clear. Under normal circumstances I would have fished my favourite chub swim by casting lobs or a slug under the trailing branches of the far bank, which entailed casting over quite thick lilies in mid-stream. On that day, however, there were a couple of additional factors I had not bargained for. First, the very hot few weeks we had just experienced had seen the formation of surface mats of thick green algae, which were caught up alongside all weed beds or overhanging foliage. Second, someone upstream of my stretch had obviously been engaged in rush cutting, since reeds and rushes littered the surface as well as the algae.

The swim I had intended to fish was therefore a thirty-yard stretch of algae interspersed with clumps of cut rushes and, to be honest, I would probably have by-passed it if I had not seen a swirl at the edge of the branches under the opposite bank. I weighed up the options, of which there were few. There was only one possibility. In the mass of surface rushes, there were lots of little gaps, no more than inches across. If I could manoeuvre an unfettered crust into one of these, I would have a chance.

At about the third attempt I managed it, using a large piece of crust on a size 2 hook to 8lb line, and, within minutes, the bait quietly sank out of sight. The resulting strike saw algae and rushes fly off in all directions, but eventually that five-pounder was safely in the net. Mind over matter, that fish.

DAPPING WITH NATURAL BAITS

Quite simply, dapping is a method of surface chubbing in which you arrange for a natural bait to rest just on the surface film, with no surplus line to cause alarm. It is particularly applicable to those overgrown areas where a more orthodox approach is not possible. Because the chub sees only the bait, the line strength is irrelevant, and in this aspect, the method is identical to margin fishing for carp.

I especially like to use the method under overhanging trees, where the chub become used to insects of all types falling into the water, and over the years I have had chub on all manner of things. Particularly effective are large moths, caterpillars, crane flies and wasps. I prefer to use these baits dead (especially wasps!) and impart life by line twitching. Two of my largest summer-caught Leam fish came on a large white butterfly and a bumble-bee.

Set up the tackle in the same way as for margin fished crust for carp, with the rod tip just

protruding from the bankside cover. Slowly lower the baited hook just to break the surface film, and then stay alert, with slack line in your hand. Takes can be sudden and violent and it is a very exciting form of chubbing that I cannot recommend too highly.

OTHER SURFACE BAITS

As well as plain breadcrust, there are many other baits that can successfully be used to tempt chub at the surface. These are useful when the fish are spooking on the bread, and especially where the attentions of small fish are tearing the crust to pieces. All these baits are fished in exactly the same way as crust.

Boilies

All bait suppliers now market floating boilies, or pop-ups, and these are devastatingly effective for chub. If you do not wish to go to the expense of buying them, you can convert your own boilies to floaters by baking them in a hot oven or in a microwave. Alternatively, mould the paste round a cork ball or poly pop before boiling.

For mounting the bait, either use a very short hair rig so that the bait is touching the hook shank or mount the bait in one of those special bait bands marketed by John Roberts for surface carp fishing.

High Protein Floater

Rather than converting your home-made paste to floating boilies, you can alternatively bake a special 'floater cake' for surface fishing. As a general rule of thumb, if you mix your boilie mix with double the normal quantity of eggs, to produce a runny mixture, and then bake it in the oven like a normal cake, you end up with a sponge-textured block of buoyant bait.

In practice, every boilie mix exhibits different characteristics, some producing lovely open-textured floater, while others give much denser results. Not all boilie mixes convert successfully to good floating mixes; it is a case of trial and error.

In my own fishing, I have very rarely gone to the trouble of producing floating cake for

A big Cherwell fish taken on a dapped, air-injected lob.

chubbing, because things like koi pellets, trout pellets or Chum Mixer are so much more convenient. However, the one floater I did make, and caught a lot of chub on, was simply a mixture of Richworth 50/50 base mix, peanut flavour and intense sweetener. This produced a lovely textured bait loaf. Like breadcrust, this is mounted by burying the hook in a chunk of the bait.

Dog Biscuits

Most dog biscuits will take chub, but the most suitable for chubbing is undoubtedly Chum Mixer. The biscuits are the right size, are very visible at range, remain buoyant for a long time, and the chub love them. I fish Mixer in conjunction with the John Roberts' bait band, and use the biscuits in the same way as I fish bottom-based particles. As each individual bait item is much smaller than a free crust sample, I introduce far more freebies when using Chum. It takes a surprisingly short time for a shoal of chub to become totally preoccupied with them, and then a couple of fish are guaranteed before the remainder become spooked.

If you cannot obtain any bait bands, Chum Mixer can simply be superglued to the back of the hook shank.

Matt Hayes baiting an Ouse run with Chum Mixer (left).

Following the hookbait's progress downstream (below).

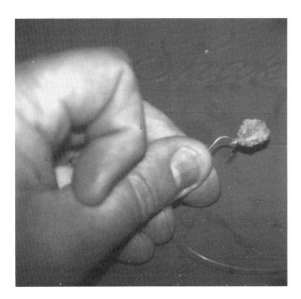

Chum Mixer mounted in John Roberts' bait band.

Koi Pellets and Trout Pellets

Fished in exactly the same way as Mixer, koi and trout pellets are the ultimate floating bait for chub, the fish going into a frenzy to get at them. I have seen the surface of shallows turned to foam by feeding fish.

When I had the pleasure of sharing a few days with Bob James on the Avon, he introduced me to the chub that lived just below the outfall of the trout stews. Those chub knew all about trout pellets, even trying to swim up the outflow pipes to get at the few pellets that had escaped the trout's attention. Being slightly smaller than Chum Mixer, these pellets are most simply fished by supergluing them to the hook shank.

Lobworms

A few years ago, I was on my way back to the van after an unsuccessful barbel session on a flooded Cherwell when I saw a good chub rise to the surface to engulf a waterlogged moth. Deciding to try and salvage a blank with a chub before leaving, I searched around for something I could use as a surface bait. All I had available that day was luncheon meat or lobs, which I had been using for the barbel. So I hit on the idea of air injecting a

lobworm and using that on the surface. In the next three casts, I had two good chub and a streaky barbel before the rest of the shoal departed.

Since then, I have not had cause to fish in that way again, but it is another idea to keep in mind. The bites were very positive, the only problem with the method being that the air gradually leaked out of the bait to make it slow sinking. This, though, could give us a deadly alternative bait when our chub are spooked on surface baits; the slow-sinking lob could be the answer.

It goes without saying that you should take extreme care when air injecting lobs, and keep the needle well away from your flesh. After use, always replace the needle guard so that you cannot accidentally inject yourself.

Breakfast Cereals

I have caught several chub off the surface on both Sugar Puffs and Puffed Wheat, using them in large quantities to attain preoccupied feeding. Being very light, they are best used on a windless day. I fish these in exactly the same way as I do trout pellets, supergluing them to the hook shank. The one difference, however, is that they have less inherent buoyancy and I add a small amount of rig foam to the hook to prevent the bait from becoming waterlogged and dragged under by the weight of the hook.

Trout pellet superglued to hook.

11 WATERCRAFT

You do not need much skill to recognize this chub swim.

Before we can catch fish we must fish where the fish are. That is a patently obvious statement, but where winter chub are concerned, I still find that many anglers are simply content to cast anywhere, as often as not with a heavy lead that anchors the bait to the river bed. No thought is given to location of the chub, and when the odd fish does reward such an arbitrary approach, the angler has no idea why.

For consistent chubbing, we must develop ways of reliably locating our quarry. Good summer swims will be equally reliable in winter, unless river conditions force the fish to move out. When they do move, perhaps from higher, faster flows, I find they only move as far as they need to find a comfortable station.

Time spent investigating the summer river, therefore, will not be time wasted, and the features to look for, apart from the whereabouts of the chub themselves, will be undercut banks, riverbed depressions, cabbage patches, underwater snags and so on. Careful appraisal of the river in close proximity to where chub are lying in summer can give invaluable clues as to where they might migrate in the higher water of winter. One vivid memory from my days on Dick Walker's stretch of the Upper Ouse is finding a warm spring by going into the river in swimming trunks. There was a respectable flow from that spring even in low water and many chub were caught downstream of this 'hot' spot in subsequent winters.

Those anglers, however, who like to concentrate on other species in summer, moving on to chub when they are at their best, the winter months, have to depend on previous experience of the river plus the ability to read the water. Only stretches of river with character and variation in flow can be read accurately. A straight, uniform and evenly flowing stretch presents different location problems. However, as many big chub are in fact taken from such featureless stretches,

possibly some of the biggest chub the river contains, they should certainly not be ignored. In these areas, the fishing is more painstaking, more a process of elimination.

If we really study the set of the various flows of a river at winter level, it soon becomes apparent that what initially appears to be of uniform flow from bank to bank is actually anything but. Even the inexperienced beginner can quickly observe that there are a great variety of current speeds, with regular divisions between fast and slow water, some marginal and some very pronounced. I have always called such divisions between fast and slower flows creases. Of all areas, these features are among the most important to note with regard to chub location.

Irrespective of current speed, the water surface itself give us vital clues to what is hidden beneath. We see that certain areas are running smoothly,

A lovely crease going across river to far bank trees.

while others are turbulent, such turbulence being either constant or intermittent. This surface turbulence can vary from minor rippling to substantial boiling, and it is obvious that the disturbance has to be a reflection of underwater irregularities of one kind or another. A constant boil or deep vortex is caused by the shelving up of the river bed or a substantial obstruction, such as a boulder or an old tree stump. In the case of shelving up of the bottom, which can also be accompanied by a diversion of flow if the bottom gravel is angled, the start of the turbulence can be a hot spot, as chub will feed at the slope, which will be a natural food trap. This, however, is very dependent on current speed, coupled with smoothness of flow. If the current is fierce enough to result in broken, boily water, chub will rarely be in residence. The only way to find out is to fish the swim by rolling a bait round to fish hard against the slope. If there are chub there, a bite should not be long in coming.

Constant heavily broken water, caused by large irregular bottom debris, is rarely worth a second look. The boils and vortices caused by such obstructions are largely avoided by chub. The one exception could be an area where a large boulder or similar rests on otherwise smooth gravel. In this case, the lee of the boulder, which often exhibits a slight depression caused by current action, could harbour fish. Such swims can only effectively be fished upstream.

It is important to differentiate between heavily broken water caused by large debris and the moderate constant ripple of shallows. The surface of shallow water will ripple even if the bottom is quite fine gravel containing small stones. Depressions in the river bed in extensive shallows can be excellent chub holding areas and what you look for here are smooth bits of surface amongst the ripple. As with rafts, do not ignore what appears to be too small a depression. I remember catching four four-pounders in successive casts from a Stour depression in shallows that was no more than three feet long and two feet wide. Similarly there was a tremendous swim on the Upper Ouse, where there was a hole four feet deep at the tail of a cattle drink. That hole was no more than four yards long but rarely failed to produce chub. Both of those swims reinforce a vitally important point. If such a depression is located in a long stretch of otherwise shallow water, it can be a natural holding spot for many fish, especially in high or flood conditions. As with our tiny summer raft, it is quite amazing how many chub can pack into a small depression.

Intermittent undulations indicate weed beds of one type or another. Submerged rushes will cause

Mid-river weed bed forming lee of quieter water downstream.

Ouse five-pounder caught upstreaming behind dead rush bed in mid-river (above).

The varying surface signals created by streamer beds.

variable surface ripple, but of a different type from that over shallows, in that it is much more broken. Also, at normal height at least, the odd rush stem will usually break surface. A substantial underwater dead rush bed will often split the flow, creating two tremendous swim types. Firstly, the roots hold back the central water, creating a lee of slacker water downstream, before the two separated flows rejoin. Slacks created behind weed beds in this manner are among the most reliable chub swims of them all. Secondly, of course, the diversion of flow across river creates inviting creases alongside the submerged rushes.

Streamer weed gives much greater variation of surface activity, as the long tresses undulate up and down in the flow. The water will run quite smoothly for a while, and then there will be a substantial boil for a few seconds as the weed rises to just under the surface. As suddenly as this, the boil will then subside. A deadly method of taking chub is to place a bait right under the trailing fronds. Cast upstream and further across from the boil, such that the bait alights on clean gravel between the beds of ranunculus, and the bait should settle in the correct place. The faster the flow, and the deeper the water, the further upstream of the boil you will need to cast to allow for the current speed.

In my experience, locating chub in streamer weed, particularly in high water, gives most anglers the greatest difficulty. Some of the very best chub rivers have long stretches adorned with ranunculus and it is vitally important to learn to interpret the surface signals if you are going to get the best out of your chubbing.

Before you start fishing, spend a few minutes just looking and making mental notes of the various surface characteristics. You will see many places where the water boils and then flattens, as the weed undulates in the stream. But what you are looking for are those narrow areas of surface which run smoothly all the time, without any boils or vortices being formed. These indicate the smooth gravel runs between beds of streamer and these are where you should aim for your bait to settle. With the correct link weight, the bait can then slowly roll round and settle under the adjacent streamer fronds.

Another favourite type of swim is where the main current suddenly diverts across river. The prime cause of this phenomenon is a shelving gravel bank, and where the current is steady a hot spot is created. The reason is obvious. Food items drifting downstream will be diverted across river by the shelf in a fairly narrow band, an abundant larder the chub are not slow in taking advantage of.

The same comments apply to junctions between fast and slow water, the crease swims mentioned earlier. Causes of such swims are legion, including bankside projections, tree stumps, bays, feeder streams, bends in the river, cattle drinks, weed beds and so on. Under normal conditions, the junction between the two flows is the most reliable area to fish.

Let me summarize this brief discourse on winter river watercraft with one sentence. If you locate an area where the current speed is evenly paced,

Leam five-pounder taken from mid-river crease.

and the surface oily smooth, there is an excellent chance you will have located chub. The cause of the swim, or its depth, is largely irrelevant. Obviously, these factors will determine the approach actually to fishing the area, but the prime problem of chub location will have been solved.

ASSESSING MORE FEATURELESS STRETCHES

There are, on all river systems, even those that are in the main fast, shallow and full of features, stretches of water which are much deeper than average, very sluggish in flow, dead straight and largely devoid of features. These lengths are much less interesting to look at, as they lack that quality known as 'character', but experience has shown that they can harbour much bigger than average chub.

On a stretch of river where there is a distinct lack of features, it is vitally important to locate those isolated features that might be present, as they could harbour the bulk of the chub population. There could, for instance, be the odd fallen branch, an occasional low growing bush at the water line or entry of a small side stream. There may be an area

The chub in this Leam swim are tight under the near bank.

of undercut bank, or a feature might have been created by a section of collapsed bank. I have known a shoal of chub to colonize a near bank area where long grass overhangs. Any feature of this type on a largely featureless stretch could be extremely significant and is well worth investigating.

Marginal bushes are important pointers, even when their foliage does not actually hang over the water. This is for two reasons. Firstly, the foliage ensures less bankside disturbance at that point and chub could colonize the near bank area for that reason alone. Secondly, bush root systems, especially hawthorn and blackthorn, often lead to bank undercutting. Before the river was dredged a few years ago, I used to fish a swim on the Leam where the undercut was several feet deep. Other anglers fished the swim by placing baits a few feet out from the branches of the blackthorn and caught very little. I used to insinuate myself right within the foliage and drop a bait only about an inch from the near bank. One winter, four different four-pound chub and a five-pounder came from that tiny area. Before embarking on a campaign at an apparently uniform stretch, it is also worth spending some time plumbing, to see whether any under-water depressions exist. Again, even a small dip in the river bed could create a hot spot, as could an area of gravel in an otherwise muddy bottom. Like

all fishing at all times, the more you know about the environment in which live the fish you seek, the more chance of success you have.

Having made the obvious comment that you should investigate thoroughly any feature that is present, it has to be said that much of the fishing in the stretches or river I have in mind will be a matter of painstaking elimination. With a perfectly uniform stretch of, say, two hundred yards, there is no way of knowing exactly where the fish will be. You have to find them either by trial and error or by creating artificial hot spots and hoping the fish will come to you. Several of the slow stretches I fish for chub have one feature in common, an overgrown far bank, usually because it is private and left to the forces of nature. One stretch of the Upper Ouse springs immediately to mind. Although there were few far bank rafts or fallen trees, the marginal far bank area was littered with old timber, branches that had broken away in storms, creating very substantial snags which were not immediately obvious to the naked eye. The technique here was to place a bait as close to the far bank as possible, casting upstream. Snagging was frequent, but the compensation was that bites were frequent also. That stretch produced several five-pounders and two sixes to my friends and I.

12 COPING WITH EXTREME CONDITIONS

Most of the advice on winter chubbing in this book is applicable to normal winter conditions, that is, conditions where the river height and flow speed is average, the water is neither too clear nor too muddy, and the weather conditions are such that the water temperature is conducive to chub feeding activity. Although chub generally will be happier feeding at a lower range of temperature than will barbel, I still like to see the temperature in excess of 40°F (4°C), and rising.

In a typical English winter, however, such ideal conditions seem to occur less and less often. The committed chub man, therefore, must be able to assess less than ideal conditions, and learn how they affect chub location, feeding characteristics and our approach to catching them.

These less-than-ideal conditions can be considered at opposing ends of the spectrum. On the one hand, we have a river that is low and clear, with clear skies and severe night frosts, such that all the slacker areas are frozen over, and on the other hand we have a river that is high and coloured in full flood. Both of these extremes are tricky for the inexperienced chub man, so let us have a look at each in detail.

CLEAR, ICY CONDITIONS

The first thing is that no experienced chub man would deny that chub are undoubtedly more difficult to tempt in ice age conditions than they are in more favourable water temperatures. Having said that, fishing for chub is still a very worthwhile proposition if you apply a modicum of logic and common sense to your fishing, and if your expectations are matched to the conditions. Even so, I have had lots of exceptionally big chub and

several large bags of fish on days that have been constantly sub-zero, proving that red letter days can occasionally occur in the most adverse of circumstances.

As with winter barbel, it is not so much the conditions on the day of fishing that are so important, but rather those that have prevailed for the previous couple of weeks. For example, if the river has been at normal winter level for some time, with consistently high pressure and severe night frosts, I would consider the conditions quite reasonable for successful chubbing. On the other hand, a sudden sharp frost after mild conditions can make chub almost impossible to tempt until their metabolism has adjusted to the new environment. Even more galling is the situation where the conditions alter dramatically every couple of days, with alternate mild spells and severe frosts, neither being sustained long enough to be taken advantage of. These 'yo-yo' conditions really are the kiss of death for most species, as the fish never have time to acclimatize properly.

For the purposes of this discussion, therefore, we are going to assume that the river has been clear and cold for a couple of weeks, at normal height and flow. Frost hangs around all day and there may even be lying snow. The slower stretches have ice margins. I have to say that I love to be by the river in these conditions as the countryside certainly looks at its winter best, and the chilly air is exhilarating providing you are well wrapped against the cold.

When conditions are extreme, there is no doubt that you should confine your chubbing to rivers you know well. It is no time for rushing off to pastures new. My choice of ice age chub swims is based on one simple premise, and that is the lower the water temperature the more lethargic

Ice margins on the Leam.

My first Leam five-pounder caught in sub-zero temperatures (below).

the usual station for the fish under normal winter conditions being on the edge of the main flow, where they easily intercept food items washed downstream. If we assume that this crease is in mid river, the slower water being under our own bank, the closer to the bank we come the more sluggish the flow gets, until it becomes very sedate in the edge. As a general rule, I would expect the chub to migrate more into the steadier flows the colder the water, tucking themselves right under the bank in severe conditions. It is very common for the bulk of the chub population to be huddled under the marginal ice when temperatures drop to such extremes.

In a biggish swim, it can be difficult to assess exactly on what line the chub will be lying on a particular day, and the method I adopt is as follows. Suppose I normally fish a crease with three swan shot and a ten pence-sized piece of crust, to keep the hookbait hovering on the edge of the faster flow. My first few casts will be with this set up, just in case the chub are behaving out of character. If, as I would expect, I have no bites, my next move would be to increase the bait size to a much larger crust sample. This is the first thing that may surprise some anglers, particularly as we

the fish are likely to be and the more likely they are to seek out the gentlest flows. I will therefore tend to fish my normal swims, but in the areas where the current speed is least. Let me give you an example.

Over the years, I have often written about the crease type of chub swim, where fast water meets slow. These are undoubtedly premier chub areas,

are discussing cold conditions. As I have said more times than I care to remember, it is not bait size that is important, so much as bait presentation. My motive for increasing bait size is simple. The extra buoyancy of the larger piece of crust ensures that the terminal rig drifts a little further round from the faster flow before settling.

If still no bites materialize, the link will be reduced to two swan, with varying bait sizes, and then to a single swan. This progression means that successively lighter and more buoyant offerings will be presented in slower and slower flows, each one coming to rest closer in to the near bank. In very cold conditions, I have often reverted to a single AAA with a large piece of crust, so that it did not settle until it was only inches from the near bank, at which time it could be several feet under marginal ice. In actual fact, this is one of the deadliest methods of taking chub in these circumstances. As well as current speed considerations, I am sure the chub view the opaque ice overhead as security against predators, much as they do rafts.

One of my fondest memories of fishing like this is on the Cherwell in the winter of 1985, which was very snowy and icy. Using a single swan shot, I presented half-inch cubes of a buoyant carp bait right under the marginal ice and took five chub, four of them over three pounds, on one of the most bitterly cold days I have ever fished. All those fish picked up the bait no more than a yard from the near bank, several feet under the marginal ice. I had to drop the bait in the clear central channel, and then allow enough slack to allow the current to trundle the terminal rig under the ice until it settled. All the bites were very positive and the fish gave a good account of themselves. The only problem was landing them, as I had to manoeuvre each chub out to midstream and then slide it over the ice into the net.

I have already touched upon bait size, but let us now look at this in a little more detail. My results have demonstrated that it is not necessary to revert to ultra-small hookbaits, although it is prudent to cut down the amount of loose feed in cold water. In normal winter conditions, I can often get through four mashed loaves a day in

loose feed. In icy weather, I usually content myself with a very occasional hookbait sample or the odd pinch of squeezed breadcrumbs. The fish are quite happy to accept a substantial mouthful, but they are not prepared to move too far for it. As I said earlier, the cold water makes them lethargic, and if you want to catch them you must put the bait to them rather than trying to move them to the bait.

If we accept that, then it makes sense to keep very mobile in our searches for cold-water chub, covering each swim very thoroughly. The more areas that see my hookbait, the more chance I have of it occasionally settling close enough to a chub for it to consider taking it to be worth the effort involved. It is a simple matter of statistics.

There has been a lot of advice over the years about the need to peer for tiny bites in cold water chubbing and quite honestly this is something I cannot relate to at all. I will concede that the real rod-wrenching pulls, when very active chub are roaming all over the river, are rare in very cold conditions, simply because of the lethargy of the fish. However, when a bait has been placed close enough to a chub so that it can be taken without the expending of undue energy, the bites are still positive enough to give a good quivertip deflection or unmistakable pull, if touch legering is being employed.

One of the contributory factors to the small bite syndrome is the concurrent advice that you must revert to tiny baits on gossamer tackle in cold water. Again, this is largely a myth, in my opinion. Chub in cold water are no different from chub in any other conditions in that they will eat anything. Provided that the bait is placed close enough to a chub, it will just as well take a single pinkie as my piece of crust. The overriding difference, of course, apart from the obvious one of bait size, is bait presentation. I will say again that this is the most important aspect of all. Whereas my ten pence piece of crust can be presented perfectly naturally using a size 6 hook and 6lb line, as its inherent buoyancy permits the use of sensible tackle, the same gear for the single pinkie would obviously be ridiculous and give a completely unnatural presentation. So we would have

Trefor weighing a good fish caught from a glide on Dick Walker's stretch on a freezing February morning.

to scale right down to correct this. To achieve as natural a presentation as my favourite crust would require probably 2lb line and a size 18 with the single pinkie. This approach in itself can lead to the tiny bite problem. Over the years the equations 'big baits equals big bites and small baits equals small bites', although obviously not infallible, have proved to have considerable merit. Of course, there is nothing whatever wrong with using the fine-line, small-bait approach if that is your wish. Certainly, some small stretches of rivers may contain chub that have become wary of large pieces of crust, as big chub are becoming a popular quarry again. What

I am trying to get across is that there is usually no need to revert to such tactics.

One serious drawback to the small-bait, fine-line approach is the one of possibly inadequate tackle strength. Just because I have said that cold-water chub are lethargic in their searches for food should not be taken to mean that they are similarly lethargic once they have been hooked. Quite the reverse is often true, and I have had some spectacular scraps with big fish under ice age conditions, scraps where 2lb line would have given me no chance at all, particularly as many of these battles were fought over marginal ice. Fishing over ice calls for hook and haul tactics to prevent

Trefor took this Cherwell specimen in a raging blizzard.

constant line friction on the edge of the ice. Also, as I have said earlier, very severe weather, where wide ice margins are present, may require the chub being held hard at the edge of the ice until it eventually beaches itself on to the ice raft, from where it can be slid into the net. Such tactics require beefier gear than 2lb line and 18 hooks.

Let me end this section with my précis on my attitude towards chub fishing in severe weather, which has stood me in good stead for thirty years. Present correctly a substantial bait, on sensible tackle, in the correct place and if there is a chub there, he will have it. What is more, nine times out of ten, he will leave you in no doubt as to his having taken it.

FLOODS

Over thirty years ago, I remember writing to Dick Walker to ask his advice on fishing a flooded river. In his reply, although he gave me a few ideas, the overall thrust of his advice was that if you find a river in flood, fish the nearest stillwater!

There cannot be many aspects of coarse fishing where I have grown to disagree with Dick, but this is one of them. I find fishing high water both fascinating and intensely rewarding, unless the conditions are totally adverse. During most floods, the chub feed avidly and memorable catches are there to be enjoyed if you know how to tackle the conditions and what to look for.

Obviously, not all winter floods are going to provide favourable feeding conditions, and so the first thing to analyse is the weather conditions that led up to the high water. I am always itching to get out on to the bank when the river rises rapidly after warm westerlies bring rain to end a dry, cold spell. As I have often written, the steeply rising temperature gradient such conditions bring turns most fish on to the feed.

There are two problems connected with chubbing when the river is rising rapidly, despite the very positive water temperature increase. The first is that the water colour is at its deepest before the flood passes its peak, and therefore only those species that thrive in muddy conditions are likely to be interested in feeding. Barbel and roach fall into this category. Secondly, the first onset of higher water flushes bankside debris into the river, so that the first twenty-four hours can be a nightmare for anglers, as the flow carries tons of flotsam with it. It can sometimes be impossible to fish efficiently in these conditions, and you will have little alternative but to wait until the rubbish subsides. Although I have many times struggled through days like this to take good barbel, the conditions are poor for chub. Also, continually winding in to clear rubbish from the line can become very tedious. Efficient angling is impossible, and you are asking for a lucky break through sheer persistence. As soon as the flood peaks, however, and the colour begins to fine off, we have superlative chub conditions.

An icy day on a flooded Cherwell. Grim conditions indeed (above).

Cheesepaste in a near bank slack of the Leam fooled this fish.

night frosts have been so severe that roads have been heavily gritted, the sudden rise in level could contain melting snow and/or road salt. Both of these factors lead to temporary deoxygenation, the kiss of death for fishing for any species. A river coming into flood with melting snow obviously will not exhibit the positive factor of rapidly rising water temperature. The super-cooling effect can take several days to

What I have just said applies to a river rising after a dry cold spell. If the cold spell, however, has been coupled with thick lying snow or the

overcome, and I rarely bother fishing a river in these circumstances.

Assuming satisfactory conditions, I believe the most important single factor in successful flood-water fishing to be current speed, coupled with smoothness of flow. One snippet of advice from Dick Walker was that he always looked for a speed of flow as close as possible to that which the fish normally inhabited, and this is something I can heartily endorse. You will notice I have made no mention of depth, and this simply is because depth is largely irrelevant in coloured water. With a comfortable, non-turbulent flow, chub will feed quite happily in two feet of water. That is why flooded cattle drinks are such reliable swims, where most of the fish will be found in water covering what is normally dry land.

Lack of turbulence is a critical factor, and few fish will stay in a boily area, where they are forced needlessly to expend energy. This is the reason I feel much of the old advice about looking for a deep circular eddy is very misleading. Such areas can be very turbulent during high water, besides acting as a collection point for swirling rubbish. No longer do I waste valuable fishing time in such places. The higher the floodwater becomes, the fewer suitable swims of gentle flow there are from which to choose, and this is when some really memorable catches are possible, as large numbers of fish pack into them to escape the full force of the current. Fond memories are catches of chub in crease swims, where the main flow is forced across river by a bankside obstruction, leaving a lee of quieter water inside, big specimens on lobworms legered in near bank undercuts, and catches of quality fish from flooded cattle drinks and back eddies. Many smaller rivers and streams consist of a series of narrow, brisk flowing channels that occasionally open out into wider, shallow and usually sluggish bays. The edges of these are only inches deep, thereby used by farm animals for drinking, hence the all-embracing description of cattle drink. Even in normal height and flow conditions, the main push of current is normally through the centre of such bays, where the edges are of much gentler flow, or even stagnant. The higher the water

level, the more pronounced this demarcation becomes. With a few feet of floodwater on, the quiet flows in the margins are arguably the best chub swims on the river.

Terrific swims I have always known as 'back eddies' are created by high water and do not exist at normal height. I am thinking here of a long straight section, with intermittent bushes or small trees, where the root systems are normally above the water line. Such areas have banks that are perhaps a little steeper than average, and the normal approach would be to fish to mid-river, or along the line of the extremity of the overhanging branches.

When the river rises, however, we have a whole new ball game. Once the root systems become submerged, two new swims are created. First, we have a raft of debris caught up around the lower branches, while downstream is a lee of quieter water. If the river is just a little high, so that rafts are present without excessive turbulence, the rafts are the places to fish. There will be a natural migration of the fish, especially chub. However, the lower branches are also the focal point for uncomfortable turbulence if the flow gets too fierce, and at this stage the fish will move out. Luckily for us, they do not move far. As a direct result of the excess turbulence, we find created behind each bush a smooth back eddy. The fish drop back into these eddies, and I can recall some terrific catches of chub from swims of this type. The technique is to fish upstream under the downstream edge of the cover.

When studying the surface of a flooded river, always be on the look-out for flat spots of appreciably slower flow than the rest. Where you see such an area in mid river, the chances are that it has been created by a bed of dead rushes, behind which are always reliable winter swims, irrespective of river height. At flood level, such a quiet oasis becomes much more pronounced, and these are terrific chub swims, particularly when the river is fining off a bit.

Once again, these swims are best fished upstream if possible, but you must be aware that a lot more lead will be required, not necessarily to hold bottom in the actual fishing area, but rather to counteract the heavy flow you might be forced to fish across. Never be frightened to pile on lead to give the required efficiency of presentation.

Remember always the principle of upstream leg-ering, in that it is a balance between all the forces

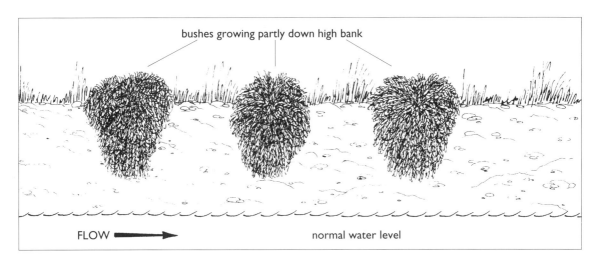

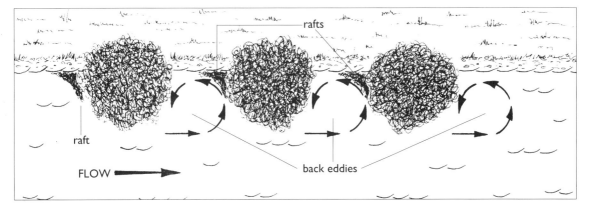

Creation of back eddies.

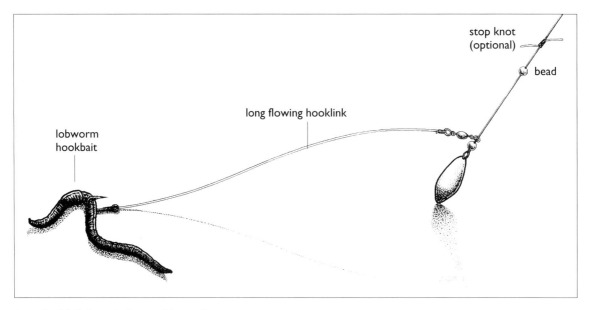

Long hooklink leger rig for searching undercuts.

at work. If the factors of current pressure on the line, weight of terminal rig, and tension in the curvature of the quivertip are properly balanced, you can be fishing just as delicately with three ounces of lead as you could with two swan shot.

Steep, high vertical banks should never be ignored by the floodwater angler, as two types of terrific swim are created in the margins. First we have the undercut bank, although generally you would need prior knowledge of the river to fish these efficiently. The water in these undercuts is of gentle flow, and is attractive to all species. In my wonderful years on the Ouse system, a couple of swims gave me tremendous chub and perch sessions in high flood. Such swims are best fished downstream, using a lead light enough to be washed right under the bank. Lobs are favoured for this presentation. One word of warning about fishing undercuts in floods. Because of their nature, high water can make such areas of bank unstable. Therefore, do not stand close to the edge or it could give way. I can still picture the angler that went in to Barbel Bend at Throop in six feet of floodwater when the bank collapsed. Had I not had my landing net handle right to

hand, that angler would surely have drowned.

Experienced chub and barbel anglers know how reliable are high banks in floods, with the bait tight against the near bank, even though the surface flows can at times appear too fast. Any student of physics knows that when water is forced through a narrow passage or tube, the speed of flow is always greatest in the centre, owing to the viscous drag created by the walls. The higher the speed of flow becomes, the more the faster flow breaks into turbulence, but the greater the effect of the drag. The difference in flow speeds thus becomes more and more marked. In an angling situation, therefore, our tube walls are replaced by the high banks and the river bed. It does not take a genius to calculate that the quietest flow will be at the junction of the riverbed and the bottom of the steep bank.

To fish such areas efficiently, it is best to use a much lighter lead than would appear necessary from the surface evidence. The reason for this is that the required presentation is hard against the near bank, not a yard away from it. First cast the bait a yard or two from the near bank. As it sinks, the quivertip will indicate excessive tension as it responds to the mid-water flows. As soon as the bait settles, however, you will notice the tip ease back into the correct fishing position. For this fishing, it is always better to fish from further upstream than normal, sitting with your back to the flow so that the line angle is as shallow as possible. In this way, the pressure on the tip is minimized and your bait presentation is enhanced.

The most reliable and well loved of floodwater swims are creases, and every species of fish will colonize these in high water. Most causes of creases are well known, but a particular cause in flood water, not present at normal flows, is a normally shallow, shelving gravel bank. With a few feet of water on, these banks tend to throw the flow across river, leaving a sedate and very enticing run downstream of the feature. One such swim on Dick Walker's stretch of the Upper Ouse was particularly reliable in these conditions. He actually christened it the Going Away Swim!

Without a doubt, the most difficult of all areas to read and fish in high flood is the streamer bed, and it involves an attitude of mind as much as anything else. Just like looking for the one flat spot behind a submerged rush bed, we are now looking for a multitude of smaller flats between streamer clumps. These can be so small that they can sometimes be impossible to spot if there is any wind ruffling the surface.

If you can see the flats, however, which are often more pronounced if you view the river from a distance initially, you have located potentially very exciting areas. The way to fish these is from as far upstream as possible, again to narrow the angle. Cast a substantial lead to alight in the flat, a lead that is heavy enough to stay wherever it settles. In high water in such swims, the line will usually be as taut as a banjo string and some of the pulls have to be experienced to be believed. Fishing in this manner is good fun when coupled with touch legering. The tremendously savage lunge of the line across my fingers is still one of my most exciting experiences in angling.

Let me end this section with two very simple snippets of advice. First, only fish a river you know well in flood conditions. If you do not know the features of the water at normal level you are going to be up against it in high, murky conditions.

Second, flooded rivers are dangerous, often with high, slippery banks. Pay attention to your safety. It is a good idea to wear a buoyancy aid under your fishing clothes. As someone who has slid down a high bank into raging floodwater, I can assure you that it is far from funny.

CREASES

In the section on fishing in very cold water, I touched briefly upon varying presentation in crease swims to present baits in different parts of the swim. Let me expand on that theme a little, into a wider discussion of how weather and water conditions influence the chub's positioning and feeding behaviour in these swims.

Trefor with an incredible catch of Cherwell chub on a cold day fishing near bank creases.

A classic crease swim on the Ouse.

Fishing creases under varying conditions (below).

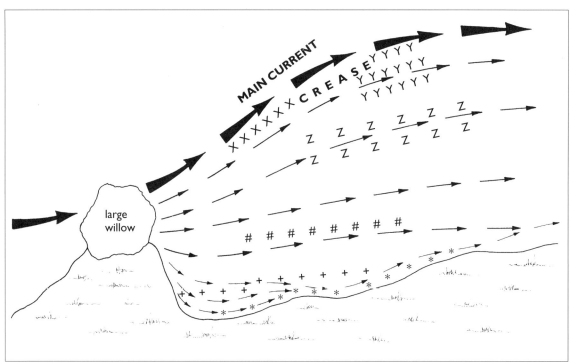

The diagram shows one of my favourite Upper Ouse chub swims, in which a large, pollarded willow on a protruding section of bank throws the main flow across river very markedly indeed.

So substantial is the bank protrusion that, even at normal flow rates, the demarcation between fast and sluggish water in mid-stream is very pronounced. Moving inshore to the near bank from the crease itself the current speed becomes progressively more sedate, being almost static close in to the near bank.

Let me now refer to the diagram and discuss how various combinations of water and weather conditions alter the chub's positioning and feeding characteristics.

If we consider first of all the situation of normal winter height, temperature and flow rate, by which I mean generally mild conditions, normal winter level, and just a tinge of colour without it being either murky or as clear as tap water, then we can guarantee that the chub will be feeding hard and actively looking for food. They will, therefore, position themselves to take best advantage of food availability in the most economic manner possible. This is best achieved at the head of the crease, right at the junction of the fast and slow currents. The reason for this is that at that point all drifting food items are concentrated into a relatively narrow band along the fastest flow. With the chub stationed just into the slacker water, they have minimum energy expenditure in moving across slightly and intercepting whatever is drifting past. The principle behind this thinking is the general rule of all wild creatures. Maximizing feeding opportunities at minimum outlay ensures survival and growth. In summary then, under these prime conditions for winter chubbing, the fish will be located largely where I have marked an X.

Let us now examine the situation where conditions are still generally excellent, with normal height and temperature, but where the current is a little sharper with slightly more colour, after a day or so of warm rain. It is important to realize that, in essence, we have exactly the same scenario as before, in that the chub will be feeding avidly. However, in accordance with the rule that, all other things being equal, the chub will adjust their position into one of comparable flow rate, the fish may now drop back to Y. At this new station, they will still be in a prime spot for picking off titbits in the main flow, but will have found a flow rate equivalent to X in the first example. After several days of sustained warm rain, although the temperature would still be

favourable, we may find a river at increased flow, height and colour. I am thinking here of, say, two feet or so above normal level. There are three circumstances that could have created this: either a very steady rise in level following persistent, light rain over many days; a fining down of the river after much higher levels or flood conditions; or a rapid rise after sustained and very heavy rain. The following comments apply to the first two of these options, which are both conducive to good chubbing. The third option mentioned would generally see very rapid colouring, plus a sudden influx of displaced bankside debris, and these are poor conditions for chubbing. Once again, knowing that the chub will still be feeding keenly, we can stick with the same principle of looking for equivalent speeds of flow to those in which we know the chub feel comfortable. At increased height, speed and colour, therefore, we look for the chub at Z. The only possible variant in the actual fishing would depend on the amount of colour present, where I might under these conditions vary from using crust to using a more pungent bait such as cheesepaste or flavoured meat; lobs are also good.

It is when water temperatures start to drop that we have to think anew, because now we are faced with a corresponding lowering of the chub's metabolic rate. This makes it even more imperative for the fish to expend as little stored energy as possible, and in low temperatures the fish will not be feeding avidly and they will certainly not be chasing baits. They will, however, take advantage of any food item if energy expenditure is virtually nil.

In this situation, the chub will tend to seek out even steadier flows than those they normally occupy, to lower their energy requirements. At normal height and flow speed, where the only negative factor is lower than normal temperature, perhaps caused by nights of light frost, I would be looking for the fish at #. The fishing technique would also take into account the factors mentioned above, in that the chub rarely chase baits in these conditions. I would therefore cut right back on loose feed and at the same time increase my casting rate, covering the line of the swim yard by yard. Remember, the chub will take the

A Leam four-pounder, taken on a freezing day, where the crust was presented right under the marginal ice in the slackest flow.

bait if it settles close to them, but will be unwilling to move far for it.

We now come to the two real extremes, severe cold, low and clear conditions, and a raging brown flood. In the first, assuming that the conditions have prevailed for a few days so that the chub have become acclimatized, the number of bites expected will be drastically reduced. In these conditions, even a bait sitting an inch from a chub's nose may not be taken for a good while, and it often pays to fish much more statically than usual. Obviously, this presupposes that you know your river, and know that the swim in question is one frequented by chub. The gentlest flows will be the places to search, and I would be searching at +. As I touched on in an earlier section, this could actually be under marginal ice.

In our full, brown, raging flood, it is hardly worth going chub fishing, and it really is time to put the barbel or roach gear to work. However, if you persist in chubbing, the best chance would be hugging the banks at * with lobworms, especially if you knew of such an area with an undercut.

I realize I have made the above description very 'pigeon holed' and simplistic. In reality, there will be many occasions when conditions do not fall into such neat sub-sections. However, my intention is to demonstrate the underlying principles governing chub location and behaviour. Get a total grasp of those, and you will be able to predict with greater and greater success where the chub will be located under any combination of conditions. And then your winter chubbing will really take off.

13 FISHING FLOOD RAFTS

A Leam four-pounder taken from under a raft at night.

Fishing for chub under rafts of flotsam caught up around obstructions such as trailing branches is obviously one of the most universally popular techniques of all, and rightly so because chub have a great affinity for surface cover, under which they feel secure. If all you want is a chub, without being too concerned about its size, there is nothing simpler than sitting slightly above the raft, and arranging for a hookbait to be presented under the debris. As many such swims are naturally created holding areas, bites come regularly to this method without any pre-baiting being carried out.

This simple, laid-back approach to a flood raft, however, has one serious drawback for the angler searching for that above-average specimen. Because the swim is a favoured holding spot, it may contain many chub of all sizes and the biggest one in residence is unlikely to be caught. Because it is the biggest and wisest, the sudden arrival of an unannounced hookbait is likely to be treated with the deepest scepticism. The smaller residents, however, have no such finely tuned instinct of suspicion and they are more likely to take the bait immediately. This results in swim disturbance which makes old granny warier than ever and even more tight lipped. We can draw a parallel here with the method of fishing for summer barbel that Trefor and I wrote about in *Quest for Barbel*. If you want to catch the biggest fish in a group you have located, the greatest mistake you can make is actually fishing for it prematurely, before it has been given the time and nurturing with pre-baiting to allay its suspicions. The principles have equal validity with groups of winter chub so let us see how they can be adapted for our raft.

To catch the biggest fish present, we must achieve two objectives. Firstly, sufficient time must be allowed for the big fish to accept the hookbait as a safe item of food without fear, with regular amounts of loose feed being available. Secondly, as much of the competition as possible, in the shape of smaller chub, must be removed from the scene, but without creating disturbance that will be counter productive to any hopes of success.

Let us assume that we have an average-sized rubbish raft in a near-bank steady glide under an overhanging willow. I know from experience that even a small swim of this type can harbour twenty to thirty chub, but for the purposes of this discussion we will assume that there are eight fish present under the debris. Five of them are between two and three and a half pounds, there are a couple of fours and one five plus. The five-pounder is the target.

The first step is to draw away from the swim as many of the lesser chub as possible, while ensuring that the big fish stays put. This is achieved by a very carefully programmed baiting sequence. First of all, I position myself perhaps twenty

4lb 11oz and 5lb 10oz Claydon Brook chub taken in successive casts on lobs fished under a rubbish raft.

Far bank Ouse raft.

yards above the raft and introduce two or three large handfuls of well-mashed bread. For perhaps ten minutes or so I steadily introduce flake samples and an occasional small ball of mash or squeezed breadcrumbs, after which I will expect the less cautious fish to be moving upstream, to intercept food particles and investigate the source of this new food supply. It is important not to keep up this baiting procedure for too long or you run the risk of attracting all the chub out of the swim, and that is not the intention. To make sure that my target five-pounder is allowed the peace to become uninhibited, I will creep down to above the raft itself about fifteen minutes after having started the upstream baiting and introduce two or three handfuls of feed directly under the rubbish. You will immediately grasp the intention. It is to split the shoal.

I then commence my actual fishing from the point twenty yards above the raft, and spend perhaps the best part of an hour steadily feeding and hopefully catching one or two of the smaller chub as they move on to the bait. During this fishing time, I will break off a couple of times to place a little more feed under the debris to keep the big fish happy.

All captured chub are carried well away from the fishing area and returned, and I always find this an exciting part of the procedure. Mentally, I reduce the odds against catching the biggest fish with each lesser companion I am able to remove from the scene.

Once bites have ceased from the upstream position, it is time to put the second part of the plan into action. This is not, as you might reasonably expect, to fish under the rubbish, but rather to fish below the raft in the small, slacker area that often exists there. There is a good reason for this. Not only does the regular feeding from upstream encourage smaller fish from the swim to move up to intercept it, but introducing the feed directly under the raft encourages chub to move downstream to catch morsels that may have drifted past them. The least likely to do this will naturally be the laziest fish which, as is often the case with humans and all other animals, is usually the oldest and fattest.

Before commencing fishing from this new station, I will introduce several bait samples under the debris. The idea now is that this limited feed is dense enough to sink and stay put without drifting downstream. While I am fishing behind the raft for any chub that have fallen back I want to be as sure as possible that the biggie stays at home.

I fish from the downstream sitting position, much as I fished from above the raft, only in reverse. The first cast will go perhaps ten yards below the rubbish and every subsequent cast closer to the cover until eventually I am presenting a bait right at the downstream extremity of the branches. It is vitally important that you fish from a good few yards below the swim, and learn how to leger upstream effectively. If you plonk yourself right on top of the swim and try to fish below the raft under your rod tip, you risk undoing all your previous good work by creating unnecessary disturbance. You will find a detailed explanation of upstream legering in Chapter 9.

After perhaps twenty minutes fishing below the raft it is time for the pay-off cast right under the rubbish, and if the preparation work has been carried out thoroughly you will be amazed at how often that results in an immediate bite from a big fish. If there is no response immediately, do not assume that there are no fish there. It is very possible that, despite all our efforts, the fishing from above and below may have temporarily disturbed the swim. What I do these days, if I have fished directly under the raft for fifteen minutes without a bite, is rest the swim for at least two hours, after introducing another few bait samples. Even better is to leave that swim until dusk when all the preparatory work could pay off with a short bout

4lb 14oz Leam chub taken from a far bank raft.

of explosive action from the big chub you have been trying to outwit all day.

The above example is an imaginary one, and as such is obviously a little idealistic. So let me end this chapter with a real life description of two hours' fishing from a recent trip to the Ouse.

At about midday, I came to a lovely little raft, which had been formed when dead rushes, driven downstream by recent floods, had draped around the dangling branches of a decrepit old willow. The raft was on the inside of one of my favourite crease swims, the current was steady and there was about four feet of water under the debris. All in all, it looked a perfect chub retreat and I reasoned that it could harbour a fair-sized shoal.

That day I was using simple legered crust and fishing exactly as I have described. After about fifteen minutes of fishing from the upstream position I started to get bites. I missed most of the bites, which were obviously from a shoal of roach that I had drawn upstream with my baiting. I did, however, manage to convert two of the twenty or more plucks into roach on the bank and two fish of about a pound and a quarter were returned well upstream of my position.

Eventually, the roach bites petered out and, at last, I had a much more positive slow draw on the tip that resulted in a muscular three-and-a-half pound chub reposing in my net. The very next cast produced another three-pounder, and he was returned with his companion, again a good two hundred yards away. The second chub saw the cessation of action from the first fishing position, and I was soon settled in the second area below the raft, after first baiting as described.

The swim below the raft was a little difficult to fish upstream as there was a fair bit of surface flotsam floating down from the recent flood, which was slowly receding. The critical balance in upstreaming is much more difficult to achieve when drifting rubbish continually fouls the line, as false bites can be a perpetual nuisance. After about four such indications, I was forced to increase the link weight to cope with the conditions. It would now take a stronger pull to shift the lead, which, though certainly not ideal, was a working compromise in the circumstances. Again, roach were not slow in attacking the baits and after at least five knocks, which I missed, there was a much more determined pull that saw the lead bounce downstream very excitingly. The chub I was expecting failed to materialize, but instead a spanking roach of 1lb 15oz was soon being lifted ashore. This was followed by another bout of plucks and trembles before a third chub then put in an appearance. Another three-pounder was soon being returned.

The cast just below the downstream edge of the raft was interesting. The bait had hardly hit the water when there was a terrific bump on the rod

Near bank Ouse raft.

tip and the line shot downstream at a rate of knots. An energetic fish roared around under my feet for several minutes with great gusto before I was able to net it and see that it was a perch of just under two pounds. In my long angling career that is the first time I have taken a big perch on legered crust.

It had therefore already been an interesting hour and a half when I eventually sat expectantly, eyes glued to the quivertip, as an enticing piece of crust hovered about three inches off the riverbed right under the raft. The first bite saw my deviating from the script, as I somehow contrived to miss it, despite the fact that it was slow, deliberate and apparently unmissable. I need not have worried because the very next cast was a repeat performance and this time there were no mistakes. Winter chub are great fighters, and this one certainly did itself proud, making several lively excursions towards the rushes before it eventually folded into the net. Despite several re-zeroings of my scales, I could not make the fish more than 4lb 14oz and as I watched it swim away I realized that I could never get tired of fishing for these worthy adversaries.

There were no further bites after landing the four-pounder, but I had a nagging suspicion there might just be another biggie in residence.

That is why once more, I settled into the swim quietly and unobtrusively just as the light was fading, and silently lowered a succulent chunk of breadcrust under the debris. For twenty minutes I sat there in the gathering dusk and rapidly falling temperature. Just as it was completely dark, I felt a small pluck on my finger, as I always touch leger in conjunction with the tip beta light after dark. I was instantly alert. Seconds later a powerful pull preluded my hooking what was obviously a very big chub indeed. For several minutes it fought deeply and slowly and then, in the beam of my headlamp, I saw a deep fish close under my own bank. The depth of flank told me that the chub was well over five pounds but unfortunately I was never to weigh it. Only a couple of feet from the net cord the fish gave a final lunge and the hook shot out of the water and wrapped itself round the low branches above my head.

Shortly after, I was on my way home and went through the day's fishing in my mind. The raft technique had worked again and I was delighted with the 4lb 14oz fish. It had also uncovered a big chub and, although I was annoyed with myself for losing it, there was always another day. Now that it had been located I would be back.

An absolutely classic Cherwell chub swim.

14 STILLWATER CHUBBING

DEADBAITING

Although I have always said that, to me, real chub fishing will always be that found in running water, and that I have always found it difficult to generate much enthusiasm for stillwater chubbing, we cannot ignore the fantastic potential for giant chub in our gravel pits. Undoubtedly, there are some colossal fish just waiting to be caught. One of angling's all-time greats, and a man who has always commanded my utmost respect, although I have often disagreed with some of his theories, is Peter Stone. Peter has told me of chub in the Oxford pits that are truly awesome, fish that may even run into double figures. Of such stuff are dreams made.

My first encounter with gravel pit chub was at Hardwick pit near Oxford, where Peter was eventually to take his seven-pounder, as well as several chub over six. Trefor and I fished the water hard during the seventies for the big pike it contained and, although we had heard rumours of big chub, we never deliberately tried for them. We saw plenty, in fact large shoals were evident

A 6lb 7oz chub that accepted a sprat.

basking under the surface on bright days, but nothing ever caught my eye that looked of exceptional size. The largest I ever spotted in the water I put at about five pounds.

In the late seventies, evidence of big chub began to build up in several ways. Both Trefor and I began to experience runs on large deadbaits that were missed, especially when using half mackerel, and we immediately suspected chub. I remember one session in particular. I was using very large mackerel tail and struck at a fast run. For a few seconds, a very large fish thrashed at the surface about forty yards out before the bait came away. On retrieval, the entire sectioned end of the mackerel was crushed flat with the flesh sucked away.

Obviously, a chub had been responsible, but looking at the width of the mackerel and the surface disturbance I had witnessed, that was no small chub.

At about the same time, the then owner of the water, who used to feed the chub off a small central island on Chum Mixer, showed me a photograph of a chub one of the caravan owners had caught off a boat on livebait in the close season. Quite what he was doing fishing at that time is another story. Anyway, although the photograph was not of the highest quality, it obviously featured a chub, and a gigantic chub at that. The claimed weight was 9lb 7oz, and the fish could certainly have been all of that. There had supposedly been an eleven-pounder landed as well to the same method, but that was never substantiated.

Having pulled out of what was obviously a very big chub, I started to hedge my bets with my pike baits, using more sardines and sprats to give me a better chance of landing any stray chub. I particularly rated sardines, and in fact did manage the grand total of two chub on them, both modest fish of about three and a half pounds. I have to admit though, that I was never really committed to the chubbing. I was piking but hoping for the occasional chub, which meant that I was not doing justice to either.

The biggest chub that I personally witnessed on the bank at Hardwick was a cracking fish of 6lb 7oz taken on a sprat, from the area where two

pits interconnected via a very narrow channel. In that vicinity, there was a gravelly beach area adjacent to extensive shallows, the location, in subsequent years, for a string of big chub to Peter Stone and others.

The big chub at Hardwick highlighted one of the best ways of fishing for them: the use of deadbaits in very shallow water at night. Peter has told me that it was common to present baits in water only inches deep, no more than a few yards, sometimes only a few feet, from the bank. As chub had often been observed patrolling the gravel shallows at first light, it made sense that they would scavenge there overnight. After all, big river chub behave in exactly the same way over gravel shallows during the hours of darkness.

The closeness of the potential quarry made it imperative to keep absolutely silent, and show no light, during the hours of fishing. So close in did the chub patrol that even an unusual silhouette could alarm the fish, and I know for a fact that Peter sat well back from the water's edge, and even lay his rods on the ground to avoid them being too visible on rod rests. Silver paper would be wrapped over the line by the rod handle, and I can well imagine the intense excitement when that suddenly rustled over the gravel on a still, dark night.

Deadbaiting for gravel pit chub with larger fish baits and treble hooks always presents a moral dilemma, in that the bait will inevitably be attractive to pike. There is no doubt at all that the chances of chub are reduced by up to 90 per cent by using wire traces, and yet we simply cannot condone a method that invites bite-offs from pike, thereby leaving potentially lethal trebles inside the fish. If we are fishing for chub with soft terminal rigs, then we have a duty to use large single hooks only, and build our rigs around them. No caring angler should ever contemplate using any rig that matches treble hooks with non-wire traces, for any species.

The only rig I would consider using for this chubbing with larger deadbaits such as sardines, herrings or half mackerel would be one that incorporates two large singles, size 4 are ideal. It is important that the hooks are only lightly nicked

Marsh Pratley deadbaiting for chub at an Oxford pit.

under the skin to enable them to come away easily when striking. For fishing at very close range, this presents few problems for casting. Indeed, for close range work on shallows the baits can be thrown out by hand. You can even wade out and place the baits in position in daylight. For longer range work, however, it is important to arrange for the rig to withstand the shock of casting without the bait flying off. This is particularly important with a soft bait like sardine, which incidentally is possibly the best deadbait for chub of all.

A simple amendment with the incorporation of PVA string solves the problem of the bait being lost in the cast. The PVA is actually used to hold the lightly lodged hooks in place during the cast. There is an even more secure alternative possible, again using PVA, to keep the hooklink slack and therefore quite free of pressure, during the cast (*see* diagram overleaf).

When using smaller baits, such as sprats or half a sardine, rigs can be made up with just one large single. A couple of friends of mine are doing a fair bit of work with gravel pit chub using smaller deadbaits, such as sprats, whitebait, bleak and small roach. They have found that fishing the bait a few inches off bottom is a deadly presentation. In the case of small whole coarse fish, this is easily achieved by leaving the swim bladder intact. Sprats and whitebaits are doctored by pushing small pieces of polystyrene into the throat.

Unlike larger baits, which can be freelined, and therefore present no resistance to a taking chub, smaller baits can only really be fished with lead, unless fishing is at ultra-close range. It is

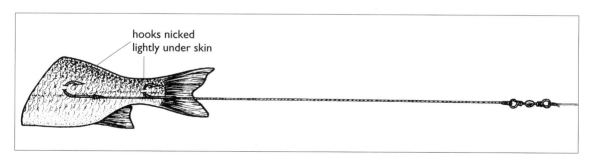

hooks nicked
lightly under skin

Double hook rig for larger deadbaits.

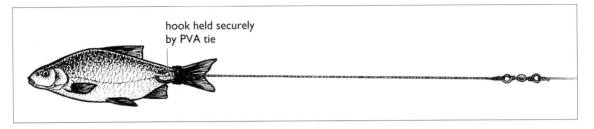

Single hook deadbait rig.

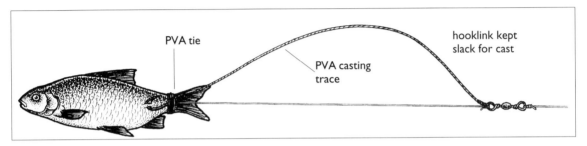

Use of a PVA casting trace for long range.

important to keep this lead to the absolute minimum to achieve the presentation. Where substantial lead is needed, for longer-range work or for anchoring buoyant baits, it should be as free running as possible. Chub seem to have an aversion to resistance when taking deadbaits, frequently dropping the bait if they feel any drag. Bolt rigs and chub deadbaiting are therefore incompatible.

If you want to fish a small, buoyant deadbait at long range, say on a distant gravel bar, PVA can be used to attach the lead to the head of the bait to prevent the hook link from tangling with the force of the cast, which is a common problem when a heavy lead precedes a much lighter bait. It also makes the whole rig more aerodynamic, thereby enhancing casting range and accuracy.

One problem to overcome with stillwater chub deadbaiting is their habit of swallowing the bait on the spot, without giving a conventional run. Many of the screaming runs on pike baits, I am sure, are caused by the fish feeling the wire and spooking. It is therefore important to arrange for the bite detection technique to warn of the earliest interest from a chub, and for this reason the amount of slack from rod to bait must be kept to a minimum at all times.

An associated problem, and an occupational hazard of the method, is the possibility of it being bitten off by the chub's pharyngeal teeth. This is very likely with monofilament, slightly less so with Dacron and least likely with the multistrand braids. As it is the softness and limpness of the hooklink material that is important, not its thickness, bite offs can be minimized by using high breaking strain braids such as Kryston Silkworm or Drennan Carp Silk. These are more resistant to shearing than Dacron. In Matt Hayes' book *Coarse Fishing* (The Crowood Press, 1995), Peter Stone confirms that he uses 45lb BS Kryston Quicksilver to overcome bite-offs.

Still on the deadbaiting theme, a more conventional approach to stillwater chubbing can be made with straightforward legering using chunks of fish flesh. My favourite fish by far, as the flesh is quite firm and does not fall apart easily, is mackerel, fished either in cubes or strips. Brian Culley and his sons have spent many successful hours fishing mackerel strip at Midland gravel pits. I understand that the method is most efficiently used when incorporating a hair rig, as the firm mackerel flesh seriously impedes hook penetration.

FLOAT FISHING

While deadbaiting seems to be the favoured method of approach for the really leviathan stillwater chub, many waters have a fairly large head of more normal-sized fish that respond to orthodox approaches. Also, of course, night fishing is not always allowed, and deadbaiting seems primarily to be successful in the dark hours.

One trait of chub, like rudd, is that they feed equally happily at all depths. This is true of both big and small fish. In fact, one of the deadliest methods for big stillwater rudd, that of using slow sinking maggots and casters under a self-cocking float, is equally effective for chub. To fish this method effectively, however, we must recognize that chub are very cautious fish, and will reject an unnatural presentation. It seems strange that a great, bull-headed fish like a big chub, that will engulf half a mackerel if given the chance, will reject a single maggot if it is sinking unnaturally fast. But that is the truth of the matter. It is therefore important to fish as fine as possible.

Another angler who corresponds with me regularly fishes a small gravel pit from which he has taken more than a dozen six pound-chub over the last few seasons. Apparently, he really struggled for a couple of seasons to get a bite, until he switched to casters. He fishes a single caster on a size 18 Drennan super spade to 2.6lb bottom. The gravel plateau from which he has taken the bulk of the fish is around five feet deep, and he fishes about a foot overdepth. Some of his chub have been taken on the drop, and some after the bait has settled on the bottom, but he reckons the most important feature is catapulting a dozen casters around the float after each cast. The idea is to have the hook bait and freebies with the same rate of sink, and his recent results certainly give testimony to the efficiency of the technique.

For shoal chub in deeper water or less settled conditions, bottom fishing with maggots under a sliding float is a good bet. Again, it is important to keep the feed going in, and a pouchful of maggots around the float every few minutes keeps the fish on their mettle. One of the best floats for this game, apart from at very close range, is the

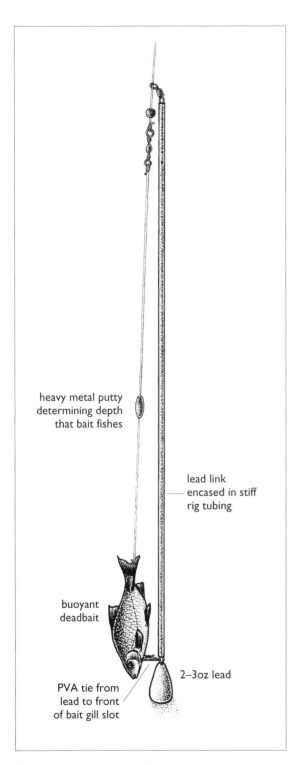

heavy metal putty determining depth that bait fishes

lead link encased in stiff rig tubing

buoyant deadbait

2–3oz lead

PVA tie from lead to front of bait gill slot

Long-range anti-tangle rig for small baits.

Drennan Missile, a special waggler that can be fished with great stability at long range in rough conditions. This crystal float has an interchangeable tip for insertion of a night light for fishing after dark. If I ever really get into stillwater chubbing, after-dark float fishing in this manner would be one of my first methods.

LEGERING

All the anglers I know who fish for stillwater chub a lot tell me that, apart from deadbaiting, float fishing techniques are far superior to legering. I do not really know why this should be, but I am not surprised at the comment. Queenford Lagoon has always been known to contain a substantial chub

population but, during my eight-year association with the water, I can only recall four or five chub picking up baits intended for bream. And remember we were fishing lobworms, which chub love.

If float fishing is out of the question and you have to resort to legering, the first obvious choice would be the swimfeeder, again using plenty of maggots. I would use a longish tail of a few feet for chub in this instance, for those fish taking on the drop.

One feeder technique well worth a try would be one utilizing a tail long enough to present a surface-buoyant bait, such as crust. If we use an open-ended feeder packed with small crust fragments, sealed with light groundbait plugs, these crusts all float to the surface around the hookbait. To ensure this happens quickly, use plenty of rusk in the groundbait plug. As well as releasing the feeder

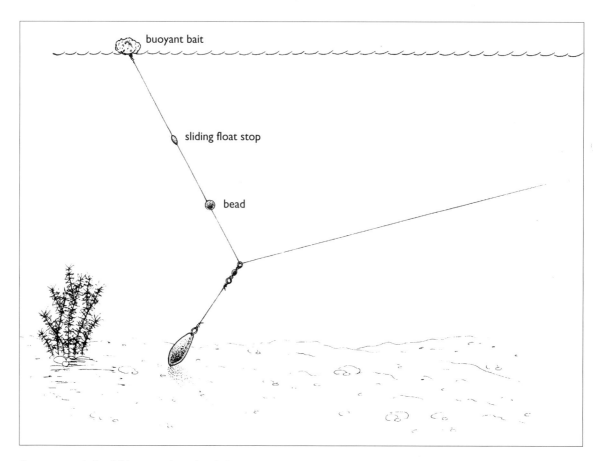

Long-range rig for fishing a static surface bait.

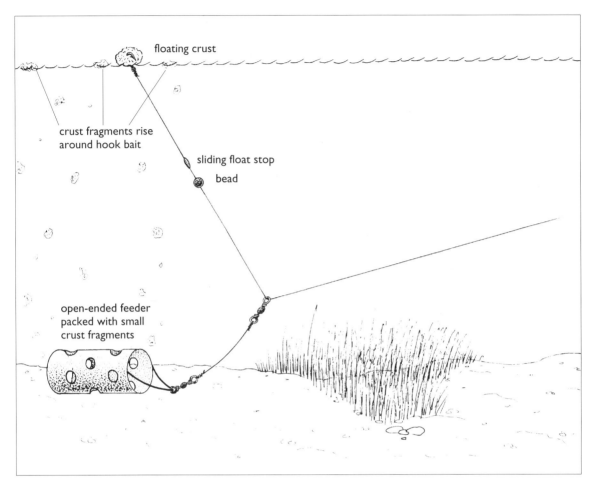

floating crust

crust fragments rise
around hook bait

sliding float stop

bead

open-ended feeder
packed with small
crust fragments

Use of feeder for attracting surface-feeding chub.

contents almost immediately it hits bottom, the rusk itself provides an additional attractive cloud. This technique is especially useful on those days when you wish to present a surface bait but the fish are at too long a range or there is too much drift to make normal surface techniques viable.

Straightforward, legered crust is another method I know to have worked, with hooklinks of from two to six inches, fishing over beds of mashed bread. However, by far the majority of stillwater chub I know to have been caught by orthodox legering came to large baits with a good smell, such as luncheon meat, especially meat that had been heavily flavoured, and cheesepaste. For these baits, it is best to fish with a tail length

of two to three feet, to avoid premature striking. Legering with short tails in stillwater gives rise to lots of 'unhittable' bites.

One legering method that can prove deadly is an adaptation of another method I have used successfully for rudd, and that is the slow-sinking leger in conjunction with a long tail and with a swingtip as a bite indicator (*see* diagram overleaf). This is particularly useful if a shoal of chub is feeding near the surface at long range. You can make slow-sinking legers by glueing half a normal bomb to the requisite amount of balsa, and then varnishing to make the bomb water repellent. Simple trials at home will give you a bomb with good casting weight that will sink as slowly as you wish.

Queenford Lagoon, home to some big chub.

After casting, watch the swingtip carefully. The slow-sinking mode takes line steadily, and the tip adopts a 45-degree angle as line is drawn through it. Any sudden change in the angle, either by the tip shooting out straight or dropping completely slack, means that the bait has been arrested in its fall. One possible cause for this is a great pair of white chub lips!

One of my favourite baits for this presentation for rudd is squeezed, slow-sinking flake, and I can see no reason why this should not be just as deadly for old Chevin.

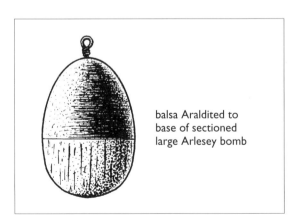

balsa Araldited to base of sectioned large Arlesey bomb

The home-made, slow-sink leger.

SURFACE FISHING

As in rivers, stillwater chub are avid surface feeders, and this is a very exciting method of taking them. Unlike in rivers, however, we have no current to assist in taking the bait to them. Chub, being so easily scared, can be frustratingly difficult to tempt on surface baits unless the presentation is spot-on.

In calm conditions, fishing at short range, particularly in sheltered bays or around marginal snags, a carefully presented bait such as Chum Mixer on light line can be successful. Excessive casting must, however, be avoided. Unlike frequent casting with light float tackle, where a constant stream of casters or maggots gets the fish into a preoccupied feeding frenzy, surface fishing has a relatively short shelf life in any one area. It is a case of one fish, or two if you are very lucky, and then moving on.

Conditions are much more favourable for surface fishing where the river current has been replaced by the stillwater wind. Now we can use drift to do the job for us, and many new possibilities are presented. The first is to attain a level of preoccupation by continually drifting freebies over the chub's heads. In the same way as for surface fishing for carp, steadily drifting a dozen

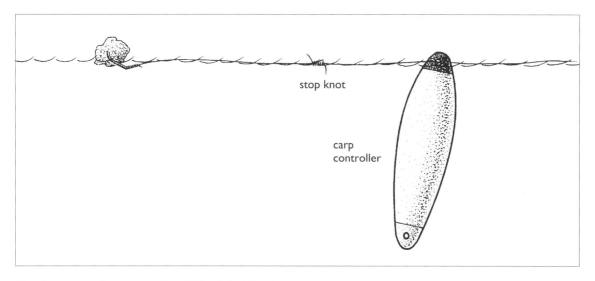

Use of carp controller in presenting drifting bait (above).

mixer biscuits down the wind every few minutes, until chub start taking regularly, is well worth a try. As with river surface crusting, make sure the line is heavily greased for this game.

Where there is a chop on the water, or where you wish to fish long range, it is helpful to utilize a carp controller.

STALKING

A great many gravel pits contain areas that have very overgrown and snaggy margins, and these are a haven for a resident chub population. Marsh Pratley was once continually drawn to an area of Queenford Lagoon we knew as the Mangrove, on account of the wildly overgrown, swamp-like nature of that part of the water's perimeter. Some very large chub inhabited the Mangrove, and the only viable method of catching them was stalking individual fish with large baits on strong tackle.

This kind of fishing is identical to stalking on small, overgrown streams, and no further elaboration is really necessary. One of the best baits of the lot in such situations is a large piece of freelined, slow-sinking flake. On one day when I joined Marsh at the Mangrove, hoping to get a photo

Marsh stalking a stillwater chub.

Efforts rewarded.

sequence of him catching a big chub, he was very unlucky. He found a group of about eight fish, two of which looked whacking great chub. The undergrowth made it very difficult to be selective, and unfortunately the chub that engulfed his flake was about the smallest in the shoal. It only weighed three and a half pounds, but Marsh and I spent an exciting hour catching it.

FISHING BOILIES

No one should doubt the efficiency of boilies as a chub bait, once they have been introduced in quantity and the fish have switched on to them. In fact, this could be the best line of attack in a pit with a good chub population. The problem with using boilies for chub is that the bait is not instant and initially you would have to be prepared for a lot of waiting. Having said that, many methods for stillwater chub require considerable patience.

I know several carp anglers who complain bitterly about the chub in their pits that simply will not leave their carp baits alone. Once caught for the first time, individual chub have been caught over and over again, thus confirming the baits' pulling power. Only last week, a friend caught a four-pound chub on a 20mm boilie, returned the fish 200 yards away, only to catch it again an hour later, on the same bait!

When fishing boilies for chub, the most successful method seems to be fishing a full-sized pop-up over a large bed of mini- or midi-boilies. Having said that, I have now caught dozens of chub in rivers on boilies intended for barbel, where I have laid down large beds of full-sized baits. More than once, the second night of a barbel boilie session has seen so many chub bites that the chances of a barbel has been virtually nil. With chub switching on to boilies in rivers, the prospects for a stillwater, determined boilie campaign are mouth-watering.

15 CHUB RIVER ROUND-UP

As virtually every river in this country will contain chub, it is an impossible task to attempt to cover them all in detail here. That is, of course, assuming I would be qualified to undertake that task, which obviously I am not: no single angler can hope to become intimately conversant with all chub rivers in a lifetime, and this chapter will inevitably contain many omissions. What follows, therefore, is a detailed look at the rivers I know well, together with stories of some of the big fish and treasured memories associated with them, as well as a more general discussion on other rivers with which I am less familiar, but where I have limited knowledge, courtesy of friends.

Wherever possible, I have included information on clubs, or general areas for the man seeking bigger chub. However, I have not attempted to include addresses of club secretaries, as this tends to change season by season, and information quickly becomes out of date. You will have to conduct your own investigative work for this information. What you will not find in this section are detailed descriptions of how to find specific chub swims. Through my many friends in big fish circles, I have knowledge of many swims on different rivers which have produced exceptional chub, but it would be breaking confidences if I revealed them. Suffice it to say that for every such swim, there are countless others as yet undiscovered. That, of course, is where you come in.

THE GREAT OUSE AND ITS TRIBUTARIES

Apart from the lower reaches of the river, which are better known for their bream, the upper and middle Great Ouse now offer the chub man superlative chubbing, with the possibility of a very big fish indeed. If you are only after chub, the upper stretches are delightful, although the chubbing is far from easy. The average size is high again, after a few quiet years, and a concerted effort could see that coveted six-pounder in the net. There has been at least one of over seven pounds caught in recent seasons. I would define the upper river as upstream of Stoney Stratford, and this is where I would expect a really exceptional chub to put in an appearance eventually. However, if you want the chance of a double-figure barbel, as well as some very serious chubbing, the middle river around Bedford is very exciting. Although I have not heard of a chub exceeding 6lb 4oz from this area, I have no doubt that a few are present, although they will certainly take some finding. My own forays into this area have been with barbel in mind, but I have taken dozens of chub in the process from several stretches. I have certainly taken enough to know that the average size does not quite match that from the upper river. However, many four-pounders and two over-fives to my barbel baits means that the quality of the chubbing certainly is not to be dismissed. Last season, a good friend had a cracking 5lb 10oz Middle Ouse chub, and that is a belting fish from anywhere.

I am not going to attempt to list the clubs that control the Ouse fishing, as they are too numerous. The best bet is to call in at the tackle shops in the main towns along the Ouse valley. Most of the angling clubs have open membership at very reasonable prices.

Although I first fished the Upper Ouse system in 1961, when I was introduced to the Claydon Brook near Buckingham, I did not actually fish the main Ouse itself seriously until 1972, when I

Matt Hayes plays a good Ouse chub (above).

Dick Walker's famous hut on the banks of the Great Ouse.

first fished Dick Walker's famous stretch at Beachampton, staying in his palatial hut. That weekend was the first and last time I met Dick, and after that enthralling initiation with the Upper Ouse, I went on to fish the river very often over the next few years, catching many good chub. Most of my trips were to Dick's stretch, which I had been told I could fish whenever I wanted, and for several seasons my best chub from the stretch was 4lb 14oz. That was to change one foul winter's day when the conditions could hardly have been worse for chubbing, as the river was rising rapidly, with filthy brown floodwater full of debris. These days, with the benefit of experience, I would not bother trying to catch chub under such conditions.

The eternal optimism of youth saw me slowly working my way downstream the opposite bank to Dick's stretch, swathed in waterproofs to keep out the heavy, cold rain. At about midday, wet, cold and still biteless, I came to Two Willows. The high bank between the two old willow trees was recessed such that a very inviting crease swim was created in high water, and that struck me as possibly the best bet for a bite under the prevailing conditions. I decided to sit in that swim until dark in an 'all or nothing' effort. I also decided to strike at anything remotely resembling a bite and, because of the blustery wind and increasingly heavy rain, relied on touch legering, with the line loosely looped over the index finger of my right hand. For about an hour I sat unmoving in those atrocious conditions, wondering whether I was displaying either tremendous fortitude or simple stupidity, when, suddenly, there was a sharp pluck on my finger. I was instantly alert and then

A famous swim on the Upper Ouse, known as Two Willows.

there was an unmistakable slackening of the line followed immediately by a steady, slow draw.

A firm strike resulted in a heavy fish rocketing upstream at a real gallop, before kiting across into the heavy flow of midstream. There it fought deep and powerfully for a few minutes, more like a barbel than a chub, using the strong current to maximum advantage. When I had managed to guide it back to the steady inside glide, the battle was quickly won and I was soon extracting my hook from a very precarious hookhold in a chub I knew to be a five-pounder at last. The appalling weather was forgotten as I steadied my scales in the blustery wind and confirmed 5lb 2oz. That chub demonstrates one vitally important point, and that is that no matter how adverse the conditions, there is always a chance while you have a bait in the water. Ironically, I could have had a brace of fives that day with a little more rub of the green. About half an hour after returning the fish, another big chub, certainly equal in size if not bigger than the first, was lost at the net when the hookhold failed.

Very interesting chubbing was also experienced in another stretch not far above Dick's stretch, which was totally different in character. It was slow, straight, of uniform flow and quite uninteresting apart from the opposite bank, which was lined with trees and waterside bushes, many of which hung in the water. A mass of fallen timber littered the riverbed under that foliage, a haven for chub. The stretch screamed big fish and, with the rest of the Coventry Specimen Group members, I decided to give it some serious attention. Our early forays saw several big chub lost in the jungle opposite. We were fishing traditional across and downstream techniques, placing hookbaits just above small rubbish rafts. It dawned on us that a hooked chub, which invariably turned downstream after taking a bait, would be in a snag almost as soon as it was hooked, so we all developed the upstream legering techniques that have stood us in such good stead since. The principle was simple. If we could get the fish to take a bait at the downstream extremity of a raft, there was a good chance it would move downstream with a bait initially, into clearer water, allowing a little time to strike the hook home and pull the chub out of harm's way. We needed a bite indication method that would allow a big chub to pick up the hookbait without immediate suspicion, and yet give a positive bite registration. Those vital seconds where we could catch a chub off guard were vital. The drop bobbin principle was the one we settled for.

After casting across and upstream, a dough bobbin was placed on the line between butt ring and reel, once the line had been drawn as tight as possible without shifting the hookbait. The bobbin had to be heavy enough to keep maximum tension in the line but not so heavy as to move the bait. As soon as the hookbait was picked up, the tension would reduce dramatically and the bobbin would drop sharply. The chub would feel nothing initially as the bait would appear unfettered. These days, of course, such fishing for slack-liners with heavy butt indicators is well known but in the mid-1970s, this was exciting new ground to me.

This new approach to our chubbing brought immediate success, and one of the first fish to succumb was a magnificent chub of exactly 6lb to my friend Merv Wilkinson. This was quickly followed by other big ones, including a fish of 6lb 3oz to Keith Walton and one of 6lb 4oz to Trefor West. Two weeks after Trefor's fish, I was fishing the next swim down, where there was a real jungle of timber under the opposite bank. I remember that the river was very low, clear, cold and sluggish. It had been sunny all day and, as the light began to fade, it was obvious that a good frost was on the cards. So sluggish was the flow that all I used was a single swan shot in conjunction with a small piece of crust. A large chunk of breadpaste did service as a bobbin, and in the first hour that bobbin dropped to the floor twice from false bites, possibly liners. That was the one problem with the method; it was so sensitive that it was very prone to false indications. The third indication, however, about an hour after dark, was the real thing, and my sweeping strike was met with a very solid resistance. After a dour rather than spectacular battle, which was somewhat spoiled by a branch being towed around, a

A chunky Ouse five-pounder.

superbly conditioned short and stocky chub sagged into the net. That fish weighed 5lb 6oz and was to remain my biggest chub from the Ouse for many years.

The drought summer of 1976 was memorable for many important lessons I learned in the presentation of crayfish as chub baits (crayfish should not be used as hookbaits these days as the crayfish plague has made them an endangered species). With the low water conditions that summer, chub were taking crays with incredible savagery and I had several full-sized crays bitten clean in half on the take. It seems incredible that a chub would be able to slice a hard-shelled crayfish cleanly in two in a fraction of a second, but it is true nonetheless. Presentation of natural baits that summer had to be on a slack line so that the chub could turn with the bait before a strike was attempted.

Those early days on the Upper Ouse also taught us a lot about floating crust presentation, not least how important pre-baiting can be, just as it is with many other forms of angling. A fond memory is lying on my stomach amongst some reeds, watching a big chub steadfastly ignoring free crust offerings as they drifted over his head. After a time, with Trefor constantly trickling the freebies in from upstream, the chub could resist it no longer and within about fifteen more minutes was taking every single offering. When Trefor finally decided it was time to put a hook in a piece of crust, the result was a foregone conclusion. Watching that sequence of events from my vantage point no more than six feet away from the fish was as much fun as actually fishing for it and taught me a lot about chub's reaction to bait and overcoming their natural caution.

During the seventies, Trefor and I fished the Ouse extensively, summer and winter, and took a great many tremendous bags of chub. One superb day I remember was when it was so bitterly cold that most of the river was frozen completely across. Despite that, we took over twenty cracking chub on large pieces of crust, each fish whacking the quivertip round with great gusto. Fond memories indeed.

Only a couple of years later, it was becoming obvious that something was seriously wrong with the river. Back in 1972, Dick Walker had told me that it was nowhere near as good as it once had been, deteriorating year by year. To be honest, apart from the absence of big perch, I had not noticed much change in the fishing myself until the summer of 1979 when, almost overnight it seemed, there were no crayfish to be found, no bullheads over the gravel, and the riverbed was becoming coated with horrible, blackish, slimy weed. The condition of the fish declined so dramatically that within months it was rare to catch a roach at all and the chub became pitifully thin. In my angling career, I have never witnessed such a rapid decline in a fishery, other than from an obvious pollution. I have never heard a satisfactory explanation of what caused the problem in those days, but I remember driving away one evening,

having caught a couple of two-pound chub that ought to have weighed double that, thinking that I might never again fish the Upper Ouse. It was in fact many years before I returned to my old haunts, when I was delighted to find that the fishing was, once again, superb. Once more, the chub were deep and thick shouldered; big perch were putting in an appearance occasionally and shoals of roach were numbered in hundreds rather than two and threes. In the last few years I have taken many big chub, exciting fish of a new strain that are short, stocky and in pristine condition. Twice in the last few years I have taken a brace of five-pounders in a day, and on one memorable evening, three fives in a sitting. The story of that catch is to be found elsewhere in this book. In the final four days of last season, March 1995, I took a total of nineteen chub, with four over five pounds and another nine over four. That is tremendous chubbing in anyone's language!

Two chub of 5lb 10oz apiece head my Great Ouse list, and there could be exciting times ahead. Several six-pounders are known to have been landed in recent seasons.

For many more years than I care to remember, the Upper Ouse has held a special place in my

Merv Wilkinson night fishing the Claydon Brook in 1968.

affections. It is my kind of river, intimate and full of character. There was a definite gap in my angling life when the river was in the doldrums during the early to mid-eighties, but now that the river is approaching its former glory, it is my fervent hope that nothing happens to change that. After my extreme pessimism about the future of the Upper Ouse only a few short years ago, I now have great hopes for the future. I may even catch a fish that at one time I would have thought totally unfeasible, a chub to beat my best of 6lb 12oz. Now that really would be something special!

I cannot move away from the Ouse system without a brief mention of the halcyon days of the sixties on the Claydon Brook. That stream still contains good chub today, although it is a pale shadow of what it once was. You have already read in the introduction the account of my 6lb 12oz fish, so let me now finish this section with a few words about a very special chub whose acquaintance I was to make four times between 1964 and 1971.

A year after landing my six-pounder, I was roach fishing with stewed wheat in a cabbage patch, when a colossal chub drifted into view over the bait, a fish I was convinced had to be over 6lb. I was eventually to catch that fish on a double lob, when it proved to weigh 5lb 14oz. Unlike my 6lb 12oz fish, which was much longer and out of condition, this latest specimen was a typical Upper Ouse specimen, short, fat and immaculate. The feature that made the fish quite easily recognisable was a slightly deformed top lip, which may have been a genetic defect as a couple of four-pounders I had taken previously had had a similar appearance.

In July 1966, I was to take two fish over 5lb in a day for the first time in my angling career in a catch of chub that I still treasure as one of my greatest angling highlights. That day, I took eight fish comprising three three-pounders, three four-pounders, and top fish of 5lb 4oz and 6lb 4oz. The six-pounder was my old friend.

I was to see him again the following January, still at the same weight, when I fished all day in the most appalling weather. I remember feeling quite rough all day and, unusually for me, fished one swim only, under the comfort of an umbrella. Just

Returning an early five-pounder to the Claydon Brook in the mid-sixties.

one bite rewarded my vigil, but the size of the fish made up for the discomfort.

Four years later, the second five-pound brace of my career featured my old friend, back down to 5lb 14oz. By a strange coincidence, I am almost certain that the other fish, a 5lb 4oz specimen, was the same one that accompanied the big one back in 1966.

THE CHERWELL

To do justice to the happy hours and memorable chubbing I have enjoyed on the banks of the Oxfordshire Cherwell would require a good-sized

Another cracking Cherwell specimen.

book in itself, and so it saddens me to say that, at present, the Cherwell certainly is not the chub river it once was. I can think of several stretches where it was not unusual for Trefor and I to see hundreds of chub in a day, and perhaps catch twenty or more between us. These days, however, some areas are completely devoid of chub. On one of the most prolific, where Trefor once took over thirty fish on crayfish in a few hours, a chub bite is now a rarity.

This information may be of interest to specimen hunters, as the present extremely low stock density seems to go hand-in-glove with a high average size. The fishing really is painfully slow. To give you an idea of exactly how slow, let me briefly discuss the stretch where I first contacted big barbel. In the mid- to late 1980's, the greatest problem to overcome in catching the barbel was the hordes of chub that devoured everything in sight. In 1987, when I first spotted my 12lb barbel, I remember one day having a swim at my feet containing one barbel and thirty chub, feeding furiously on a hemp carpet. It was becoming noticeable in 1989, when many of my big barbel first came to net, that the numbers of chub were declining, although we still caught plenty. That

year, I took the biggest I had ever seen there, at 4lb 14oz. The stretch had never been known as one for big chub.

A couple of years ago, as far as I can tell, only a handful of chub were caught from that stretch in the entire season, and that included several repeat captures. But all the fish were big, mostly five pounds plus.

Unlike a great many rivers at the moment, which have a thriving crop of young, vigorously growing chub as well as an increasing number of big ones, the chub population of the Cherwell seems far from thriving. However, this is almost certainly a cyclical phenomenon and the river will shortly regain its former chub glory, as has happened with the Upper Great Ouse.

Most of the clubs controlling fishing on the river Cherwell are open to anyone, although there are isolated short private lengths. I suppose the cream of the fishing would be controlled by Banbury, Kidlington and Oxford Alliance, and joining one or all of those associations will give you access to many miles of bank. Included in those miles are lengths or river that have produced many big fish for Trefor and myself. One of those areas is where I came so close to my first Cherwell six-pounder.

The story starts in the winter of 1981. I had enjoyed a good day's chubbing at a normally very slow stretch, having taken five fish of just under five pounds each, when I was startled by a voice behind me. It was an angler by the name of Dave South, who I had first met when tenching at TC. Dave was very agitated and I soon discovered that he had taken a very big chub but his scales had broken. As he had never taken a chub of over four pounds before, he wondered whether I could bring my scales and do the honours. I will never forget his words. 'I reckon it might make five pounds,' he said.

With a mental image of a possible five-pound chub in my mind, it came as quite a shock when Dave eventually produced a monstrous fish from his sack, a chub which I knew instantly would easily beat six pounds. In fact, it weighed six and a quarter, and I do not believe I have ever seen an angler as dumbstruck as Dave was that evening.

It was two years later when I was eventually to meet up with that fish again, this time in my own landing net. As I remember, it was a bitterly cold, frosty day and I had originally intended to go to a far more prolific stretch, where bites would be more frequent and I would be on the move more. One of my intuitions had intruded on logical thought, however, and dawn found me walking the banks of the slow stretch. I continued to follow my instincts and remember stopping abruptly at the head of a run of pollarded willows, knowing exactly where I had to place my first bait. What made this decision the more surprising was that a pair of swans were browsing only feet away from where I knew the bait had to settle. As I was tackling up, I introduced a few flake samples, soon to be followed by a large crust bait. I reckon that bait settled almost right underneath the closer of the two swans.

Only about two minutes later, I was on my feet. The light rod I was using bent into an alarming curve as a mighty chub battled for his freedom. He kept deep for a good while but when he eventually broke surface, I knew immediately it was the six-pounder I had weighed two years previously. It was not to be, however, and despite zeroing the scales twice, the dial stubbornly refused to budge from 5lb 14oz. That chub is the biggest I have taken from the Cherwell by far, and my joint-fourth biggest ever.

Personal best from the Cherwell – 5lb 14oz.

THE THAMES

I freely admit that I have never really got to grips with Thames chubbing, as the adjacent river Cherwell has always commanded my attention when I am in the Oxford area. My Thames trips have been odd, one-off sessions over the years, and you can never do justice to any fishing in that manner. I find the heavy boat traffic on the river intensely irritating, and it hampers my enjoyment.

The only areas of the Thames that have received my attention are those in the immediate Oxford area and the stretches either side of Tadpole bridge, where the Trout Inn is located. The stretch above the Trout, to Rushey weir, was the venue I visited most often and, in truth, is still one of the top rated areas for Thames chub. Although it has been many years since I last fished there, I understand that there is a very good crop of fish up to and over four pounds, with several five-pounders and an occasional six reported most seasons. I have heard reports of a near seven-pounder from this area, but have not been able to substantiate that. This particular stretch of river is, I believe, now day ticket, with tickets available on the bank, making it a popular venue with the casual visitor.

Below the bridge, around two miles of the right-hand bank are controlled by the Trout Inn itself, and this stretch really is a superb mixed fishery. Again, the chub are an agreeably high average weight, with plenty of five-pounders being taken each season.

Around Oxford itself, most of the Thames fishing is controlled by the Oxford Alliance, which anyone can join. If you are serious about Thames chubbing, this club is a must.

The river at Oxford undoubtedly produces numbers of 5lb-plus chub each season, but has been the subject of several rumours of giant chub in recent years. However, as these rumours never included photographs, the stories of the captures rarely rang true and I am becoming more cynical the older I get; I never believed a word of any of them!

If you want to know about Thames chubbing, from men who know how to catch them without embellishing the truth, give my old friends John Everard or Peter Stone a ring. Both have impressive records with the river.

I know nothing of the lower Thames, so will not attempt to give any advice. The only thing I can say is that a good friend who lives in the Henley area tells me that the river there is producing good chub. It is also producing carp to over 30lb. One of those would add an extra buzz to your chubbing. Leisure Sport control about three miles at Henley but, again, boat traffic can be a nightmare.

THE WENSUM

I first fished the river Wensum in 1981 when my friend Dave Plummer moved to Norfolk, and quickly began to extract some really serious chub from the river. On our early forays, to the areas in the immediate vicinity of Norwich, Trefor and I took many tremendous bags of chub of a remarkably high average weight. Most days saw several four-pounders between us, and by the end of the 1986/87 season I had taken no fewer than nineteen chub of over five pounds from the river. While it is true to say that the majority of these were taken at night on large meat baits intended for barbel, the best two, both weighing 5lb 7oz were caught quite deliberately.

The first of these was in fact my first Wensum five-pounder and was the highlight of a fabulous March week which had seen Trefor and Dave both take five-pounders, with Trefor taking a brace of fives on a very memorable, if wet, night. My five-pounder was enjoyable in that it resulted from deliberate bait movement to induce a bite. I had been fishing a crease in perfect conditions without response, and decided to increase the link weight and present a bait initially in the faster flow of mid-river, before dislodging the terminal rig and allowing it to trundle downstream on to the crease more naturally. The first cast to this amended presentation did the trick, and Trefor was soon congratulating me as he weighed my first Wensum five-pounder. The second 5lb 7oz specimen will live in my memory for ever, as it came on a night when I also took a brace of fives, both again from bait induction.

Joint biggest chub from the Wensum, at 5lb 7oz.

What a night that was! A brace of fives from the Wensum.

This time I had been barbel fishing, but it soon became obvious that the swim was full of chub, most of them reasonably small. I had been in the habit of using very big meat baits in that chub nursery, ignoring all the little taps, and waiting for a solid thump from a barbel. That night, how-ever, the constant bangs and bumps on the rod tip eventually got to me and I decided to induce a bolder bite by quickly winding the meat upstream. In that I succeeded, but what a fish it was that resulted. Instead of the two-pounder I had been expecting, I was soon watching the needle on my scales settle at 5lb 7oz.

Not content with that, my very next cast saw a repeat performance, with a fish of only five ounces less. I recall Dave Plummer and John Bailey, who were fishing with me that evening, describing a certain part of my anatomy as golden!

An unlikely date for my second brace of Wensum five-pounders was 16th June 1988, and I fully admit that both came to baits intended for barbel. I had baited several known barbel swims with hemp and corn and, in mid-afternoon, several barbel had been spotted surreptitiously coming and going over the bait carpet. At 5pm, my quivertip suddenly plunged around but, instead of the barbel I was expecting to see, a big chub shot from under the tangle of branches. That fish was soon being weighed at 5lb 6oz, a great start to a new season.

Later that night, well after dark, and after taking two good barbel, I was again to land a five-pound chub, of 5lb 2oz this time. That memorable June day was the fifth time in my career when I had taken two five-pound chub in a session.

At the time of writing, it has been several seasons since I last fished the Wensum, for no other reason than that other projects have taken precedence. Friends that are active there, however, tell me that the quality of the chubbing is still superb. Six-pounders have been taken in recent seasons.

Apart from the relatively short stretch of river downstream of Costessy Mill, where the original Wensum barbel syndicate was based, my knowledge of the clubs controlling the various sections is limited to Norwich and District AA. The books for this club are available from Norwich Angling Centre. The staff there will also be able to guide you towards many of the free stretches of the Wensum around Norwich. One of these is the stretch at Drayton Green Lane, where Trefor and I took many big chub a few years ago.

THE LEAM

It was to the banks of the River Leam, a tributary of the Warwickshire Avon, that I was taken on the first ever fishing trip of my career. That day the quarry was gudgeon, but the river quickly took an unshakeable grip on my affections that lingers to the present day. As my experience grew, the prolific chub population became my favourite quarry, although the river was never known for big fish. In fact, as recently as the mid-seventies, even a fish of over four pounds was a rarity. At that time, roughly coincident with the flooding of Draycote reservoir, Leam chubbing underwent a metamorphosis. Four-pound chub became common, and for a few blissful years Trefor and I managed to keep a lid on some of the most exciting chub fishing I have ever experienced. A five-pound chub from the Leam became our target, a fish that would have been unthinkable only a few years before, and I was eventually to break that magical barrier in February 1980, with a fish of 5lb 3oz.

The lessons Trefor and I learned on the Leam in those years form the basis for our knowledge of chubbing today. One of the most important was that it was not always under bushes and trees that the fish would be found, but in the runs, creases and glides in open water. We learned how to interpret current flows, which gave us a distinct advantage over other anglers who came to fish the river. In those days, the Leam contained

My young son Chris fishing the Leam in 1973.

more rafts and overhanging bushes than almost any other chub river of my acquaintance, and yet many of them rarely contained chub. Lacking our hard-won knowledge, most other anglers persevered in seductive-looking rafts, and continually blanked.

It is an interesting fact that my first five-pounder, the 5lb 3oz fish mentioned, taken from under a raft that I fished on instinct that cold February morning, was from the only bite I ever experienced in the swim in over thirty sessions!

It was following my instincts that led to my taking what is still my biggest Leam chub, in March 1983. There was this uniform, steady glide that looked good but that had always failed to yield me a bite over the years. So much so, that I had taken to walking straight past it. On that particular March day, I had already walked the stretch at dawn, pre-baiting a dozen swims. The glide had not been among them and I had certainly had no intention of fishing it. But when I approached that section of bank to fish the next pre-baited area I experienced this overpowering feeling that I ought to fish the glide. What is more, I knew exactly where the bait had to be presented and, sure enough, only moments after my legered crust settled, the quivertip plunged around and a powerful fish surged across to the far bank. A few minutes later, I was peeling the folds of my landing net back from the outline of a tremendous chub that proved to weigh 5lb 10oz.

Most of the Leam is a typical small chub stream, with plenty of character, but the exception is the lower reaches around Leamington itself, which are much more sluggish and of uniform flow and depth. These areas are less interesting to look at, but the man seeking an exceptional Leam chub would be well advised to concentrate his efforts here. I know of two genuine six-pound-plus fish caught here in recent seasons.

One of my most remarkable Leam sessions was close to Leamington on this sluggish water. One particular length gave very few bites indeed, on average less than one a day in the late eighties, but they were usually from fish in the high four-pound category. When I was working on some theories about loose feeding techniques, I

A 4lb 14oz Leam fish taken on a wet and windy July day.

devised an approach requiring several hours of pre-baiting in an attempt to attract chub to the selected feeding areas while segregating the large chub from the 'also rans'. I had already had an encouraging response to my theory on the Cherwell, and took the new approach to the Leam. For several hours, I walked the banks, progressively baiting and rebaiting six selected swims. In between baiting sorties, I relaxed with some far from serious perch fishing. About four hours after my arrival, I was finally in position to introduce my first chub bait, and only moments after that first cast I was locked in combat with a worthy adversary indeed. That chub weighed in at 5lb 5oz, a dramatic reward for my patient preparatory work.

After some self-portraiture, the chub was slipped back and I moved to the second swim. Moments later, I was regretting not having retained the fish in a sack for a while, as I looked with disbelief at my scales. The second bite of the day had yielded a chub of 5lb 2oz. Never in my wildest dreams did I ever expect a brace of fives from the Leam, and I know of no other angler to have achieved that feat.

At the time of writing, there are some huge chub being caught up and down the country, and in that context I cannot see the Leam seriously challenging for top chub honours. The chubbing there is, however, still very good, with a high expectation of four-pounders and every chance of a five. The clubs that control the best Leam fishing are Leamington and Warwick, both with open membership. If you are looking for the peace and quiet of traditional small stream chubbing with the chance of a big fish, those clubs are well worth joining.

THE DORSET STOUR

For more years than I care to remember, the Dorset Stour has been one of my favourite chub rivers, the first five-pounder of my career having been taken from just above Iford bridge in 1962.

During the 1970s, Trefor and I haunted the banks of the Stour at the famous Throop fisheries during the winter months, and throughout those memorable years took dozens of super chub, with a high percentage of over four pounds and a fair few of over five.

Throop Fisheries, of course, needs little introduction, and some gigantic chub have been taken here in recent seasons, with confirmed fish of over 7lb. Apart from individual heavyweight chub, large bags of chub are taken on the float, trotting either maggots or flake, and the fishery really is superb for both specimen hunters and pleasure anglers alike. The manager of the fishery, Glen Sutcliffe, is very pleasant and most helpful, and will go out of his way to advise visitors as to methods and where to fish. Be warned, however. He rightly insists on the fishery regulations being strictly adhered to, so break them at your peril.

During recent years, as is the case with many rivers nationwide, the average Throop chub is far heavier than its counterpart in the years when Trefor and I were fishing it hard. Those days, a six-pounder was a rarity, whereas today fish of this weight are caught quite often.

Compared to chub of this stature, my own Throop best is relatively modest, taken in March 1974. I had spent three days on the river with a match-fishing friend from work, who had expressed a wish to see what this specimen hunting was all about. Fishing large pieces of bread crust on size six hooks, or 'shark tackle' as Fred described it, we shared a tremendous bag of good chub, about thirty fish all told, with half of them topping four pounds.

In early evening of the final day, my personal tally stood at nineteen fish to 4lb 14oz, and I settled in one of my favourite swims at the tail of pig island for the last hour. After baiting with two large handfuls of mash, I rolled a crust bait to settle on the downstream gravel and sat back to wait. For over half an hour I fed the swim steadily, periodically casting further downstream. As the dusk closed in, there was a sudden lunge on the rod tip and I was firmly tethered to a hard-fighting chub that made the clutch sing, a fish that took the scales to 5lb 6oz. Twenty years on, that is still my biggest Stour chub. It is high time I rectified that situation and perhaps this coming winter, when I intend some serious Stour chubbing, I will be able to do just that.

Apart from Throop fisheries, most of my Stour chubbing has been carried out on stretches of river controlled by either Ringwood or Christchurch angling clubs. So extensive are the river holdings of these two clubs that I would advise anyone with serious intent on chubbing in the south of England to join them. For the fishing available, the price of each book is very modest. First of all, let us have a look at the Stour lengths controlled by Ringwood and District AA. The club's holdings on the Stour are so extensive, comprising fifteen separate fisheries for a total of twenty-one miles of bank, that space forbids a comprehensive breakdown of each area. So I will give a general appraisal of the chub fishing to be had on the club stretches of this wonderful river.

The upstream stretches are grouped around the towns of Stourpaine and Blandford Forum, and there are eight separate venues from which to choose. Generally speaking, these stretches are underfished, which is surprising, as the river here contains some very big fish indeed and most of the venues are delightful.

Big chub, as well as enormous roach, are exciting targets, but are certainly not easy to find. The specimen hunter, however, will find the effort worthwhile because there are certainly chub to well over 6lb to be caught.

Most of the big roach succumb to large pieces of breadflake, either trotted or fished in conjunction with open-ended feeders loaded with liquidized bread, a method that also takes its share of good chub. I had a chub of 5lb 5oz recently on feeder-fished flake intended for roach. My old favourite legered crust is still a superb method for chub, fished with loose-fed mashed bread. Legered cheesepaste has also been a good Stour chub offering.

As the lower fisheries, from Longham down through to Christchurch, are where barbel are far more established, these stretches get the bulk of the angling pressure. This is not surprising as, on the right day, the fishing can be fabulous. As well as lots of barbel, however, chub well over 5lb, with some over 6lb, are taken regularly. Probably the most common approach in these lower beats is the blockend feeder, which takes good fish of all species. The anglers who know the river well, however, still swear by bread for the bigger chub.

The stretch where good chub are very prolific is at Bounds Farm, where there is a bonus for the big fish man, in that night fishing is available with the appropriate permit. Bounds also teems with eels, and you are well advised to steer clear of meaty baits, especially at night. A good ploy would be to fish particles over hemp.

One last point to make about the Ringwood club is that members may fish Throop fisheries on presentation of their club book to the Throop fishery manager, without additional cost. Please be aware, however, that you must book in first and not just go straight to the river.

Although its Stour holdings are not as extensive as those of the Ringwood Club, Christchurch Angling Club controls six stretches of this superb river, the most upstream being at Gains Cross, and two super lengths at Wimborne, these being the Leaze and that at Canford Bridge. At each venue, the average chub is very impressive. Many five-pounders and a handful of sixes have been taken in recent seasons. These stretches are by no means easy, but the size of the fish makes them a popular target for specialists.

Moving down to Longham, we have the stretch above the weir at Highmead and the stretch below the weir at Dudsbury, downstream to the New Road bridge. The Highmead water is particularly noted for its superlative roach fishing, as well as for the presence of some very big chub. The Longham area is also where the head of barbel starts to increase quite dramatically, and this is particularly the case on the Dudsbury stretch, probably one of the most popular CAC river holdings. Large shoals of barbel can be found on this stretch and I have taken up to a dozen fish in a day on the feeder. This is the stretch where, in the late eighties, I saw one of the biggest chub of my life, a fish that unfortunately defeated all my attempts to catch him.

At Christchurch, another superb stretch is that from Iford Bridge to the lower end of the Throop boundary. All the usual species are present to good size, but there are some truly massive chub. A confirmed seven-pounder has been taken here in recent seasons. In the last two seasons, only three days fishing at Iford bridge has yielded me eleven chub, with ten of over four pounds and one fish of 5lb 4oz. That is some average!

Apart from the two clubs mentioned, I have had odd days chubbing the Stour on lengths controlled by the Wimborne and Southampton clubs, as well as the free stretches at Muscliffe and Parley. There are undoubtedly some huge fish around the Wimborne area, and several friends have reported six-pounders there. My best is a modest 5lb 1oz. The free stretch at Muscliffe, which abuts the top boundary of Throop, is well worth a look, containing as it does a large head of chub to decent sizes. Night fishing is also available. Although I have never taken a five-pounder at Muscliffe, I have a very fond memory of six fish in an hour at around midnight a few years ago, all chub of between 4lb 6oz and 4lb 14oz, that accepted huge chunks of meat intended for barbel.

THE HAMPSHIRE AVON

When I first became interested in big fish angling in the late fifties, the chubbing on the Hampshire Avon, and in particular the Royalty, was legendary. Each year saw a colossal number of five- and six-pounders taken, and the occasional fish of over seven. Two good friends of mine, Peter Rayment and Don Stockton, of the Birmingham Specimen Group, now both sadly deceased, told of days spent trotting the Royalty when numbers of fives would be taken. If my memory serves me correctly, Don took the best recorded catch with, I believe, six five-pounders and two over six in one session.

By the late sixties and early seventies, Avon chubbing was declining alarmingly, largely on account of a parasite that I first read of in an article by Dick Walker. I shall never forget a chub I took on maggots from the Severals at the time. It was twenty-three inches in length and weighed just over three pounds. An Avon chub of that length in good condition should have easily exceeded six pounds.

For years thereafter, the Avon was ignored as a chub river, specialist anglers fishing it only for its barbel and roach. A few years ago, however, healthy, stocky chub once more started to make an appearance, and initially isolated reports of big fish from several stretches quickly became an avalanche. While it is still possibly premature to say that the river has regained its former chub glory, it is not far off, as six-pounders are now being taken regularly, and I know of three confirmed sevens. Once again, exciting Avon chub days are with us.

As is the case with the Dorset Stour, the two clubs who control the cream of Avon fishing for the ordinary angler are Christchurch and Ringwood, although there are a multitude of syndicates and day ticket fisheries available. As I know little of these from personal experience, I shall confine my comments to the two clubs mentioned.

The CAC Hampshire Avon holdings are truly impressive and a man could spend a lifetime fishing these alone and still never know it all. Starting upstream around Fordingbridge, there are two mouth-watering stretches, one at Horseport in Fordingbridge itself, just below the famous East Mills fishery, and the other at the equally famous Sandy Balls holiday centre, the other side of East Mills. Some of the most massive coarse fish of the Avon are to be found in this section of river, and many five pound chub are taken every season. Do not try and fish at Sandy Balls, however, if you are not particularly fit and healthy, as the footpaths to the river are exceptionally steep.

Below Fordingbridge, we enter the renowned Somerly Estate waters, from the upper boundary at Bicton to the lower boundary at Lifelands Weir, just above Ringwood. Included in these fabulous miles of river are famous names like Gorley Corner, Ibsley Bridge, Ellingham Bridge and, of course, the much-publicized Lifelands stretch itself. As well as the main river, the Somerly estate holdings also give access to some super winter fishing on the Avon carriers, principally the Ellingam and Woodside carriers, and the Ashley and Kings streams.

The chub fishing at all of these venues is quite magnificent at times, with scores of five-pounders taken each season, and many of over six. Because the area is quite popular, as the stretches are close to Ringwood, many of the fish are rather shy, and light feeder tactics score. At Lifelands, trotted flake is popular with roach men, and many huge chub also fall to these tactics.

It is on the lower river, from Avon Tyrell, through Dudmoor, Sopley and Winkton to the upper boundary of the Royalty, where the barbel population increases and becomes largely dominant. The chub on the lower river, however, after some years in the doldrums, are now magnificent, several six-pounders having been reported in recent seasons.

Without a doubt, Ringwood and District AA control some of the finest sections of the middle Avon available to the club angler, their waters producing many of the specimen fish that grace the pages of the angling weeklies each season.

The most upstream Avon fishery is Shallows Farm, at Breamore, where the club control one mile of double bank. This stretch, although by no means easy, contains a good head of chub of high average size, with many five-pounders and a few sixes having been reported. Good methods are blockending with plenty of maggots, or roving with large bread baits. Moving downstream, we come to the famous stretch at East Mills Manor, near Fordingbridge, where some of the most colossal Avon specimens of several species have been taken in recent years. East Mills has an incredible pedigree, having produced chub of over 6lb, barbel over 13lb and roach over 3lb, as well as big pike, carp and bream. The upper boundary of East Mills is on the opposite bank to the well-known stretch at the Sandy Balls holiday complex, where many giant barbel have been taken.

Downstream of East Mills are, first, Fordingbridge Park Recreation Ground, and then Redbrook, two fairly short stretches. The general fishing available is the same although not quite as prolific as East Mills. One interesting fact about Redbrook, however, an Avon stretch where you are allowed to night fish, is the common occurrence of big carp picking baits up. Several twenty-pounders have been taken, and one of those would certainly liven up a chub session.

Members fishing Redbrook must take extreme care at night, as the stretch runs primarily through a permanent water meadow. Walking and fishing is off walkboards and platforms.

Possibly the most famous Avon stretch of all is next downstream, at Ibsley. What angler has not heard or read of Dick Walker's exploits at Ibsley in the company of Colonel Crow? Ringwood control two miles of the river here, and I would say that it is probably one of the more difficult stretches on which to catch fish consistently. Ibsley is quite heavily fished, and the fish are correspondingly educated to anglers' wiles. There is no doubt at all that some of the biggest fish of the Avon reside here, and that is the reason why many good anglers go back again and again, often suffering many blanks in the process. Like East Mills, Ibsley has produced all Avon species to enormous weights.

This is one Avon stretch where you may have to resort to very light hooklinks to catch consistently. Three seasons ago, I had several big chub here, to

5lb 5oz, and had to drop to 3lb BS hooklink to get bites. The blockend feeder is by far the most popular method here, but trotting flake and roving with crust baits have produced many good fish.

Downstream of Ringwood is the well-known and heavily fished stretch known as the Severals. Two miles of river are available, the lower half being restricted to Ringwood members only, but the upper half is also available to day-ticket anglers. The Severals has always been best known for its prolific head of barbel, but over recent years the quality of the chubbing has been quietly and steadily improving. Those anglers in the know are reporting an increasing number of big chub, young fish that are short and stocky, worlds apart from the pathetic, flaccid creatures of only a few years back.

The bottom boundary of the Severals abuts the top boundary of a very scenic half-mile stretch at Avon Castle, which I have walked but never fished. Apparently, there are some very big chub to be found at this lower end of the fishery.

An interesting feature of the Severals fishery is the backwater which runs alongside it, known as the Bickerley Millstream, and which fishes particularly well in flood conditions. Occasional specimen chub respond to roving tactics.

We cannot move away from the Avon, of course, without mentioning the Royalty. Best known for its barbel, Royalty chub have been a neglected quarry for years. When Trefor and I used to fish the Royalty regularly during the mid-eighties, it was rare for either of us to catch a chub of any size. In recent seasons, however, that has changed with a vengeance. Not only are Royalty chub a worthwhile quarry again, but the fishery offers the prospect of possibly among the biggest chub on the entire Avon. The last few seasons have seen a good number of six-pounders and one of over seven.

To summarize, the Hampshire Avon offers the serious chub man some of the most exciting prospects of huge fish in this country. But be warned, the Avon is a far from easy river to fish. You must be prepared to serve your apprenticeship on its banks; get to know its moods. A colossal chub could be your reward.

THE SEVERN

There is no doubt whatever that the River Severn contains some colossal chub, and I have seen photographs of two authentic six-pounders in the last couple of seasons. This is true from the upper reaches right through to the lower. The upper Severn, in fact, is remarkably underfished, but anglers who are patiently plugging away up there are getting some exciting results.

Many clubs and private associations have a stake in Severn chubbing, but the club with the most extensive holdings on the river is obviously the giant Birmingham Anglers' Association.

The BAA holdings on the Severn are impressive, from the upper river just south of Welshpool, to the lower river, north of Gloucester. All told, thirty-eight separate lengths are involved, with individual lengths including as much as three miles of bank.

The entire BAA holdings can be considered these days as one long chub and barbel swim, and there are huge fish as far upstream as Underdale, near Shrewsbury. Much above that, although barbel are still present, the river is a better bet for really big chub.

Below Shrewsbury to perhaps Holt Fleet, which includes some famous venues such as Knowle Sands, Quatford, Hampton Loade,

Trefor playing a good fish on the Bristol Avon.

Arley, Trimpley and Stourport, the river is classed as the Middle Severn, and most sections are notable for their large heads of barbel, as well as for enormous fish in some sections. The middle river is also gaining a reputation for larger and larger chub, and five-pounders are now common. In recent years, it is the lower river around Worcester, comprising famous stretches at Severn Stoke, Upton, Kempsey and Bushley, that have attracted feverish attention from specimen hunters, particularly those intent on enormous barbel. Several huge chub have accepted barbel baits in these areas.

Other clubs well worth joining if you are interested in the lower river are Worcester DUAA and Tewkesbury Popular AA. A good head of chub is present on all stretches, with every chance of a five-pounder, and the odd much bigger fish. Good areas on the Worcester book are Diglis Weir, Clevelode, Upton and Beauchamp Court, while Tewkesbury have a good stretch at Upper Lode.

I cannot relate a story of a big Severn chub myself as I have never taken one, but from what friends who are regulars on the river tell me, the next few seasons could see some really enormous fish putting in an appearance. I will follow their results with interest.

THE WYE

I have only fished the Wye once in my life, at Ross, so I am not qualified to offer any advice on Wye chubbing from first-hand experience. What I do know from others is that there is an enormous head of chub in the river, including some big ones. Ross on Wye itself is known as an area where the chub run very large.

There have been many rumours in recent years of exceptional chub from the Wye, although I have not seen any photographs of fish that appeared in that category. It is a river, however, that is wide open to exploration by chub anglers, particularly as some of the salmon beats are being opened up for coarse fishing. Dramatic advances are being made in some of these areas by anglers

seeking big barbel, and I would not mind betting that very big chub could reward some pioneering.

THE BRISTOL AVON

Although the Bristol Avon teems with chub, it does not, at the moment, appear to hold any attraction for anglers seeking really big fish. Trefor West, who has fished the Avon for barbel as much as anyone in recent years, has yet to take a chub of anything more than average size. Trefor has fished intently at several different venues, and had there been really big chub present, he would certainly have caught one by now.

Readers will remember a supposed record chub from the Avon a few years ago. I never believed the claimed weight of the fish at the time, and I still do not. Let me just say that in my opinion it owed as much to a fertile imagination as it did to accurate weighing!

THE WARWICKSHIRE AVON

The BAA controls thirty-two separate lengths of this delightful river, from Stratford-upon-Avon downstream to its confluence with the Severn near Tewkesbury.

Throughout its length, the river is a fine mixed fishery, although the once large numbers of average sized chub seem to have declined somewhat in recent years. The chub are fewer in numbers but of greater individual size, a common phenomenon with many rivers at present. Looking at some of the more popular lengths in a little more detail, Avon Meadows at Stratford-upon-Avon is excellent, as not only does it contain a very good head of chub, but it also holds the occasional very big fish. In recent seasons, several five-pounders have put in an appearance.

Another excellent area is Welford-on-Avon, where there are also some useful chub, as indeed there are at Bidford. Some of the most extensive chub shoals are to be found at Bidford, making the stretch one that contains chub of both quantity and quality.

The angler looking for sport from good chub as well as shoal-sized barbel could do worse than fishing at Cleeve Prior or Marlcliff. Specimen hunters are starting to extract some very useful fish. Below Evesham and running down to Tewkesbury, a number of extremely big chub are present, although they take some finding. Rumours persist that the lower Avon now holds some massive fish. The biggest fish appear to favour the snaggier swims.

I have done very little Avon chubbing personally, but most of what I have experienced has been on the more upper reaches, controlled by either the Rugby or Coventry clubs. To be honest, the chub fishing there cannot be described as anything more than average, the fish on the nearby Leam being far more impressive. My biggest Warwickshire Avon chub was little over four pounds, although that is probably an unfair comparison, as my hours spent chubbing the river have been strictly limited.

THE WAVENEY

Although I have never fished the Waveney myself, it is one of those rivers I have always intended to give some attention. The reason is simple. The Waveney undoubtedly contains some of the most enormous chub to be found anywhere in the country.

One of the best chub anglers in this country is Alan Rawden, and Alan has taken many huge chub from the Waveney, including one of just under seven pounds. As well as this fish, there is substantiated evidence of other fish of over seven, making the river right at the top of any specimen chub angler's list.

My information on the clubs controlling Waveney fishing is rather sketchy, but I understand that two clubs worth joining are the Bungay Cherry Tree AC and Harleston, Wortwell and District AC. One good stretch I do know of is the free stretch at Bungay Common. Although it is extremely popular, that particular venue has produced monstrous chub in the past and is well worth taking a look at.

THE YORKSHIRE RIVERS

As with the Waveney, my personal experience of the chub rivers of Yorkshire is nil, although I could not fail to realize how much Yorkshire chubbing has blossomed in recent seasons. No one could have overlooked the fact that large numbers of huge fish have come from the Swale, which has largely overshadowed the other rivers. In fact, the Nidd, Ure, Ouse, Wharfe and Derwent have all produced good chub to well over six pounds, and the Tees has yielded the current record, making Yorkshire a paradise for the big chub man of the nineties. I understand that joining the Leeds and DASA and the Tadcaster AC will give access to many terrific venues.

The area is also blessed with a host of cracking day-ticket venues at very reasonable prices, almost all of which have produced chub in excess of 6lb. On the Swale, there are good stretches around Topcliffe, including Cundall Lodge Farm and Cundall Hall, and a terrific stretch extends a mile either side of Thornton bridge near Helperby. Also near Helperby is Myton Grange Farm, which has not only produced individual monster chub, but on occasions, multiple catches of specimens.

A cracking day-ticket stretch of the Ure is at Boroughbridge.

THE KENNET

The Kennet is rapidly becoming one of the most exciting chub rivers in the country and it is a river I intend to give more serious attention in future. All along the river, chub weights have increased dramatically and Len Arbery, who has extensive knowledge of Kennet chubbing, is of the opinion that the fish may be gorging on immature signal crayfish, with which the river now abounds. The presence of these crustaceans is not, however, good news. In some stretches of the Kennet, as in other rivers, they are reaching plague proportions, and several clubs are having to address the problem very seriously. At times, especially in the summer months, signals can make serious bottom fishing virtually impossible.

Whatever the truth of the matter, however, the undeniable fact is that Kennet chub are now extremely impressive indeed. The club controlling long stretches of this fabulous river is Reading and District. Possibly the most famous day-ticket Kennet fishery is, of course, the stretch at Aldermaston Mill. Below the roadbridge, one mile of double bank is available, as well as fishing being allowed in the house grounds themselves. This area includes two super weirpools.

The chub at Aldermaston are awesome, although the intense angling pressure means that many of the monstrous fish reported to the angling press are recaptures, and a few certainly have not been weighed as accurately as they might have been. There is no doubt, however, that several chub of over 7lb have been landed, and there are reports of fish topping 8lb. It is difficult to establish how many different fish are involved in these reports.

What I know for an absolute fact is that there are many different five-pounders and several different sixes at Aldermaston. A good friend of mine had three six-pounders last season alone. As far as he can tell, they were all different fish.

The only drawback to Aldermaston Mill is the angling pressure. However, if that is not off-putting, there is no doubt that the venue offers the chance of chub of a size possibly unmatched anywhere in the country at the moment.

OTHER RIVERS

Let me finish this look at chub rivers with some very general comments on other rivers I know to contain good chub, but of which I have no first-hand knowledge, and neither do my friends. First of all, there is the Trent, which has produced monstrous chub in some sections and very mediocre fish in others. I have never been able to get excited about Trent fishing, but if you would like more information, you could do a lot worse than contact Archie Braddock. Archie has fished the Trent for many years.

Another good chub river I have never fished is the Cam, which I understand is now producing five-pounders regularly. A contact of mine who has written to me recently after reading my articles is concentrating on the Cam and has taken several big fish. He has actually sent me a photograph of a 5lb 10oz fish he had taken, and it looked in cracking condition.

In Norfolk, the River Yare is worth a look for good chub, and I understand that the Norwich club controls some fishing on this river. Another river I have never fished is the Lea, which has produced chub to over 6lb. Good areas, I understand, are at Kings Weir at Wormley and the Leisure Sport venue at Cheshunt.

Also worth a visit is the Lugg, which I have fished just once in my life, many years ago. I have no information as to big chub in the Lugg, but it has always held a healthy crop of four-pounders and the occasional five.

Very good chub are also to be found in the upper Welland. Living where I do in the Midlands, it is amazing that I have never fished the river in my angling career. Rumours persist of six-pounders in the Welland, but two very good angling friends of mine, who know the river well, say that the largest chub they know of is around 5lb 12oz.

Midlands rivers that seem to produce mediocre chub only are the Teme, Nene and Warwickshire Stour, although the latter two have scraped the occasional five-pounder. On the Teme, a four-pounder appears to be exceptional.

In Lancashire, the only chub rivers I have any knowledge of at all are the Ribble and the Dane, and that knowledge has only come to me from my good friends Martin James and Graham Marsden. Martin's chub exploits obviously confirm that the Ribble is a river well worth devoting some time to, although I have no knowledge of day-ticket availability or club memberships that I can pass on to you. As far as the Dane is concerned, Graham has told me that the chances of a big chub there are fairly remote. Apparently, a four-pounder is a rarity.

Martin James displays a good Ribble specimen (overleaf).

16 LAST CAST

Contained within the pages of this book are the knowledge and experiences gleaned from a lifetime's love affair with the chub. I have held nothing back, and my only wish is that you should have enjoyed reading it. Hopefully, something within its pages will have given you inspiration.

To quote an old cliché, the book has been a labour of love. I wonder how many times in its

And then I came to the most mouth-watering swim.

writing I have suddenly drifted off, as another fond chubbing memory came flooding back.

At the opening of the book, I set the tone by describing the capture of my personal best chub, taken in the summer all those years ago. I would now like to close in a similar vein, leaving you in contemplation of the sheer joys of winter chubbing with the story of a recent winter's day.

It was good to be alive on such a beautiful March morning; it was sunny, springlike and totally windless. Catching fish would be a bonus on such a lovely day.

As I walked the lonely banks, with only the dabchicks and a distant vixen for company, my mind lingered on the events of the previous evening when, from a new stretch of river, I had taken four lovely chub to 4lb 14oz. Even after more than thirty years' chubbing, my heart still raced in contemplation of the day ahead.

After an unproductive half-hour in the first glide, I decided to explore much further upstream, to an area I had never before fished. Soon, I was lost in a wonderful wilderness, the head-high reedmace and rushes growing in wild profusion a mute testimony to the lack of previous human intrusion.

And then I came to the most mouth-watering swim. A large raft lay upstream of a sudden left-hand bend, the raft featuring an underwater obstruction that threw the main flow completely across river. The difference between the brisk current and the near bank slack created by the obstruction would be obvious to the most inexperienced chub man; there just had to be fish there.

Baiting was simplicity itself, merely involving dropping mash at my feet at the junction of the flows, such that it drifted across river from my sitting position. I adopted the procedure of baiting steadily for ten minutes while I enjoyed a sandwich and a cup of tea. Apart from the murmuring of the willows in the light breeze, my world was one of silent serenity in the winter sunshine.

When eventually I lowered the first crust offering, no more than a rod length out, it was taken almost before it settled. In short order, the first chub of the day was being returned a hundred yards away. It weighed 3lb 13oz.

The second cast in the swim went five yards down the crease, and again there were only moments to wait. Soon, a bigger fish of 4lb 3oz was being returned in the same slack as his companion.

The third and last fish from that swim, twenty minutes later, was the highlight of the day. I had progressively fished the crease until eventually landing a bait at its extremity under a large willow on the opposite bank. The bite was impressive, the rod literally smashing round as something big and powerful snarled away under the willow branches. It was several minutes before I was to get my first look at the fish, but that it was a bit special was evident from the frequent buzzes from the clutch as the chub took line. Eventually, however, it was beaten, and a magnificent fish sagged in the mesh. Moments later, I was confirming that it was over the magical five pounds, 5lb 4oz to be exact.

In mid-afternoon, having searched four other good-looking areas, I arrived at a swim where a large rush bed protruded to mid-river. Just the odd dead stalk above water level was the giveaway. Behind this obstruction was a lovely slow, smooth glide. Again I adopted the procedure of pre-baiting the glide, this time by depositing my feed right into the rush bed, so that particles of bread filtered through into the slack. After a few minutes of this treatment, my first crust bait was propelled upstream right behind the dead rushes. The response was instantaneous, a dramatic kickback of the tip heralding an exhilarating battle with another great fish of 4lb 12oz.

The last fish of the day, well after dark, was taken back in the glide from where I had caught three good chub the previous evening. The first two pulls in the swim, from, I suspect, roach, were missed but eventually, thirty yards down the run, another good pull resulted in a solid resistance from yet another four-pounder, 4lb 7oz this time.

The previous day's chubbing had been great, with three four-pounders, but today had surpassed it. Again, there had been three four-pounders, but topped off by a five. I was in buoyant mood as I began the long, sweaty march back to the van.

What, I wondered, would tomorrow bring?

INDEX